Understanding Chinese Society

For Tina

Understanding Chinese Society

Norman Stockman

Polity Press

First published in 2000 by Polity Press in association with Blackwell Publishers Ltd.

Editorial Office:
Polity Press
65 Bridge Street
Cambridge CB2 1UR, UK

Marketing and production:
Blackwell Publishers Ltd
108 Cowley Road
Oxford OX4 1JF, UK

Published in the USA by
Blackwell Publishers Inc.
Commerce Place
350 Main Street
Malden, MA 02148, USA

ISBN 0–7456–1735–2
ISBN 0–7456–1736–0 (pbk)

A catalogue record for this book is available from the British Library and has been applied for from the Library of Congress.

Typeset in 10.5 on 12 pt Sabon
by Kolam Information Services Pvt Ltd, Pondicherry, India
Printed in Great Britain by MPG Books Ltd, Bodmin, Cornwall

This book is printed on acid-free paper.

Contents

Acknowledgements

When people ask me how as a rogue sociologist I became interested in China, I tell them a rambling, picaresque story, if they can be bothered to listen. Among the cast of characters is Stan Rosen, a political scientist from the University of Southern California, whom I happened to meet in Beijing in 1987 when studying Chinese language at Beijing Normal University. He was interested at that time in street traders, and we spent some time together eating melon at street stalls and chatting about social studies of China. On one walk he prompted me to practice my Chinese by making inquiries about booking a room at a nearby hotel catering (as it turned out) exclusively for Chinese people, an incident that provoked more merriment than embarrassment. Perhaps on the same walk he asked, in passing, as one does, whether I had thought of 'doing a China book'. I hadn't. You should, he said. Clearly the remark stuck in my memory, working away at my subconscious. So here it is, my China book. My thanks to Stan Rosen for his initial encouragement.

The book emerged from teaching a course called 'Chinese Society' for the past ten years. It is a short course on an immense subject. Ten cohorts of students have passed through the course, and together we have grappled with the problems of understanding the twists and turns of revolutionary social change in twentieth-century China. The book could not have been written without those students, their enthusiasm and never-ending questions. As I did, they start off knowing almost nothing about China and, as I did, they assume that almost everything about Chinese society is very different from the western societies of Europe and America that they live in or have some familiarity with. Then they begin to find aspects they can recognize, and go through a stage in which all societies appear essentially the same, variations on a set of common themes. There is truth in both of these extreme positions, and we continue to oscillate between them and to search for more satisfactory middle ways.

The debts that I have accumulated in writing this book are extensive and unrepayable. My most general indebtedness is to the scholarly communities of sociologists and other social scientists who have conducted the research on which the generalizations and interpretations in this book rest. Part of the information I report derives from my own research activities and my own personal experience in China. A much greater part comes necessarily from the detailed investigations and analyses of a wide range of scholars, each expert in their own fields of study. I have, as is customary in academic circles, given full acknowledgement of the source of all specific research findings and all major contributions to analysis and argument, and I hope that readers will be encouraged to follow up the leads provided in my suggestions for further reading and in the full bibliography. They will quickly discover what should in any case be obvious, that I have been forced to simplify and condense the carefully and subtly wrought books and articles of many scholars into short paragraphs, sentences, or sometimes merely a phrase. The result, I hope, remains intelligible, but it cannot do justice to the complexity of empirical materials and their analysis that is now available in the scholarly literature, whether originating from within China or without.

I am indebted more specifically to my Chinese colleagues on particular research projects, especially Sheng Xuewen of the Institute of Sociology, Chinese Academy of Social Sciences, and Ding Jinhong of the Institute of Population Research, East China Normal University. Both of them patiently explained to me many aspects of everyday life in China as well as the workings of social processes, and Sheng Xuewen opened up the possibility for one of my most fruitful visits to China in 1992.

I should like to thank also the committee and members of the University of Aberdeen Chinese Studies Group which has been in existence since 1989. Ever since the group's first public meeting, held fortuitously on 6 June 1989, and crammed with visiting Chinese students and scholars distraught at the news emanating from Beijing, the enthusiasm of the group's members has made it possible to invite very many distinguished scholars to Aberdeen. I am grateful to all those members of the China studies community who have visited Aberdeen over the years and allowed me to pick their brains.

Collection of material for the book benefited greatly from the award of a Visiting Research Fellowship at the Institute of Development Studies at the University of Sussex in July 1996, generously sponsored by Gordon White, whose death in 1998 sadly robbed the China social science community of one of its most imaginative researchers. This fellowship also gave me the opportunity for stimulating discussions with members of the Institute.

I should like to acknowledge the support of the British Council in funding my trip to China in August–September 1997, and to thank my hosts and colleagues at Fudan University, Shanghai, for making the visit instructive and intellectually profitable.

Conversations with many people, both in person and by e-mail, have helped me to grapple with the topics dealt with in this book, and it is invidious to mention some and leave others out. None the less, I would particularly like to thank the following: Bob Benewick, Bian Yanjie, Flemming Christiansen, Vincent Yiu-kong Chu, Delia Davin, Stephan Feuchtwang, Rance Lee, Garland Ching-Mui Liu, Lu Hanlong, Caroline Hoy, Lu Jianhua, Geoffrey MacCormack, Tang Ning, Rodney Taylor, Wang Jufen, Heather Zhang, Zhang Ming and Zhao Minghua.

At Polity Press, Rebecca Harkin and Sue Leigh have acted as sympathetic, encouraging and helpful editors. I should also like to acknowledge the thorough work of Harriet Evans who, as a reader of the manuscript, provided very stimulating criticism and valuable advice and suggestions for revision. Another reader, who remains anonymous, also made useful comments. The final version, and any remaining inaccuracies or infelicities of interpretation, are of course my responsibility.

Finally, I owe a special debt of gratitude to Tina for her unflagging support. For too long now she has had to endure the excuse: 'I can't do that, I've got to work on the book.' She put up with it with reasonably good grace, and will be pleased to get a respite from 'the book'. As I will. Until the next one.

Notes on Romanization and Names

The Chinese language is written in characters that need to be transcribed into the roman alphabet for the benefit of readers of English and other languages. The internationally recognized standard system for this transcription is now the Hanyu Pinyin system used by the PRC. This book mostly follows this convention. However, the reader will also encounter other transcriptions, in particular the Wade–Giles system named after the two British sinologists of the nineteenth century who invented it. This is used in most writings published before the 1970s, and is still used by some historians, as well as in English-language texts produced in Taiwan. Quotations and bibliographical items therefore sometimes contain words and names in this system. Thus readers should realize that Fei Xiaotong (pinyin) and Fei Hsiao-t'ung (Wade–Giles) are the same person, as are Mao Zedong and Mao Tse-tung. Similarly *guanxi* (pinyin) and *kuan-hsi* (Wade–Giles) are both the commonly used word for social connections (see chapter 4). There was also a postal system for transcribing place-names: Beijing (pinyin) is the same city as Peking (postal). Cantonese names and place-names are often transcribed to represent the different pronunciation of Cantonese; hence it is common to use Sun Yat-sen (rather than the pinyin Sun Yixian), Chiang Kai-shek (rather than the pinyin Jiang Jieshi), and Canton (in pinyin: Guangzhou for the city, Guangdong for the province).

Chinese people's names usually consist of a family name (mostly one syllable, but occasionally two, as in my own given Chinese name Situ Nuoman) and a personal name (either one or two syllables). The family name is traditionally placed first. Examples are MAO Zedong, DENG Xiaoping, FEI Xiaotong, JIANG Qing. However, the situation is complicated by the fact that many Chinese scholars, especially but not exclusively those who work outside China, adopt the custom of placing their family name after their personal name in their publications, name-cards, and so on. For example, BIAN Yanjie now publishes in English under the name Yanjie Bian. In the bibliography, I omit the comma after the family name where the Chinese author retains the traditional order of names.

1

The Study of Chinese Society

The turn of the millennium is witnessing a radical change in perceptions of the world. The world of nation-states and power blocks, the division of capitalist and communist political economies, of industrialized and developing societies, of private and public spheres and sectors, which formed the framework of social thought up until the late 1980s, is giving way to a new global formation whose contours are still unclear. Politicians and electors, managers and workers, tourists and consumers, teachers and students, all find themselves in a world where old uncertainties are being overlaid by new ones. Those of us who work in the realms of social science and social thought are having to rethink and regroup even more than in previous decades.

In few spheres is this rethinking more active than in the case of China. For the first decades of the People's Republic, relations between China and the outside world were sparse. Few foreigners had been to China or knew much about it. China after 1949 had been transformed from a weak and divided country, prey to western and Japanese imperialism, Christian missionaries and orientalist curiosity, to a communist regime shut off from the world except for its actual or potential allies in the communist or developing world, which after 1960 ceased to include the Soviet Union. The Chinese seat at the United Nations was occupied by the American-supported regime on Taiwan, and diplomatic links with the Communist People's Republic were shaky. The regime closed down most trade relations with the outside world and abolished inward investment. The world's media had little access to developments in China, nor did Chinese people have access to the world's media, and the first thirty years' post-war growth of the television audience took place without China either as viewing subject or, to a great extent, as object.

All of this has been transformed in the last twenty years or so, and the transformation proceeds at ever-increasing pace. More and more tourists, students, business people, media workers and researchers have taken the opportunity to visit China or to include China in their range of operations. The PRC, having replaced Taiwan at the UN in 1971, plays an increasingly important role in world and regional affairs. China has joined the global economy, transnational corporations have invested in China on a major scale, many residents of affluent industrialized countries now possess consumer items made in China, and some even possess some pension fund or personal investment holdings in the Chinese economy. China news appears regularly in the world's media and TV programmes and films made in China by foreign or Chinese companies bring an increasingly wide range of images of China to the world's viewers. Conversely, more and more Chinese people have the opportunity to travel or trade outside their country and to learn about global affairs through a variety of media. China, to a considerable degree, has joined the growing globalization of society.

Teaching and research in the social sciences are adapting to these new conditions. For a long time, China could appear on the curricula or the research agenda only in a small number of specialized institutions. Social science textbooks often ignored China altogether. Libraries outside the realms of sinology or international relations held few books on China, partly because there were few published. Most students could go through degree programmes in sociology, anthropology, economics or political science without encountering China. In the English-speaking world (which must provide the main readership for this book), and elsewhere too, this situation is changing. In North America, Britain and Australasia, national research agencies are encouraging the growth of knowledge of Chinese developments. Many universities have well-developed Asian Studies programmes with a strong emphasis on China. There is a rapid growth in the publication of monograph and periodical literature on China in the social sciences.

Yet China still appears to occupy a place on the margins of the social scientific consciousness. For some very good reasons, which will be explored later, China remains a subject for specialists, and has penetrated the mainstream of the social sciences only slightly. In major textbooks of sociology, for example, China appears, if at all, under certain specific headings, such as family life, population growth and control, or political and social revolution. Alternatively, China may be treated primarily as a developing society, and discussed under such typical rubrics as rural development or socialist industrialization. In recent years, China has also appeared in discussions of post-socialism, as a case of transition to a more market-led economy, albeit still under the control of a communist party, unlike most of the societies of the former Soviet bloc. This is all very worthwhile, and far better than ignoring the society altogether. Yet such textbook presentations give a very partial view of Chinese society, as an example of very specific problems or issues, rather than as a complex society with a structure of interrelated institutions and processes.

At the other end of the academic scale lies the highly specialized research literature reporting the findings of the most recent detailed research on particular aspects of social life. This is not easily accessible to the non-specialist, in a number of respects. First, it may not be easy to get hold of, for it will be held only by specialist libraries and mentioned only in specialist review periodicals and catalogues. Second, it may be difficult to decipher if the reader lacks detailed and complex background information about Chinese history and institutions. And third, it may be too advanced for the student reader in terms of the theoretical frameworks or methodological techniques employed.

Textbooks are beginning to appear that aim to bridge this gap between the specialist research literature on China and the general run of social science courses, their teachers and students. The present book is a contribution to this genre, drawing on a range of social scientific research and especially on sociological and anthropological investigations. It is based on the conviction that there are good reasons for incorporating China more fully into the mainstream of these disciplines. In the next sections of this chapter, some of these reasons will be briefly reviewed.

A fifth of the world's population cannot be ignored

The most superficial argument for giving greater emphasis to China in general sociology is simply that it is a very large country with a very large population. The land area, smaller only than Russia's and Canada's, measures 9.6 million square kilometres, according to PRC official statistics. The population is many times as big as either. The last full census in 1990 gave a mid-year estimate of 1.134 billion people, and the latest available population estimate[1] at time of writing was 1.259 billion. One could go on; everything about China is large.

Size, in sociology, is certainly not everything. The development of sociological theory and research has responded more to the patterns of geopolitical and cultural domination than to the size of populations or territories of given societies. Major theoretical arguments in sociology and anthropology have often been carried on in relation to studies of relatively small societies, such as the Nuer. None the less, the size of China's population is now important in bringing the society to the attention of social scientists, since the incorporation of China into global economic, political and strategic systems has made its impact increasingly felt in all these respects. Similar processes of globalization are affecting many other societies, even in the same region, but size determines that we will pay more attention to China.

The rise of Pacific Asia

Another reason why China is increasingly capturing our attention rests on the apparent reshaping of the world's economic and political patterns. The regional power-structure of the world has shifted many times in the course of history, and the dominance of European and American empires in the nineteenth and early twentieth centuries has until recently provided the background to contemporary assumptions about the world system. The rise of the Soviet Union and its satellites in the middle part of the century generated a bi-polar view of the world, summed up in the idea of the Cold War. Decolonization reduced the overt world grasp of the imperial powers, but theorists of development identified continuing asymmetries of economic and political power and labelled them in terms of theories of 'dependency' or 'the development of underdevelopment'. Still it was the rich industrialized countries of North America and western Europe which seemed to hold the advantages in the world system. But from the 1960s commentators increasingly came to identify a shift to the East, with the rise to economic prominence first of Japan and then of the 'newly industrialized countries' or 'NICs', and especially the 'four little tigers' of Hong Kong, Taiwan, Singapore and South Korea. Once China, too, 'opened its doors' to the world, the stage was set for a variety of future scenarios in which the 'East' figures as the new powerhouse of the world.

The image which has most strongly captured the imagination is that of the 'Pacific'. The Pacific is increasingly seen as the new centre of economic and technological dynamism and of strategic power in the world, and appears in a number of apocalyptic book titles, such as *The Pacific Century* (Linder 1986) or *Pacific Destiny* (Elegant 1990). Concepts such as 'the Pacific Rim', 'Pacific Asia' or 'Asia-Pacific' are widely used in journalistic as well as social scientific commentary on the restructuring of the world system. For example, Preston (1998) builds his analysis of this restructuring around the notion of a 'tripolar global industrial–capitalist system' incorporating the Americas, the European Union, and Pacific Asia. With China as the largest and most populous country of Pacific Asia, and with the Japanese economy, although still the largest economy in the region, in the doldrums, it is not surprising that China is increasingly seen as a major 'player' in the various power games that make up the global system.

China has indeed become in recent years a centre of increased economic and strategic power, and this is not a negligible cause of increased sociological interest in Chinese society. Chinese economic growth rates in the 1980s and 1990s have outstripped those of most of the rest of the world, and China's military might is an increasing concern to its neighbours. China is also seen as a new land of opportunity, for example by the many Australian school students who now choose to learn Chinese rather than a European language. The economic down-turn at the end of the 1990s may have punctured some of the more inflated claims for the Pacific as a new global centre, which in any case had their critics.[2] The reshaping of the global system will continue in some form, however, and will continue to draw sociologists away from their American- and Europe-centred views of the world.

The only major communist society left

The year 1989 appeared to signal the end of communism. The regimes ruled by communist parties, most notably the Soviet Union and its satellites in eastern and central Europe, collapsed from within under the burdens of economic inefficiency, loss of self-confidence of the ruling Communist elites, and forfeiture of any legitimacy they might have had in the eyes of their citizens. Communism, which had once been a world-wide movement dominated and to some extent united by the party of the Soviet Union, but which later exhibited fundamental divisions such as those which gave rise to the Sino-Soviet split

of 1960, had conquered more territory and ruled over a higher proportion of the world's population than any other ideology since the
rise of Islam. It ruled in the name of a theory of history which placed
the destiny of the world in its hands, as active representative of the
interests of the universal class, the proletariat. It claimed to be building a new kind of society in which class domination and exploitation
would be abolished and the ideals of the French revolutionaries,
liberty, equality and fraternity, would become reality for all, not just
ideological disguises for the benefit of a small ruling class.

Yet the reality of 'really existing socialist societies' was a rigid and
inefficient state-owned and state-planned economy, a monopolization
of power and privilege by the officials of the Communist Party, and a
heavy apparatus of ideological repression and control. Such a society
could be kept stable only by isolating it from alternatives. When this
isolation could no longer be maintained, the regimes collapsed. What
followed was a headlong rush towards electoral politics and party
pluralism to replace the monopoly of the Communist Party over state
power, and towards privatization and marketization of the economy
to replace state ownership and planning. Believing (wrongly) that the
former Soviet regimes were converging on American-style capitalism
and liberal democracy, Fukuyama (1992) ironically proclaimed this
form of society, not communism, as the 'end of history'.

Up to the time of writing, the People's Republic of China has not
followed the lead of the former Soviet societies. It remains, in certain
senses, a communist society. It was never a replica of the Soviet Union,
and it has changed in many ways in recent years. But in two main
respects it has remained communist. It is governed by a communist
party which does not allow electoral challenge to its monopoly of rule,
except to a very minor degree. And its economic resources are still
predominantly state- or collectively-owned, despite a large and growing private business sector. The regime also remains publicly committed to the construction of a socialist society, albeit one with
distinctively 'Chinese characteristics', and to the leading role of the
Communist Party and to the truth of Marxism–Leninism as adapted
to Chinese circumstances by Mao Zedong and Deng Xiaoping.

It is impossible to predict how enduring this form of political
economy will turn out to be. It has already survived powerful challenges, most notably from the movements of popular protest in 1989.
One of the many uncertainties in writing this book has been the
thought that, weeks before publication, the Communist Party would
give up or be deprived of its monopoly of power and would lose an
election to a party committed to total privatization of the economy

and liberalization of all aspects of culture. It would be foolish to rule out the possibility of such a course of history or to write about China, as many did write about the former Soviet Union, as if its presently existing institutional framework were destined to last into the indefinite future. Yet, until it ceases to be the case, it does remain the case that the CCP has managed to adapt economically, politically and culturally to conditions which proved to be too much for communist parties in other states. The continuing rule of the Chinese Communist Party marks China out for distinctiveness at the beginning of the twenty-first century.

Social stability, social change and revolution

The foregoing paragraphs offer some explanation for the fact that China attracts increasing interest in recent years, and go some way to suggest that the study of Chinese society should be embraced by the mainstream of sociologists and not just left to China specialists. Yet so far we have not discovered any good reasons for this proposal that lie within the discipline of sociology itself. Why might sociologists in particular pay more attention to China? An answer to this question requires some reflection, necessarily simplified, on the nature of sociology.

Western sociology arose in an epoch of rapid social change, when processes such as capitalist industrialization, urbanization, and the formation of modern class structures with their attendant inequalities and conflicts, were arousing growing concern among the peoples of Europe. Those who had the time, energy and detachment had for centuries past asked questions about the principles of collective human life, and their ponderings had created and been incorporated into the scholarly disciplines of moral and political philosophy, jurisprudence, theology, and others. The diversity of human customs in different times and places had long provided stuff for speculation. The rapidity of the changes to what came to be called modernity, together with the model of the natural sciences as a revolutionary new way to tackle the intellectual study of social life, stimulated the emergence in the late eighteenth and nineteenth century of the new social science disciplines of economics, political science and sociology. Of these, sociology asked the most general and wide-ranging questions, seeking an understanding of the conditions of stability and change in society, questions which had both a theoretical and a pressing practical significance.

The scientific study of society could, however, proceed from either of two opposed points of view, and this generated debates about the social sciences which have lasted to the present day. One could on the one hand assume that underlying all the disturbing and contentious phenomena of modern industrial capitalism there were natural laws of social life and social change waiting to be discovered by social scientists, which would explain the inevitability of these processes, to which the citizenry had no choice but to adapt. This is a viewpoint that might be expected to be attractive to those sections of society which benefited disproportionately from the patterns of inequality found in modern society. Or on the other hand one could assume that all the processes of social life were essentially made by human action and could potentially be altered by human action. This is a line of thought that might be expected to appeal to more disadvantaged groups in society; those whose chances in life were injured or restricted by social forces could in principle hope and struggle for liberation from those social forces. This opposition, between a functionalist (or 'positivist') perspective with an interest in the conditions of social stability and a critical perspective with an interest in social change, continues to underlie both theoretical and practical argument in sociology.[3]

The investigation of social change, and especially radical or revolutionary social change, lies at the very heart of sociological thinking. Although there have been major social changes in all societies in the world in the twentieth century, China must have a special place in sociologists' attempts to grapple with these fundamental issues of their subject. China has been ruled for the second half of this century by a party committed to radical social change. The CCP gained power through military struggle, mobilizing its supporters with images of a new society in which the working masses would be liberated from the shackles of the old. This language of 'old society', 'new society' and 'liberation' lies at the core of the Communist Party's project and the justification of its rule. The army which created the military conditions of that rule was and is called the 'People's Liberation Army' (PLA), and the CCP's gaining of power over almost the whole of China in 1949 is called 'Liberation', both in official discourse and often still in popular parlance. From 1949 onwards, at every available opportunity, the new rulers of China told themselves and the rest of the people that they lived in a 'new society' which was to become utterly different from the old one. This combination of features – the military overthrow of one regime and the installation of a new one committed to drastic reconstruction of social institutions and of struc-

tures of power and inequality – is precisely what is meant by the word
'revolution' (Krejcí 1994: 7). China is not the only example of revolutionary social change in the twentieth century, far from it, and in many
respects its revolutionary experience has been similar to that of countries such as the former Soviet Union; but it is arguable that China is
the largest and most powerful country that has also taken revolutionary transformation further and deeper than even the USSR. Certainly
that would have been the claim of some of its leaders, who came (with
whatever justification) to identify the USSR as just another capitalist
society.

China specialists in the West, having tended hitherto to take the
division between pre-communist and communist China for granted,
have increasingly come to challenge the view of 1949 as a fundamental break in Chinese society. The historian Paul Cohen has referred to
what he calls 'the 1949 barrier'. According to Cohen (1988: 519), in
the United States 'for the most part different people study the pre- and
post-1949 periods. They ask different questions, rely on different
sources, read different books, and often attend different conferences.'
Taking as his theme the nature of reform projects in different historical periods, and the relationship between centralizing and decentral-
izing forces in the Chinese state, Cohen points to what he sees as
similarities and continuities over the span of the last hundred years. A
similar argument is put forward by Hooper (1992), who argues that
continuity from the past is often neglected, partly because of the
'barrier of 1949'. For example, Hooper herself originally shared a
tendency to assume that the Communist regime had made enormous
changes to gender relations, but after living in China for a while it
became clear to her that she 'had seriously overestimated the extent of
change and seriously underestimated the continuities from the past'
(p. 92), issues which were taken up systematically by later research. A
related line of thought, also bearing on the 1949 divide, suggests that,
far from having revolutionized society, Communist policies and the
social processes they encouraged actually stabilized society in some
respects and prevented change that would otherwise have occurred.
An example can readily be found in the field of urban–rural relations
and the process of urbanization. Right up to the present day China has
retained an atypically high proportion of its population in the countryside, for reasons clearly related to the Communist regime's policies,
dating from the 1950s, of control over population movement. A rate
of urbanization more typical of developing countries has only emerged
since the authorities have relaxed the implementation of household
registration regulations and since rural people have had both the

incentive and the freedom to look for work in the cities. The key point of change here is not 1949 but rather 1978, the beginning of the post-Mao phase of economic reforms (K. Chan 1994). All of these substantive issues will be taken up in more detail later in this book;[4] what I am stressing here is that, even while disputing the regime's official claim to have constructed an entirely new society in 1949 (a claim that has in any case been modified in recent years), sociologists can find in China questions of social stability and social change which lie at the core of the discipline.

Questions of social continuity and social change in China will be a major theme of this book. It will chart the main contours of continuity and change in the major institutional areas of twentieth-century Chinese society. It will also try to identify the main factors and forces which have been responsible for both continuity and change, giving full weight to the claims and reality of revolutionary transformation promoted by the Communist Party and regime, but without assuming in advance that Communist policies and initiatives have been the only cause of change. However, given that the CCP has remained in power for the last half-century, during which it has attempted to transform the society in the direction of what its leaders always described as 'socialism', a particular concern will be to understand the relationships between social changes and the expressed aims of the party and regime. As will be seen, these aims have been continually disputed and reinterpreted, both within the party and outside it. None the less, certain general themes remained salient to the various versions of the socialist project: the dismantling of traditional hierarchies, the elimination of extremes of wealth and poverty, the democratization of culture. While there can be no simple interpretation of 'success' and 'failure', these egalitarian and emancipatory goals remain a benchmark against which to set the reality of social change in China.

An important issue here concerns the possibility of demarcating sociological interpretation from ideological justification. The collapse of the Soviet Union and the transition of its constituent states towards 'market economies' and electoral multi-party 'democracies' gave rise in the capitalist West to forms of Cold War triumphalism, the 'I told you so' of those who had long proclaimed that socialism was impossible and that there was 'no alternative' to the market and the ballot-box. Fukuyama's work has gained celebrity as a model of that tendency. It has clear affinities with the functionalist–positivist perspective in sociology mentioned earlier, which easily slides over from a sociological perspective into a self-justification of the rich and powerful in capitalist societies. The strategy of this book is to attempt to avoid this ideological pitfall. It would be easy to interpret the shift towards market processes under the Chinese economic reforms in a similar vein, as a further demonstration of the inevitability of capitalism. And it would be easy to interpret any other 'failures' of the CCP's revolutionary project (for example, to abolish all of the main inequalities between men and women) as a demonstration of 'natural laws' of social life which cannot be gainsaid. The present text will attempt to avoid such interpretations. Rather, if it transpires that 'liberation' has not proceeded as far as optimistic communists may have hoped, sociological explanations will be sought in the tendencies to self-perpetuation and self-maintenance of social institutions, explanations that none the less hold out the possibility (in principle) of emancipation. In particular, emphasis will be placed on the difficulty of transforming society against the opposition of powerful social interests. The fact that these powerful social interests now include the CCP itself is another irony of history.

Whose study of Chinese society?

In the previous sections the focus has been primarily on western sociology, rooted in the specific historical experience and intellectual traditions of Europe and America, and on the approaches that western sociologists might take to the study of Chinese society. In this discussion one set of voices has so far been kept silent, the voices of Chinese sociologists themselves, for whom the study of Chinese society is the study of their own society. It is time to open this question directly: what is the nature of indigenous Chinese sociological study of Chinese society and how should western students relate to it?

The first part of this question requires a brief excursion into the history of Chinese sociology.[5] There is a long tradition of social thought in China which, as in the case of western philosophy, might be seen as a forerunner of sociology. In chapter 4, the main elements of this essentially Confucian tradition will be outlined. However, some Chinese scholars at the end of the nineteenth century, including Yan Fu and Liang Qichao, developed a strong interest in European and American sociology and other social sciences and branches of social thought, many of the major works of which (such as Spencer's *Study of Sociology*) were translated into Chinese.[6] Some universities, especially those run by western missionaries, established courses and departments of sociology, beginning with St John's University in Shanghai in 1906, and many students also went abroad to study, gaining sociology doctorates mainly from American universities. After the First World War there was a rapid growth of empirical research in China, often relating to social problems and social policy, and scholars also wrote books and articles attempting theoretical interpretations of Chinese society. Sociology flourished in China throughout the 1930s. The most famous figure, both in China and the West, who was involved in both of these tasks from the 1930s on, is Fei Xiaotong,[7] but there were many others. During the Japanese occupation of eastern China, sociology research units were set up in the far west of the country, especially in Yunnan, and some important research was done and young sociologists trained. At the end of the war, some of these sociologists moved back to their eastern universities, others (such as Francis L. K. Hsu (Xu Langguang) and, later, C. K. Yang (Yang Qingkun)), moved to the United States where they had previously studied and where they spent the rest of their careers. In 1952, after the Communists came to power, sociology was condemned as a bourgeois subject and its practitioners as reactionary tools of imperialism (as they had been also in the Soviet Union) and departments and institutes of sociology were closed down. In 1956, sociologists took the opportunity of the more liberal atmosphere of the 'Hundred Flowers' movement to campaign for the re-establishment of sociology, but they were unsuccessful. Although many trained sociologists were reassigned to work in social research, especially the ethnographic study of national minorities, the university departments and academic research institutes of sociology remained closed for more than twenty years.

The banning of sociology was one small part of the attempted revolutionary transformation of culture in China, which will be the subject of chapter 7. In general terms, this project of cultural revolution rested on a Marxist interpretation of culture as the expression of the dominant class. Cultural beliefs and hierarchies both stem from and reinforce the economic and political power of the dominant class in a given mode of production. Hence, if power is to be transferred away from the former owners of the means of production to the masses of working people, the elimination of the cultural hegemony of the former ruling classes will also be required. The interpretation of sociology as a bourgeois subject was, at least in part, simply the outgrowth of the general judgement that academic scholarship, teaching and research were structured in the interests of the former propertied class and had to be transformed. However, two specific aspects of sociology also came into consideration. The first, that sociology was a foreign import, a form of cultural imperialism, will be explored further in a moment. The other stemmed from the fact that, as a discipline laying claim to the scientific study of social structure and the dynamics of social change, sociology appeared to be in direct competition with Marxism, the doctrinal basis of the Communist Party itself. This was accentuated by the political affiliations of some of the leading sociologists. Few of them were actually supporters of the Guomindang (the Nationalist Party, which had ruled China until the Japanese invasion of 1937, had then been involved in triangular armed struggles with the Japanese and with the CCP, and had finally lost the civil war in 1949 and fled to Taiwan). But many prominent sociologists were members of the Democratic League, a reformist party which (along with several other 'democratic parties') was allowed after 1949 to coexist in a state of uneasy subordination to the CCP. When leading sociologists attempted to promote the revival of their subject with the argument that sociology could make useful contributions to the development of Marxism, they may if anything have made things worse for themselves by drawing further attention to the potential tension between sociology and Marxism (Wong Siu-lun 1979: 109).

While the academic discipline called 'sociology' was banned as bourgeois, the study of Chinese society continued in other forms. The development of an explicitly 'Marxist sociology' had begun in the early 1920s when CCP members had taught it in Beijing and Shanghai, but this was suppressed by the Nationalist government after 1927 (Cheng and So 1983). The adaptation of Marxism to Chinese circumstances continued in areas controlled by the CCP, and Marxism–Leninism in its Maoist interpretation provided the conceptual framework for the study of Chinese society, while Mao's own participatory investigations into the conditions of life of peasants[8] provided the model for research practice. This continued after the CCP gained power in 1949. Wong Siu-lun (1979) argues that what had been abolished in the 1950s was merely one version of sociology, the western academic version, based on the institutionalization of specialized professional research seeking theoretical synthesis and claiming to exercise critical autonomy. The Chinese Communists established a different version of sociological work, one which L. C. Young (1974) described as 'mass sociology', in which thousands of partially trained amateurs (Wong called them 'bare-foot sociologists') collectively conduct social investigations aimed at solving particular social problems under the guidance of the Communist leadership. Academic sociology was condemned as elitist; 'mass sociology' was seen not only as egalitarian, sharing social knowledge among much wider social circles, but also as a more appropriate use of scarce resources in a developing society. Education in Marxism–Leninism–Mao Zedong Thought and participation in social investigations produced a population with a strong consciousness of the workings of society, as if 'everyone was a practicing sociologist' (Cheng and So 1983: 479).

The end of the Cultural Revolution and the shift of power to the more pragmatic and technocratic leadership of Deng Xiaoping heralded the reintroduction of specialized sociology. From 1979, the Chinese Sociological Association and provincial associations were re-established; an Institute of Sociology was set up in the new Chinese Academy of Social Sciences, most provinces and metropolitan cities have their own sociology research institute within their academies of social science, and many universities have established departments of sociology (Dai 1993). The twenty-seven-year break in the teaching of sociology left many problems in staffing these departments and institutes with trained sociologists. A survey carried out for the State Education Commission in 1986 by sociologists at Nankai University in Tianjin attempted to quantify the demand for sociology graduates over the period of the Seventh Five-Year Plan (1986–90), including the projected requirements of academies of science, Party Schools, journalism and publishing, administrative departments, large enterprises and educational institutions, and concluded that the country's capacity to fill the demand was very low (Investigation Group 1989). None the less, the reconstruction of specialized sociology has proceeded apace, and the published output of Chinese sociologists is now very considerable, covering a wide range of empirical research areas as well as theoretical discussions. A number of sociology journals are now published and several hundred monographs in various areas of sociology have appeared in print.

The revival of sociology in the 1980s was accompanied by considerable discussion of the discipline's western origins. As mentioned earlier, the fact that sociology had originated in the imperialist West had been another stick to beat it with during the Anti-Rightist campaign of 1957. Not that it was a completely new issue even then: the extent to which China could or should adopt western intellectual categories and procedures had been a matter of controversy since the mid-nineteenth century. Some had argued that western imports could be restricted to the area of technology, in the belief that western military superiority rested merely on technical factors, while the essence of Chinese culture could be maintained intact. Others maintained that Chinese culture was irretrievably moribund, and that only complete 'westernization' could enable China to rebuild its power and stave off imperial conquest (as if this cultural westernization would not itself be a kind of conquest). Sociologists and anthropologists were exposed to this problem in an acute form, since they had to decide whether the theories and concepts which had been developed in Europe and America to explain and understand the social patterns of liberal industrial societies could also be used to grapple with the problems of China's overwhelmingly rural and traditional society. The sociology courses set up by Americans in the 1920s and 1930s and the translations of American textbooks of sociology appeared to Chinese like Fei Xiaotong to offer little help in the understanding of China's social structure or social problems, and so they set out to try to create a Chinese sociology. Communist intellectuals, on the other hand, decided that Marxism (another western import) had more potential as a framework that could be adapted both for the understanding of China's problems and for their solution, and that there was no need for western imperialist sociology.

Those who took part in the revival of sociology in the 1980s thus had to steer a difficult course, to avoid reopening the attack on their subject as either anti-Marxist or anti-Chinese or both. Hence the appeal of a tendency in Chinese sociology which goes under the slogan of 'the sinification of sociology'. Throughout the 1980s, debates took place in conferences and journals over the possibility of creating a specifically 'Chinese sociology', one that would be best suited to understanding the specific character of Chinese society and its problems, and able to guide its leaders and citizens along the correct course of social development. It would be inappropriate here to try to give a fuller account of these debates,[9] though some of the specific features that are supposed to distinguish Chinese society from others will be discussed later in this book. It is worth pointing out, however, that such an attempt to 'indigenize' sociology is by no means unusual in developing societies.[10] Some contributors to the debate over sinification also looked forward to a future stage of globalization, in which Chinese sociologists would engage in mutual dialogue with sociologists across the world in a common endeavour to build a global sociology (Chan Hoiman 1993).

This brings us directly back to the second question posed earlier: how can western students who want to engage in the study of Chinese society make use of Chinese sociology? More generally, what sources can the western student of Chinese society use?

In the first place, this question concerns the accessibility of the writings of Chinese sociologists, and has an obvious answer. This book is written in English, and directed towards non-specialist, English-reading students. The writings of Chinese sociologists are mostly written in Chinese, and relatively few of them are translated. Even publications in Chinese are not easy for outsiders to come by. They are not widely marketed outside China, and are sometimes not even widely available within China. Specialist libraries in the West have holdings of the journals published by academies of social sciences as well as some of the books published in China. The distribution of such materials can also depend on personal contacts between Chinese and western sociologists.

However, the propagation of Chinese sociology outside China is developing along various channels. Some Chinese writings are translated in China and published in English; the journal *Social Sciences in China* contains translations of selected articles from the Chinese publication of the same name. A useful translation service is provided by the American-published journal *Chinese Sociology and Anthropology*, in which western and Chinese experts co-operate to provide selected translations on specific themes. Another channel, growing in importance, is the physical mobility of Chinese sociologists outside China. Chinese sociologists attend conferences held in the West (so long as they can obtain a passport from the Chinese authorities, a visa from the host country's authorities, and funding for travel, none of which is guaranteed), and their papers are given in the conference language (often English) and published in conference proceedings. Chinese sociologists are awarded visiting fellowships in western countries, including those specifically earmarked for Chinese scholars under programmes of international scholarly exchange, and the research they do during their visits is often published in English. Chinese sociologists have also entered into collaborative research projects with western colleagues, the results of which are published in English or other western languages. Some Chinese sociologists have decided to pursue academic careers outside China, hold university posts in the United States, Australia or elsewhere, and may move relatively freely between China and their new place of work.

In the foregoing paragraphs I have assumed that 'Chinese' sociologists are those from the People's Republic of China. The question of 'which China' and the relation of the PRC to Chinese communities elsewhere will be taken up in the next chapter. Sociology is practised in Chinese places such as Hong Kong[11] and Taiwan and, for reasons deriving from British colonialism and American foreign policy, is more likely than that from the PRC to be published in English and become accessible to western scholars and students. There is in addition the research on Chinese society carried out by members of overseas Chinese communities, who may themselves be migrants or later generation descendants of migrants; in America, some of these 'American sociologists of Chinese descent' in 1981 set up the North American Chinese Sociologists Association (NACSA) to exchange information among themselves and to promote relationships with sociologists in China and south-east Asia.

The issue, however, is not only one of accessibility, but also of the political context in which such sociology is written and may be read. Despite the relative liberalization which made the reinstatement of sociology possible, sociological research in the PRC has remained subject to political supervision and to politically orientated funding constraints. Sociologists have been trained and continue to work within a framework of Marxism–Leninism–Mao Zedong Thought, and this influences their use of theoretical concepts and their interpretation of research results. Research topics tend to be chosen with an eye to what the authorities require and permit, especially as sociology was readmitted as a legitimate discipline solely in order to investigate problems facing the society. This does have the advantage that approved research projects should gain the co-operation of relevant organizations, such as branches of government ministries, units of local government and other kinds of work-units, but it does constrain sociologists to operate within a framework of official discourse. Research methods are influenced partly by a prevailing scientistic (or positivistic) philosophy of science, partly by a concern to use scarce resources effectively, and partly by the need not to overstep political limits; thus there is a tendency to rely on large-scale sample surveys rather than on research within an ethnographic or interactionist framework (Rosen and Chu 1987). Western sociology is referred to sparingly and selectively, partly because of limited access to it on the part of Chinese sociologists, who are faced with the reverse problems of language, funds, and knowledge discussed above, as well as political censorship. Increasing communication and exchange of personnel with the West are gradually easing some of these constraints, though the direction of change is not all one way. Political control over the activities of sociologists increased for a while after the military repression of the large-scale popular protests in 1989, in which students and scholars as well as other sectors of the urban population were heavily involved.

Political influences on sociology are by no means confined to China and are also evident in liberal democratic societies. Interpretative frameworks within sociology tend to move alongside shifts in the political climate, and research funding is also affected by political and commercial interests. However, a public commitment to freedom of speech and scholarship, sometimes written into constitutional or legislative proclamations and upheld by relatively autonomous universities, permits a greater degree of pluralism in sociological writing than is possible in China. If anything, western sociology is faced with the opposite problem of extreme diversity of sociological perspectives, whose proponents talk past or ignore each other rather than advance sociological understanding through mutually beneficial dialogue. The fact remains that western sociology has the capacity to be critical of official doctrine or hegemonic discourses, and can publish research results which run counter to the interests of the powerful. This is more difficult in China, where this critical task is taken up more often by journalists in the genre of reportage than by sociologists.[12]

The upshot of this discussion is that there are some limitations to the extent to which western sociologists can rely on indigenously produced sociology for their understanding of Chinese society. None the less, much of the research of Chinese sociologists is invaluable, and I will make as much use of it as possible. References will be restricted to those works of Chinese sociologists which are reasonably widely accessible in English, and can therefore be consulted by interested readers. Those who do follow up this expanding literature will be in a position to judge it for themselves. In doing so they will be engaging in transnational dialogue and cultural globalization.

The other main kind of source which will form the basis for this book consists of the writings of sociologists from outside China who have specialized in the study of Chinese society. They, too, have faced difficulties in conducting research on China. In the pre-communist period, some significant research was carried out by missionary-sociologists and others, and their writings are still often referred to. Since then, for much of the period up to the death of Mao, China was simply inaccessible to western researchers, and research had to be based on documentary sources available in the West. Sociologists also resorted to a technique which had been developed by specialists in Soviet studies, namely interviewing Chinese émigrés in such places as Hong Kong and America, and some valuable work came out of this approach (Parish and Whyte 1978; Chan et al. 1984; Whyte and Parish 1984), though the representativeness of such informants remains questionable. From the late 1970s, this constraint was eased, but western sociologists have still had to work predominantly under official permission and supervision (Wolf 1987: 28–56). Those who work in China under official programmes of scholarly exchange must receive an official invitation from an academic institution, which presupposes an acceptance of their research project. Collaborative research can face the western researcher with problems of accommodation to an official discourse with which he or she has little sympathy; Greenhalgh (1994a: 9) for example, conducting research on the one-child family policy,[13] states that her Chinese 'co-researchers were clearly part of the dominant discourse and practice. Employed in a prestigious, state-run university, their role was not to produce independent evaluations of the merit of fertility regulation, but to assist the state in its policy efforts.'

It would, however, be wrong to over-stress the contrast between a Chinese sociology incorporated into the state policy process and a western one orientated to the unrestricted search for truth and enlightenment; to the extent that sociological research in the West is state-funded, it too is subject to political pressures in the identification of thematic priorities. Western research on Chinese society finds itself in a particularly politicized situation, which the reader must decipher as best he or she can. Although many sociologists have maintained a detached or critical stance, social scientific writing on China (as elsewhere) has sometimes had in common with journalism a tendency to respond to short-term shifts in the political agenda. I have already mentioned the '1949 barrier' with the widespread assumption that the PRC represents an entirely new society. A swing to the opposite assumption, that essentially nothing has changed and that what appear as communist patterns are really just continuous with the past, based perhaps on inherited cultural traits that are essentially Chinese, would be equally tendentious. An example is found in the interpretation of the Great Proletarian Cultural Revolution. Many writers in the early phases of the Cultural Revolution saw it as truly democratic movement aiming to continue the fundamental transformation of Chinese society and culture, whereas in the last decade or so the consensus has crystallized that, as the Chinese leadership itself puts it, the Cultural Revolution was ten years of complete disaster, and it is very difficult to escape the discourse that has been erected on this judgement (Gao 1994). Similarly, the events of June 1989, when detachments of the People's Liberation Army were sent in to suppress by force the 'democracy movement' in and around Tiananmen Square, gave rise to a volte-face in the journalistic approach to the Chinese economic reforms and their supposed architect Deng Xiaoping, and also to considerable academic discussion on the significance of the 'massacre' (or whatever one calls it, the term chosen symbolically revealing the political stance of the speaker) for social scientific interpretation of Chinese society (Dirlik and Prazniak 1990). The question posed by one analyst, 'do we need to reassess the Chinese regime after the events of mid 1989?' (Brugger 1990), also carries considerable ideological ambiguity.

Overview

All in all, the study of Chinese society is more than your average minefield for the unwary, and one ambition of this book is to help the student tread through it without the loss of too many limbs. This survey is also, however, necessarily selective. In the last few years there has been a small explosion of research in China by social scientists of all kinds, and it is now impossible for any one scholar to keep pace with it all. The following chapters attempt to provide an introduction to the main directions of research and interpretation in the main institutional areas of Chinese society. Chapter 2 considers the general scope of the phrase 'Chinese society', in historical, geographical and ethnic terms. China has a long history, it is often said, but how should we understand that history and the place of contemporary China in it? Is 'China' just the PRC, or should we also include Taiwan, Hong Kong, and the communities of overseas Chinese throughout the world? Are the Chinese people the same as 'the Han', who are supposed to make up over 90 per cent of the population of the PRC, and what is the place of the many 'minority nationalities' in Chinese society? Chapter 3 tackles the distinction between rural and urban society in China. Chinese society is often held to be unusual in having such a high proportion of the population living in the countryside. But what are the main dimensions of urban–rural difference? Have they been exaggerated or diminished in recent times? What are the reasons for the great migration to the cities which has been occurring in the last decade? What significance does it have for social change in China?

Chapter 4 takes up the relationship of individual, group and society in Chinese culture. Are Chinese assumptions about individual and society as distinctive as is often claimed? How should traditional Confucian social thought be interpreted in sociological terms? Has the Communist regime transformed these relationships and created a new type of Chinese person? Is Chinese society becoming more individualistic? This leads on in chapter 5 to a consideration of the institution that is frequently held to be the core of Chinese society, the family. To what extent have traditional patriarchal structures been transformed in the twentieth century? How have relations between the sexes and the generations changed? Does the family still play the same role in the reproduction of social structure as it once did?

Chapter 6 provides an overview of the main structures of economic and political power in Chinese society. Has the Communist regime transformed the structure of power? What are the main forms of ownership and control of material resources in China, and how does this relate to state power? Has the reach of the state into people's lives been extended during the twentieth century, and is this reach diminishing once again in the period of economic reforms? Chapter 7 continues the theme of the restructuring of social power in the study of cultural change, cultural continuity and cultural revolution. The Communist Party attempted to remodel Chinese culture through control over the education system and the mass media and aimed to revolutionize the common sense of the society, destroying the cultural hegemony of former dominant groups and classes. How successful was this project of cultural transformation? What are the main cultural tendencies in the recent era of greater liberalization and exposure to global culture outside China? Chapter 8 examines the changing class structure and patterns of inequality in China. Which were the dominant classes before the revolution and were they destroyed? How should we understand the structure of inequality in the different phases of post-revolutionary society? Which are the important resources that are unequally distributed, and how is this inequality maintained or changed?

Chapter 9, finally, raises some general questions concerning the overall structure of Chinese society at the turn of the century. Is it becoming more pluralistic and differentiated? Is there emerging a segregation of economic and political power and institutions, often held to be the underlying structure of modern capitalism? Can we see the emergence of 'civil society'? What is the relationship between 'public' and 'private' realms in contemporary Chinese society?

Further Reading

Preston (1998) provides a critical discussion of the changing place of Pacific Asia in global society. Wong Siu-lun (1979) is a thoughtful study of the position of sociology in China from pre-revolutionary times to the Cultural Revolution, while *International Sociology*, vol. 8, no. 1 (1993) contains a symposium of papers on sociology in China since the post-Mao reforms.

Web-sites

There are many useful Internet web-sites with information on contemporary China. The following are some of the gateway sites providing access to a wide range of detailed home pages:

Australian National University Asian Studies WWW Virtual Library:
http://coombs.anu.edu.au/WWWVL-AsianStudies.html

China Education and Research Network:
http://www.cernet.edu.cn/

China Resources:
http://www.chron.com/voyager/china/resource/

Internet Guide for China Studies
Institute of Chinese Studies, University of Heidelberg:
http://www.univie.ac.at/Sinologie/netguide.htm

2
Which China?
Whose China?

What are we to mean by 'China', 'the Chinese' and 'Chinese society'? How are we to identify and to put limits on what we are talking about? These are questions of geography (where is China the place?), territoriality (where is China the state?), ethnicity (who are the Chinese?) and culture (how do the Chinese live?). And in addition they are questions of history, since the answers to all of the above vary over time. Societies exist in history; social continuity and social change can only be conceptualized in frameworks of time. Although this is true of any society, it is especially salient for China, where claims to continuity stretch over longer expanses of time than is the case for many other societies, where written and standardized historical records exist for longer periods than elsewhere, and where (it has been argued) the tradition of dead generations weighs heavier on the minds of the living. For many, both in China and outside it, this is the core of China's predicament: that its long history, both in reality and in imagination, is a prison from which it is very difficult (but essential) to escape (Jenner 1994).

The aim in this chapter is to show that the sociological problem of social continuity and social change in contemporary Chinese society can be raised in a number of different ways, depending on the conceptual framework within which that society is historically located. It is a kind of consciousness-raising exercise, a sensitizing to a range of concepts which are often used to identify Chinese society and the patterns of its past, present and future: barbarism and civilization;

order and chaos; tradition and modernity; old society and new society; feudalism, capitalism and socialism; empire and republic; unity and disunity (or diversity); majority and minority; oriental and occidental. These concepts, moreover, are not just different ways of describing continuity and change in Chinese society, they are also imbued with social values and political programmes, so that arguments about the appropriate framework for understanding Chinese society are often also arguments about how China should be changed.

Dynastic history

For nearly two thousand years, the conventional way of structuring Chinese history was in terms of a succession of dynasties, imperial royal houses who gave their names to their periods of rule. Nowadays modern historians treat these names merely as convenient markers of periods of history, so the student will get used to seeing references to 'Tang times' or 'Song commercial expansion' (rather as English history talks of Plantagenets or Tudors). For the ruling classes of imperial China, however, the idea of dynasty contained an entire social theory, based on assumptions about the normality and legitimacy of imperial rule (Loewe 1966). Periods of unity and stability, when imperial authority was generally recognized by the whole population, when food was plentiful and the people satisfied, when the borders of the empire were secure and the barbarians beyond the walls were subdued, were treated as the normal state of affairs. The intended effect was to lend legitimacy to the royal house that could maintain unity and prosperity, a legitimacy resting on the perpetuation of an ancient form of government with its roots in a golden age which, though it could never be entirely reborn, could at least serve as a model to be aspired to.

This way of understanding history was, as Jenner (1994) stresses, backward-looking. It did not recognize change, just cyclical repetition. As a theory of legitimacy, however, it did allow for rebellion. The ruling dynasty could lose the Mandate of Heaven by poor government, which was indicated by bad harvests, floods and other natural disasters, civil strife and foreign invasion. In such circumstances, rebellion was justified and the establishment of a new, more capable and vigorous dynasty was legitimate. This model of regime succession has continued to have resonances in more recent times. It could provide a framework for understanding the decay of the Qing dynasty in the nineteenth century, which proved itself incapable of dealing satisfactorily with internal rebellion and foreign aggression. It could legitimate the overthrow of that dynasty, even in traditional terms, and the subsequent attempts to create a new stable and competent form of government. Even the Communist victory in 1949 and the re-establishment of unity, peace and the beginnings of prosperity could be seen as the early days of a new and vigorous dynasty. Despite their Marxist theorizing and their rhetoric of a new society, the Communists have often been ambivalent about the idea that they are a new dynasty. The traditional model also provides a language for critique of the Communist regime; during the 1989 protest movement, for example, the accusation that the Communist leaders were behaving like emperors carried the additional implication that they were bad emperors who were not ruling in the people's interest (Calhoun 1994).

The new orthodoxy: Marxism

If dynastic history emphasized continuity and repetition, the Marxist theory of history and society which provides the official doctrine of the ruling Communist Party stresses discontinuity and progress. Marxism was first heard of in China in the early years of the twentieth century, though among revolutionary opponents of the Manchu empire it initially faced strong competition from both nationalist and anarchist ideas. Marxist theories became more common in the discourse of younger intellectuals and students during the 1910s, when they were popularized by the magazine *New Youth*, and particularly after the Bolshevik revolution in Russia. The founding of the Chinese Communist Party in 1921 provided a forum for the discussion of Marxism, as a theory of history and society as well as a programme for revolutionary social change. With very few of the original writings of Marx or Engels available, Chinese Marxists had to come to terms with Leninist interpretations propagated as orthodox Marxism by representatives of the Comintern. Some leaders of the CCP, such as Secretary-General Chen Duxiu and, later, the so-called Returned Students who had studied in the Soviet Union, completely accepted the main tenets of Leninism, which implied that material conditions in China were too undeveloped to allow for a socialist revolution and that peasant rebellion had little to contribute to revolutionary struggle. Others, and most notably Mao Zedong, came to the conclusion that Marxism had to be adapted to the specific circumstances of China. With the rise to dominance of Mao at the Zunyi conference in 1935, his 'sinified Marxism' became the new orthodoxy, at first within the party and then, from 1949, within the People's Republic as a whole, although this did not prevent conflicts between alternative interpretations of the implications of Marxism for Chinese policy and development. The orthodoxy of Marxism meant that for some decades to come it provided the concepts and language within which arguments over social interpretation and struggles over political programmes had to be carried on.

Although Marx himself denied towards the end of his life that his analysis of European history could be generalized to the whole world, orthodox Marxism of both the Soviet and Chinese types saw history as a fixed sequence of five modes of production: primitive communal, slave, feudal, capitalist and socialist. Chinese Marxists had to decide how to adapt this periodization to the facts of Chinese history. Complex historical debates have taken place among Chinese historians over when, if ever, primitive communism gave way to slavery and slavery to feudalism, which need not concern us here. More important is the identification of the stage Chinese society had reached in more recent times. Mao accepted the orthodox sequence and argued that China had been a feudal society until the incursion of western imperialism after 1840, when it had become a 'semi-feudal, semi-colonial' society (Mao 1967: II, 309). Orthodox theory required that societies pass through the stage of capitalism, during which the forces of production are developed and class antagonisms intensified, before socialism comes on the agenda. Chinese Marxism therefore had to identify elements of capitalism in China before the establishment of the PRC; for some it was sufficient that western imperialism had stimulated capitalist production and trade, but for others it was important to show that capitalism could have developed in China even without this foreign stimulation. Mao himself was equivocal on the matter (Knight 1985a); in earlier writings he had accepted that a stagnant China had only been pushed into capitalist development by foreign intervention, but in the 1950s revised versions contained the idea that a gradually commercializing Chinese economy would have allowed the 'sprouts of capitalism' to grow anyway, and Chinese historians expended considerable efforts to find evidence for these sprouts as early as the Ming dynasty.

The importance of correctly assessing the pre-revolutionary mode of production in China was that it provided doctrinal justification for the building of socialism after 1949. However, there has been little consensus within the Communist Party over how socialism should be built. It is convenient to identify three 'visions of socialism' (Solinger 1984b), between which there have been debates and even violent struggles. The first (which could be labelled 'Stalinist' and which drew on the experience of the Soviet Union) held that the transition to socialism occurs when private property-owners are expropriated and the means of production taken into the hands of the whole people and controlled by the state, whose historical task is to construct a rationally planned economy, continue to develop the productive forces and thereby lay the foundations for an egalitarian communist society. The second (which could be called 'market socialism' and in the early stages drew on the attempts in Yugoslavia to construct an alternative model of socialism to that of the USSR) saw this programme as premature in a poor and underdeveloped society such as China's, and believed that the transition to socialism is a long drawn-out process requiring co-operation with bourgeois forces and a mixture of capitalist and socialist methods to develop the productive forces, especially the use of market mechanisms to ensure incentives and the rational allocation of scarce material resources. The third (which was essentially indigenous to China and can be labelled 'Maoist') was based on the assumptions that the transition to socialism is fraught with contradictions and potential reverses, that the expropriation of the propertied classes does not spell the end of class divisions, that even the Communist Party bureaucracy which administers the planned economy has the potential to become a new exploiting class in conflict with the working masses, and that the revolution has to be renewed or 'continued' (Starr 1979) to prevent the restoration of capitalism (Knight 1985b).

These different visions of socialism (and their associated interpretations of history) have varied in their predominance at different times since 1949. In the early days of the People's Republic, when the Communists were still establishing and consolidating their rule, elements of both central planning and market socialism could be seen. The mid-1950s saw a rapid shift towards the collectivization of agriculture. Then in 1958 Mao launched the Great Leap Forward, a renewal of the revolution through a mobilization of the masses to take industrialization into their own hands (the enduring image is of peasants melting down their cooking pots to smelt iron in their yards). Considerable dislocation and widespread famine ensued, the results of which could even be identified in the skewed age distribution of the population in subsequent decades, and the proponents of central planning regained the upper hand. A second burst of Maoist populism to continue the revolution came in 1966 with the Great Proletarian Cultural Revolution, with its attack on experts, technocrats and planners, who were often criticized for 'taking the capitalist road'. The

Maoist faction, with its centre in the Shanghai 'Gang of Four', retained control until 1976, when Mao died and his adherents were overthrown. Since 1978, when a major programme of economic reform was set in motion, the dominant vision of socialism ('Socialism with Chinese characteristics') has been that of market socialism, with the means of production still predominantly (even if only technically) in the hands of the central state or local governments, and market mechanisms of prices and wages increasingly used to stimulate efficiency and growth.

Marxism continues to provide a framework for official statements of strategy and for ideological debates. The period of the Cultural Revolution, now judged as 'ten years of disaster', is often attributed to the residues of 'feudal' thinking in the party and among the people. The aim of the post-Mao leadership is 'socialist modernization' (see below) and this is held to require a pragmatic appropriation of the techniques of more advanced societies, including those of capitalism. A key source of inspiration and legitimation is now found in the speeches of Deng Xiaoping, who died in February 1997. During his 'southern journey' (nanxun) of early 1992, Deng spoke of the need to experiment with a variety of methods that would stimulate economic growth. 'Deng Xiaoping Theory' was endorsed by Jiang Zemin at the 15th National Congress of the Chinese Communist Party in September 1997 as a continuation of the sinification of Marxism begun by Mao Zedong. Although 'Leftist' critics of market socialism have been much weakened, they have not been eliminated, and adherents of both Maoism and of a planned economy can use Marxist categories to argue that the present economic line is tantamount to the restoration of capitalism.[1]

Orient and Occident

The orthodox Marxism of the five modes of production appears to be a universal theory of history which would apply throughout the world. Knight (1983) has argued that Mao's 'sinification of Marxism' accepted that Marx had formulated universal laws of the development of human society, but that these laws need to be specified in detail for the conditions of particular national societies. But there is another line of argument that can be derived from Marx's writings, that appears to challenge the universality of the theory more decisively, namely that oriental societies were traditionally characterized by a quite different economic and political structure from those of Europe and that the sequence of historical stages which he and Engels had identified in European history might therefore not apply to the ancient civilizations of Asia. At several points, Marx even mentions the idea of an 'Asiatic mode of production' (Marx 1970 [1859]: 21), and this notion has generated, in China and elsewhere, considerable debate and argument (Brook 1989). Influenced by an image, widespread among European scholars, of Asiatic society as static and unchanging, with vast numbers of self-sufficient local communities mired in tradition and ruled over by a despotic government, Marx formulated the idea that the material conditions prevailing in Asia, and especially the (supposed) lack of private property in land, prevented the dialectic dynamic found in Europe. China (and India) could not break through into the capitalist mode of production (which was a precondition for the revolutionary transition to socialism) on their own; they would need to be prodded into change from without, by the spread of capitalism through imperialist penetration or conquest.

Marx's earliest writings on Asia were based on some knowledge of Mughal India. As time went on, however, he tended to generalize the idea of 'Asiatism' to encompass a variety of societies which were not even geographically located in Asia, such as those of Mexico and Peru before the Spanish conquest, and this generalization has continued to plague later Marxist discussions of the Asiatic mode of production. It was carried to even further lengths by the non-Marxist Wittfogel (1957) in his idea of 'oriental despotism'. Anderson's (1974) conclusion, that as a contribution to historical scholarship the notion of an Asiatic mode should be entirely rejected, seems well justified. In the Chinese context, however, it has continued to be debated, in part at least as a coded way of pursuing political arguments (Rapp 1989). Reformers have from time to time resurrected the idea of the Asiatic mode of production as a way of criticizing the legacy of despotic state control which they believe to be evident in China. It can be a relatively risk-free means of implying the need for greater political reform and democratization, although the party authorities have sometimes felt under threat from such debate and banned discussion of the Asiatic mode. The themes of the Asiatic mode, and particularly the emphasis on state control of irrigation and river control as the basis of oriental despotism, were given wide public expression in the popular television series *Heshang* (River Elegy), first shown in 1987–8.[2]

The Marxist concept of an Asiatic mode of production is merely one version of a deep-rooted tendency in European thought to contrast oriental and occidental cultures and societies. Marx himself was only building on a long tradition, as conveyed by such writers as

Montesquieu, Adam Smith and Hegel. The critique of this discourse stimulated by Edward Said (1978), even though Said was mainly concerned with western writing on the Islamic world, should put us on our guard. In sociology, the contrast of western and eastern society, or at the very least the uniqueness of the West, was a fundamental tenet of the work of Max Weber, and given its clearest expression in the introduction to his collected essays on the sociology of religion (Weber 1930 [1904–5]: 13–31), which contain his studies of the religions of China and India as well as the essays on the Protestant ethic and the spirit of capitalism. His assumption that the West developed a distinctive form of rationality and hence of rational capitalism, which has brought about the dominance of Europe and America in the world, continues to be discussed in western historical sociology (Schluchter 1981), though has also been subjected to criticism from a variety of perspectives.[3]

A distinctively sociological approach to the issue of 'orientalism' has been taken by Jack Goody.[4] Goody views the 'East–West' question from the standpoint of an anthropologist with his fieldwork roots in sub-Saharan Africa, among a tribal people with little in the way of an elaborated state or class structure. Turning then to issues of comparative and historical sociology, Goody sees greater contrasts between African cultures, on the one hand, and the agrarian civilizations of Europe and Asia on the other. These 'Eurasian' societies developed stratified class systems and state formations as part of the bronze age urban revolutions, along with the introduction of literacy, metallurgy, plough agriculture, the wheel, and systematic written forms of knowledge. Because 'the major societies of Eurasia were fired in the same crucible' (Goody 1996: 226), they have certain similarities when contrasted with sub-Saharan Africa, despite the considerable differences among them which scholars of various kinds have fastened on. There are similarities in their kinship systems, deriving in part from the interest that parents have in ensuring that their children (both sons and daughters) preserve or improve their position in the stratification hierarchy (Goody 1990), and in other aspects of their culture, such as their cuisines or their cultural use of flowers, which reflect their more highly stratified societies. Not that the differences between the oriental and occidental societies of Eurasia are insignificant; but they are variations on common themes. In particular, Goody is highly suspicious of both culturalist and institutionalist attempts to explain the greater development of the West in recent centuries; there is something to explain, but the relative development of the East and the West should rather be seen as swings of the pendulum. In a longer time frame, the eastern cultures, especially China, were in any case, until about five hundred years ago or less, wealthier and had more elaborate patterns of culture and knowledge than the societies of Europe. Once again, different historical perspectives cast the nature of Chinese society in a different light.[5]

Modernization

The contrast between a dynamic West and an unchanging East is part of a mode of thought that gave rise in the sociology of the 1950s and 1960s to 'modernization theory'. If the cyclical repetition of dynastic history was the orthodoxy of imperial China, and the revolutionary succession of modes of production was the orthodoxy of Chinese communism, modernization theory became the orthodoxy of western and especially American sociology, as a sociological theory of history in general and of Chinese history in particular. Somewhat ironically, the concept of modernization is now also fundamental to the new doctrinal orthodoxy of the leaders of the Chinese reform programme.

There are many different versions of modernization theory, which cannot be discussed in detail here (Harrison 1988). Most such theories posit a basic distinction between two forms of society, the 'traditional' and the 'modern'. Traditional society, as the name implies, rested on the passing on from generation to generation of traditional forms of behaviour, which gained authority from having 'always been done that way'. Somehow, within the interstices of this traditional society, arose the idea that things could be done differently. 'Modernity' signifies a radical break with tradition, a casting off of chains, a lifting of anchors, and a striking out into an uncertain future. It requires people to refuse to accept the authority of the past, and to be prepared to use reason to think through alternatives and decide on what appears to offer the best prospects of success in coping with whatever problems face them. This emphasis on reason and experiment, in some versions of modernization theory, places science and scientific technology at the core of the process of modernization. The increasing salience of the social institutions that promote a scientific view of the world, the modern university and research institute, and the knowledge professions of engineering, medicine and the like, is central to modernization, as is the decline of those social institutions that transmitted and upheld traditional authority, such as traditional religion and hereditary leadership. Beyond that, the growth of the competitive market economy, which displaces traditional methods of meeting economic needs and places a premium on the discovery of new needs and new techniques of meeting them, and of rational bureaucratic organization, which establishes the search for the most efficient way of managing collective human affairs at the expense of procedures hallowed by time, is also characteristic of modernity. Most abstractly, Parsons generalized Tönnies's distinction between *Gemeinschaft* and *Gesellschaft* into his account of the 'pattern variables', with orientations towards particularistic, affective, diffuse and ascriptive features predominant in traditional societies, and universalism, affective-neutrality, specificity and achievement-orientation predominant in modern ones. The latter orientations imply also a highly differentiated and complex institutional structure in modern societies, with individuals capable of switching flexibly between the requirements of roles in specific institutions and dealing with others only on the basis of characteristics relevant to that particular institutional context.

The emergence of modernization theory in American studies of China can be seen at its clearest in the work of Marion Levy (1963 [1949], 1966) in sociology and Levenson (1958–65) in history. A basic contrast is drawn by both writers between 'traditional Chinese society', which had existed for more than two thousand years and which was maintained in essentially the same form until the mid-nineteenth century, and Chinese society since that time, which had been undergoing ever more thorough processes of transformation. Traditional China was a highly developed agrarian civilization, with complex institutions capable of maintaining themselves intact and providing as high and as reliable a standard of living for its population as existed in any pre-industrial society. Its political structure was able to rule over a large territory and people, to maintain internal peace and harmony through a complex legal framework administered by a well-organized and differentiated bureaucracy. Its economic structure was based on highly efficient labour-intensive family farming and handicrafts, with state-controlled infrastructure and famine relief in case of bad harvests, a wide range of crafts producing luxury goods for a relatively small upper class, and an increasingly commoditized and hierarchical market system. Its cultural system was based on respect for literacy and scholarship, and upheld a complex tradition of philosophical and practical learning concerning the place of humanity in the cosmos and the nature of social and political life. None of this precluded change and development: sophisticated modernization theorists like Levenson and Levy knew better than to accept the old European image of unchanging China. Yet this change was always 'change within tradition', to use a phrase popularized by the doyen of American historians of China, John

K. Fairbank, and his colleagues (Fairbank et al. 1965). The strength of tradition could be seen either in intellectual or in social structural terms. In intellectual terms, which was the main focus for Levenson, tradition was upheld by a belief in the essential rightness of the Chinese way of life and philosophy, as enshrined in the ancient books which formed the basis for the education of rulers and bureaucrats. In terms of social structure, which was the main focus for Levy, tradition was maintained by the predominance of kinship as the key institution of Chinese society, so that particularistic and diffuse commitments to kin defined the rightness of behaviour in all social contexts, and prevented the development of the universalistic and functionally specific rational attitudes of modernity.

The main factor which undermined traditional China, according to this interpretation, was the intrusion of the already modernizing West. 'Pre-modern social changes' (Rozman 1981: 484ff), especially the growth of population in the eighteenth century coupled with the failure of government to adapt adequately to population growth and the increasing commercialization of the economy, meant that even without the western intrusion the traditional institutions would have had to change. But the incursion of western armed force and enforced trade stimulated the beginnings of an unstable period of transition, followed by a series of attempts at modernization, first by the last imperial rulers in two phases of reform from above in 1898 and 1905, then by the Nationalist government of Chiang Kai-shek from 1927, and finally by the Chinese Communists after 1949. The failure of the earlier of these attempts was reflected in the increasing backwardness of the Chinese economy and the inability of its rulers to maintain the unity and integrity of the state. War and civil war opened China up to uncontrollable and unpredictable external influences, even the possibility of conquest. The success of the Chinese Communists in establishing a stable regime initiated a new, modernizing drive, but one which retained many pre-modern elements: a refusal or inability to incorporate many aspects of the institutional framework of the most modernized societies, such as a democratic political system, a competitive market economy, a public sphere allowing open exchange of information and ideas, and a modern system of education and research, and a relatively undifferentiated social structure which, according to the theories of Talcott Parsons, implies a low adaptive capacity to an uncertain environment. According to the conceptual framework of modernization theory, Chinese society at the death of Mao remained relatively backward and unmodernized, the transition to modernity incomplete (Rozman 1981).

Modernization theory has, of course, not gone unchallenged within the sociology of development and the theory of social change. Nor has the use of modernization theory as a framework for understanding history and social change in China passed without criticism. The very dichotomy of 'tradition' and 'modernity' has been held to overemphasize the stability of Chinese society before the incursion of the West, over-stress the impact of that incursion, and underestimate the potential diversity of paths of social change (Cohen 1984). Marxism has been at the forefront of critiques of modernization theory, and the two are often taken as incompatible. It is therefore ironic that the concept of modernization is now a cornerstone of the Chinese regime's expressed programme for the future of China, and that modernization theory is given increasing attention by Chinese sociologists. Zhou Enlai first formulated the programme of the 'Four Modernizations' in 1964, but this did not become central to state policy until the reformers gained control after 1978. The 'Four Modernizations' slogan refers to modernization of agriculture, industry, science and technology and national defence. This catalogue appears to give privileged status to developments in the spheres of productive techniques and military technology, backed by the force of advanced science, and hence to be congruent with the materialism of Marxism. In western theory, too, modernization is sometimes defined as the institutionalization of the scientific and technological revolution (Rozman 1981: 3), and non-Marxist modernization theory can also rest on materialist premises (minus class struggle and the dialectic). Yet Chinese sociological reflections on modernization go way beyond this materialist starting-point, and see 'the development of science and technology as an impetus to the development of the whole society', a many-sided process involving 'the advancement of social organization and political democratization', 'the modernization of social values and ways of life', and 'changes in the forms of human settlement – urbanization' (Li Lulu 1989). Most recently, Chinese sociologists have begun to apply to the analysis of Chinese modernization the concept of structural differentiation which is directly derived from Parsonian and post-Parsonian versions of modernization theory (Li Hanlin 1991; Sun et al. 1995).[6]

Which Chinese society?

So far in this chapter we have considered different historical frameworks within which Chinese society, its continuity and change, can be situated. There remain a number of other questions concerning the identification of Chinese society, raised at the beginning of this chapter, all of which have a historical dimension, but also territorial and cultural dimensions. Is 'Chinese society' bounded by the territorial borders of the Chinese state, and if so which state, and at which period of history? Is membership in 'Chinese society' defined by an ethnic conception of 'Chineseness', in which case which or whose ethnic conception? These territorial and ethnic questions overlap, as is apparent if 'China' is conceived as the place occupied by people who see themselves as 'Chinese'. What then of the position of people who occupy part of that territory but do not see themselves, or who are not seen by others, as Chinese? The rest of this chapter is devoted to exploring these questions.

The question begins with the territorial borders of the People's Republic of China. The present-day borders, approximately the same as those of the imperial state of the Qing dynasty, are the result of a long process of expansion and consolidation of rule over the empire whose rulers considered it to be the 'Middle Kingdom', the centre of the civilized world. This expansion and consolidation involved coming to terms with peoples and rulers who did not define themselves as Chinese. Some non-Chinese people, such as the Mongols and the Manchus, conquered the middle kingdom and came to be the new rulers, often adopting Chinese ways of life (Eberhard 1966). In the case of others, such as the peoples who lived in the western parts of what is now the PRC, the empire treated local rulers and their peoples as tributary states and eventually incorporated them into the empire as provinces ruled from the capital. The large number of 'minority nationalities', discussed further below, live predominantly in those western regions.

The process of imperial expansion brought with it border disputes over territory and peoples, and many of these continue to the present day along the long inland frontier with states of the former Soviet Union, including Russia, and of central and south Asia. Many 'minority nationalities' live on both sides of the borders, and move regularly across them, especially traders and those pastoralists who lead nomadic lives. There are also two territories on the other, eastern side of China, which raise particular issues in relation to the identity of 'Chinese society', since they are inhabited by people many of whom do consider themselves and are considered by others to be 'Chinese', namely Taiwan and Hong Kong, and it is important to give some further consideration to these two situations.

Taiwan

Taiwan (along with the whole of China) is currently claimed by two governments, and its history over the past century has stamped its social institutions with distinctive characteristics. Settled in the seventeenth century by people from the neighbouring mainland province of Fujian, who also encountered native aboriginal populations, Taiwan was brought under imperial administration as a number of counties within that province. Following China's defeat in the Sino-Japanese war of 1894, Taiwan was ceded to Japan and remained a Japanese colony from 1895 to 1945, during which time it experienced considerable infrastructural and economic development under Japanese direction. The Japanese withdrew after their surrender, and were shortly afterwards replaced by the refugee government and supporters of the Nationalist Party (Guomindang), which had been defeated by the Communists in civil war. The 'mainlanders' established their domination over the island and its people, in the process bloodily repressing protests against their rule. They set up a one-party government which also claimed to be the government in exile of the whole of the 'Republic of China'. This claim was accepted by the international community led by the United States, which supported the Nationalists diplomatically (the Republic of China held a permanent place on the Security Council of the United Nations) and economically, in no small part because Taiwan was a useful anti-communist base for American operations in the Korean War. It was, of course, rejected by the Communist government of the PRC, which treated Taiwan as a rebel province, a part of the PRC temporarily under the control of the defeated side in the civil war in alliance with the capitalist enemy. In these geopolitical circumstances, Taiwan experienced considerable economic growth, becoming one of the major industrial and trading areas of East Asia (one of the 'four little dragons'). The anomaly of Taiwan's claim to represent the whole of China became, however, increasingly glaring, and the PRC took over Taiwan's seat in the UN in 1971, shortly followed by the visit of President Richard Nixon to China in 1972. Taiwan now occupies a peculiarly ambiguous situation in the world system, having very little diplomatic recognition and represented in other countries mostly by trade and cultural offices (Yahuda 1996). It remains a centre of economic power (Gold 1986), and an important source of inward investment into the PRC. Residents of Taiwan are now able to travel to the PRC and engage in economic co-operation with PRC enterprises. Rhetorically, the PRC government follows the policy of 'one country, two systems', periodically threatening to take over Taiwan by force, but also encouraging peaceful and friendly relations with its 'compatriots'. Within Taiwan, the authoritarian one-party system has relaxed to allow greater political pluralism (Tien and Chu 1996), and a spectrum of views is now expressed, from support for reunification with the PRC through maintenance of the status quo to outright independence as a separate nation-state (Cabestan 1996).

In the period up to 1978, when sociologists and anthropologists from outside China had little opportunity to conduct research within the PRC, Taiwan was often chosen as a site for investigation, partly in its own right, but partly also as a surrogate for the mainland, on the assumption that China was culturally and ethnically homogeneous and that Taiwan represented what Chinese society had been and might become without communist rule, a viewpoint which would be supported by GMD authorities. Since then, it has become unnecessary to use Taiwan for this purpose, and it has become possible to treat Taiwanese society as one variant (or many, given its own internal diversity) on Chinese themes, to study its specific features and distinct trajectory (Gold 1996), and to investigate economic, political and cultural interrelationships between Taiwan and other components of what is coming to be referred to as 'Greater China'.

Hong Kong

Hong Kong lies in the far south of China, at the mouth of the Pearl River. Hong Kong island appears to have been little settled in the early nineteenth century when traders, especially in opium and tea, chose the Pearl River as their point of access to Chinese markets. Resistance to such trade by the Chinese authorities was broken down by force in the first Opium War of 1840, and the British exacted a price in a treaty which ceded Hong Kong island to the British crown in perpetuity. Hong Kong became an important base for trading operations in South China, and fortunes were made by British companies based there. It was also a centre for Protestant missionary activity in southern China, and the residence for many years in the mid-nineteenth century of James Legge, the Scottish missionary and sinologist who made the Confucian classics accessible to the West in his series of translations and commentaries still used today. In 1898, with China increasingly weakened and defeated in wars, Britain took a 99-year lease on a stretch of mainland known from then on as the New Territories.

Other western countries took similar leases on Chinese territories at around the same time, all of which eventually found their way back into Chinese control over the years, except for Macao, a Portuguese colony.[7] Hong Kong and the New Territories remained primarily a trading port and a military base through the early part of the twentieth century. It was occupied by the Japanese during the Second World War, and retaken by Britain at the time of the Japanese surrender.

When the Communists gained control of the mainland, Hong Kong became a place of refuge for fleeing opponents of the regime, including a considerable number of capitalist businessmen, many of whom came from Shanghai (Wong 1988a). With their entrepreneurship and a large labour supply provided by other refugees from the mainland regime, backed by a free-trade, low-tax, British colonial policy, Hong Kong was built up during the 1950s to 1970s into a major urban economy based on manufacture and trade. This economic expansion continued into the 1980s and 1990s, though now mainly in commerce and financial markets, since manufacturing operations have mostly been transferred to Guangdong Province, where labour is cheaper and the economic reform policies of the PRC favourable to such investment. The New Territories, which used to be the agricultural hinterland for Hong Kong island, have now become increasingly urbanized, and Hong Kong imports much of its agricultural requirements from the mainland and elsewhere. In terms of average per capita income, Hong Kong is now one of the wealthiest places in the world, though its prosperity was dented somewhat by the problems experienced by Asian economies in the late 1990s. In 1984, with the end of the 99-year lease looming just thirteen years away, Britain and China signed an agreement that not just the New Territories, but also Hong Kong island, would revert to Chinese sovereignty, and this duly took place on 1 July 1997. Under the policy of 'one country, two systems', the Chinese government pledged to maintain Hong Kong's thriving economic and financial framework intact for fifty years from 1997, with consequences that will gradually become clear in the coming years.

With its distinctive history, Hong Kong society has developed in distinctive ways. As in the case of Taiwan, the New Territories became a research location for anthropologists who had no access to the mainland in the early decades of Communist rule, and some classic studies of Chinese peasants and the dynamics of village life were carried out (Baker 1968; J. M. Potter 1968). The urban society was also a focus for sociological research and, with the growth of sociology in the Hong Kong universities, analyses of the specific character of Hong Kong social structure were advanced. One of the most widely discussed theories was that of Lau Siu-kai (1984), who argued that Hong Kong was a 'minimally-integrated socio-political system', in which an atomistic society based on principles of 'utilitarianistic familism' coexisted uneasily with the bureaucracy of the colonial government. However, with the increasing integration over the last twenty years of the Hong Kong and southern Chinese economies, with the increasing salience of links between Hong Kong residents and their kinsfolk in the villages and towns of Guangdong Province and elsewhere, and with appointed representatives of the Chinese government now holding formal power in Hong Kong, it is increasingly unrealistic to treat Hong Kong as a separate social system, however much its distinctive features may be perpetuated into the future.[8]

Chinese overseas or overseas Chinese

Further problems of defining Chinese society are raised by the fact that many people of Chinese origin or Chinese descent live outside the territories of the People's Republic, Taiwan or Hong Kong. Migration beyond the Chinese borders (as contrasted with expansion, conquest and sinification of the conquered people) has a long history. Chinese traders settled all over south-east Asia from at least the fifteenth century, and this proceeded apace in the nineteenth and twentieth centuries (Fitzgerald 1972). The population expansion and social disturbances of the eighteenth and nineteenth centuries created pressure for migration and the industrialization of Europe and America provided opportunities. War and civil war in the twentieth century have also been the occasion for emigration. People of Chinese descent are now to be found all over the world, often occupying specific niches within the economies and societies of their place of residence. One estimate of the number of these 'ethnic Chinese' (*huaqiao*) puts the figure at approximately 55 million. Large numbers are citizens of states other than China, by birth or naturalization, but they often constitute a distinct ethnic group (though, as we will see below, the ethnic unity of the Chinese, whether in China or overseas, cannot be taken for granted and poses specific sociological problems), and many live in demarcated settlements such as the Chinatowns of such cities as London, New York, Vancouver, Manila or Yokohama.

The question arises of whether such people consider themselves, or are considered by others, to be ethnically Chinese and part of a Chinese society dispersed around the world. The question is complex and the answers, necessarily tentative, vary depending on which part of the globe one examines, whether Singapore, Malaysia, Canada, Britain, Hungary, and so on (Pan 1991; Wang Gungwu 1991; Benton and Pieke 1997). Part of the answer depends on the nature of social relationships between people of Chinese descent in the rest of the world and those living in China. Kinship relationships are often maintained or re-established, sometimes in the form of 'roots-seeking', sometimes in the classic form of migrants sending remittances to the folk back home, sometimes through contribution to the rebuilding of ancestral halls and village temples. Economic and trading links may be important, with considerable sums being invested by overseas Chinese in China since the opening of the economy to the outside world from 1978. Chinese people overseas may be drawn into the politics of the Chinese region, organizing and giving support to political parties or movements in China, Taiwan or Hong Kong. Many Chinese who left China in the early days of the Communist regime have been encouraged to return since the swing in policy away from radical Maoism. Finally, many Chinese such as business people or media communicators now lead cosmopolitan lives, moving freely from country to country as citizens of the world or servants of global capitalism.

Nationality and ethnicity

A final set of problems in defining 'Chinese society' concerns the questions of national identity and ethnic composition. Here is another minefield where it is necessary to tread warily. The official doctrine of the PRC, elements of which are widely repeated in general studies of China, holds that the Chinese population is composed of fifty-six 'nationalities' (*minzu*); every member of the population is allocated to one of these *minzu* and this classification is entered into each person's identity papers. The Han *minzu* contains the overwhelming majority of the population, around 92 per cent, and the other 8 per cent is made up of minority nationalities (*shaoshu minzu*) with populations ranging from a few million to a few hundred thousand. Most of these minority *minzu* are located in the remote and mountainous areas of western China, except for the Hui people (identified in relation to a presumed Muslim origin), who are found all over China. Minority nationalities are accorded specific rights under the Chinese constitution (though not the right to secession from the state), and are often treated in distinct ways under laws and regulations, such as the.regulations promoting the one-child family policy. The Chinese authorities claim to have progressive policies towards the development of minorities as well as the protection of their distinctive customs.

However, every part of this official picture is open to question and further analysis, as recent sociological discussions of ethnicity and nationalism would lead one to expect (Calhoun 1997; Jenkins 1997). The expansion of the Chinese empire to the west, north and south brought within the scope of Chinese rule a variety of 'peripheral' peoples (Harrell 1995) of different origins, languages and cultures. Over the centuries, as Harrell argues, these peoples have been the objects of various 'civilizing missions'. The Confucian rulers of the Middle Kingdom identified these peoples as more or less 'civilized' according to their degree of literary culture and their capacity for being transformed by Chinese rule. The Communist regime has continued this civilizing mission within a new framework of social thought. After the Communist Party gained state power, the minority nationalities were identified by a bureaucratic procedure of expert testing of group applications for official recognition. The experts were supposed to use the four criteria laid down by Stalin as defining a nationality: common territory, language, economy and psychological nature; and the groups thus recognized were also allocated to their appropriate point on the scale of historical development defined by the successive modes of production of Marxist theory. In practice this procedure was infected by assumptions of Han superiority, by pre-existing Han beliefs about which ethnic groups really exist, by complex interrelationships between peoples with fluctuating senses of their group distinctiveness, and, most recently, by strategic claims to distinct ethnicity designed to gain benefit from newer state minority policies. Of over four hundred claims by groups to be accorded the status of a minority nationality, only fifty-five have been recognized by the state authorities, other claims are still being examined, and some groups which were originally deemed to be Han are seeking to be re-designated as non-Han (Wu 1990). The result is a series of often tense disputes over whether a group of people is or is not a minority nationality, and an inevitably politicized anthropology of the non-Han peoples in peripheral regions.

In the case of some minority peoples there is a long history of resistance to Chinese rule which has flared up again periodically since 1949, mostly in the inner Asian frontier provinces of Xinjiang, Ningxia, Qinghai, Inner Mongolia, Yunnan and Tibet (A. P. L. Liu 1996: 189–222). Resistance has been particularly intense in western areas with high concentrations of Muslim populations; large-scale rebellions took place in the 1880s, Muslim warlords took control of territories in the 1920s, collectivization in the 1950s sparked opposition, and further rebellions have taken place during the 1980s and 1990s. The rise of Islamic consciousness in central Asia and the Middle East has provided support for separatist movements.[9] In Tibet, a major rebellion took place in 1959, and its suppression resulted in the escape of the Dalai Lama to India. Tibetan revolts against Communist policies such as of those of the Cultural Revolution have continued, led predominantly by young Lamaist monks and nuns from the countryside, although Tibetan Communist cadres are also reported to support Tibetan separatism. Separatist movements have also appeared in Inner Mongolia in the 1990s. Among other minority nationalities, however, especially in the south and southwest, Chinese policies of economic development, including the growth of tourism, have provided local leaders and economic elites with an interest in co-operating with the central state.

The identity of the majority Han people also raises questions for analysis. As Elvin (1973) remarked, the great longevity of an empire the size of China presumes a degree of cultural unity as well as a range of technological and institutional conditions, but that cultural unity itself cannot be taken as something primordial; it had to be constructed. Over the centuries, the imperial state elites were active in promoting cultural unity across ever larger territorial areas, through such means as the standardization of the written script, the unified system of examinations for entry into the civil service and the Confucian curriculum on which these examinations were based, and the building of similar City God temples as well as those dedicated to Confucius in all seats of local administration. The elites came to be orientated to a common culture and way of life, as expressed in dress, architecture, ritual and etiquette, family life, scholarship and public service. However, as anthropologists such as James Watson (1993) and Myron Cohen (1991) argue, a shared sense of what it meant to be 'Chinese' was also created by the activities of ordinary people in villages and towns all over the territory of the Chinese empire. Shared notions of the correct way of carrying out the most important life-cycle rituals, especially of birth, marriage and death, came to be accepted by villagers as defining who was Chinese and who was not, while at the same time allowing for local variations and local customs which reinforced strong emotional ties to native places. Cohen stresses that peasant cultural forms were often modelled on those of the elite, while local elites also incorporated local variations into their 'Han' practices, thus a unified culture spanned major class divisions in imperial Chinese society. Over the last century, however, modernizing elites, whether imperial, Republican or Communist, have attacked these traditional cultural forms as obstacles to China's modernization and the building of a rich and powerful state. Intellectuals have turned away from Chinese traditions as the basis of Chinese identity. Whereas there was once a unified and common culture which defined what it meant to be Chinese, being Chinese is now a problem and demands a quest. That quest will vary across many dimensions, including those of gender, region, generation, religion and class, in ways that are still being investigated by social scientists and cultural commentators (Dittmer and Kim 1993; Tu Wei-ming 1991).

Issues of cultural identity and cultural transformation will recur at many points later in the book. However, the entire discourse of Han and non-Han can also be questioned. Gladney (1994) argues that the idea of *han minzu* itself is a distinctively modern one, and came to prominence because of Sun Yat-sen's desire to gain widespread support against the Manchu overlords of the late Qing empire. Cultural differences between northerners, southern Cantonese, Shanghainese, and so on, which had always remained strong, were a potential threat to the unity of the revolutionary Chinese, and the stress on an overarching Han identity aimed to counteract such a possibility. Chinese solidarity was also strengthened by racialized accounts of the Han nation, in which late nineteenth-century western biological theories of racial hierarchy were adapted to Chinese circumstances (Dikötter 1997). Once the idea of a Han national identity had gained ground, the space was available for 'minority nationalities', so long as these did not threaten Chinese unity, and this space was filled by the theory of nationality taken over from Lenin and Stalin, which, as seen above, was used in the 1950s to identify legitimate minority nations, less evolutionarily developed than the Han and therefore dependent on the Han to lead them towards the modern world.

Like any collective identity, then, that of the 'imagined community' (B. Anderson 1983) of the Han people is also a constructed one and open to contestation. One such contestation derives from spokespersons for a rival collective identity, that of the Cantonese, inhabiting wide areas in the south of China and the origin of the majority of overseas Chinese. Cantonese speak a distinctive form of the Chinese language which is not mutually intelligible with the official national language *putonghua*, and are both the subject and object of mutual stereotyping.[10] Proponents of Cantonese distinctiveness have reconstructed the official and widespread interpretation of the historical spread of Han culture southwards from its original centre around the

Yellow River, and have accorded the southern peoples greater autonomous cultural force in historical development (Friedman 1994).
Few go so far as to promote Cantonese separatism, though the greater
economic development of the coastal areas, especially around the
Pearl River delta, has given this region distinct economic interests in
a degree of autonomy from the centre which are pursued by a variety
of economic and political agents (Vogel 1989). As we shall see in later
chapters, issues of regional and local autonomy are prominent in
China today, and may be intensified by divergent collective identities
(Goodman and Segal 1994).

Conclusion

It would be inappropriate in a work of this scope to try to provide
detailed historical and geographical background to the study of Chinese society, and also unnecessary, since there are many sources of
such information for the interested student.[11] This chapter has aimed
to guide readers through some of the issues involved in the historical,
territorial and ethnic construction and demarcation of Chinese
society. Many of the lines of thought started here will be continued
in later chapters: the problem of the 1949 frontier between the old and
the new society, and the phases of modernization; the characterization
of the mode of production in China; the relationship of the People's
Republic to its global economic, political and cultural environment,
both Chinese and non-Chinese; the extent and character of China's
social and cultural uniformity or diversity, and the mechanisms of its
social integration and divisions. The next chapter explores one major
dimension of variation within any society, that between rural and
urban contexts of social life.

Further reading

Spence (1990) is probably the best available single-volume history of
late imperial and modern China. Duara (1995) is prominent among
those who more critically problematize the interpretation of Chinese
history, as are the contributors to Hershatter et al. (1996). Tu Wei-
ming (1991) contains essays on various facets of Chinese identity,
both within China and elsewhere in the world. Essays in Dikötter
(1997) present interpretations of the Han Chinese as a form of racialized identity, while those in Harrell (1995) analyse aspects of ethnicity
and ethnic relations.

3

Rural and Urban in China

Introduction

China is a vast territory, and much of the population still lives in rural areas and gains its living from the land. It also has a long history of urban formation with many ancient cities and towns, and modern industrialization and the growth of state administration has been accompanied by further waves of urbanization. Over the course of the twentieth century, urban–rural difference has been a major dimension of social experience, social conflict and social inequality, and it has been the focus of fluctuating government policies. The idea of a deep-rooted conflict between the country and the city has been a key doctrine of the Chinese Communist Party, although for practical as well as theoretical reasons the interpretation of this conflict has differed markedly from that of orthodox Marxism, with policy consequences whose impact can still be felt to the present day. This chapter explores the changing relationships of rural and urban in Chinese society in the context of economic, political and social transformation.

Urban and rural division in China and the West

Much sociological theorizing has assumed that there is a fundamental difference between rural and urban society. The grand narratives of development and modernization, as well as Marxism, have built upon distinctions of traditional and modern society, of *Gemeinschaft* and *Gesellschaft*, in which the process of urbanization and the marginalization of various forms of rural life were key elements. This conventional wisdom of a sharp rural–urban contrast has been much debated in the last half-century of western sociology, yet it had considerable validity in European history. It is not merely a question of settlement sizes and population concentrations. The cities of Europe have for thousands of years been seen as distinct centres of religious significance and political power. From the time of the ancient Greek city-states, city life has been associated with a distinct social status and form of government. In many European countries the burghers of cities claimed rights of self-government and specific forms of representation in assemblies and parliaments. Whereas the institutions of serfdom embodied an opposition of free and servile, the urban mode of life was often held to be synonymous with freedom. Cities were seen as the fountain of civilization in contrast with the backwardness of rural life.

According to Mote (1970, 1977), this Eurocentric conception of the significance of cities did not apply in traditional China. China did not lack large concentrations of population; in fact Chinese cities were among the largest in the world even in Han times, and contained considerable proportions of the Chinese population.[1] But Mote's argument, which is echoed by many other writers,[2] was that urban and rural society were not structurally or culturally separated, and that a distinct urban population, way of life and culture did not develop in China until perhaps the later nineteenth or even twentieth century. There were close relationships between cities and the surrounding countryside, and many city-dwellers identified strongly with 'their' native (not necessarily natal) village where their ancestors were buried and worshipped. Many residents of cities were sojourners, living in the city temporarily (though possibly for long periods) to pursue trade or a craft, leaving wives and children in the village to maintain family continuity and to serve the older generation, and returning when possible for festivals. Even in the later nineteenth and early twentieth centuries, a considerable proportion of the population of such cities as Beijing, Hankou or Shanghai consisted of men and women living apart from their families, often in accommodation related to their employment (Gamble and Burgess 1921; Rowe 1984; Wakeman and Yeh 1992). Furthermore, the inhabitants of cities did not, as so often in Europe, develop a corporate identity as a collectivity of burghers claiming rights and liberties, especially the right of self-government. Instead, organizations of people stemming from the same native place, called *huiguan*, played a major part in city life, exercising social control, providing welfare services, arranging burials or transportation of the dead back to the native place, and increasingly entering into the politics and power structure of growing cities such as Shanghai (B. Goodman 1995). The ideals of the upper classes involved land ownership and rural living, and their residence oscillated between town and country. Towns and cities were indeed elements of the power structure of Chinese society, but not as autonomous 'containers of power' (Mumford 1961); rather, they were subject to the national system of administration and law enforcement, and were organized into units, for example counties, which combined towns or cities with a large rural area, often under the same name. Nor were Chinese cities major elements in the structure of religious organization or sacred power. Temples of the state Confucian cult or of Buddhism or Daoism did not represent the city culturally or dominate the city horizon architecturally; important temples and shrines often had a rural location. There were no physical structures or architectural forms that marked the city off from the small town or village; cities might be more opulent and more extensive, with a wider range of crafts, trades, and cultural activities, but they were not a distinct form of social life.

There were, however, differences between kinds of places. A number of hierarchies or continua between cities, towns and villages existed in traditional Chinese society. One of these was the hierarchy of state administration, descending from the capital city through provincial and prefectural capitals down to the county town.[3] Administrative cities and towns were walled, for reasons of defence as well as for symbolic reasons, and contained the residences and offices of state officials, as well as school-temples of the state religion and of the City God. The lowest level was the county town with the office of the county magistrate. The magistrate was responsible for administration and law enforcement in the county, a large area with a large population. There was no official administrative structure below the level of the county town, and the magistrate had to use unofficial channels to negotiate with local elites in small towns and villages and to carry out his functions.

The second hierarchy linking village to town and city was economic. According to Skinner (1964, 1977),[4] agricultural products were transferred up the hierarchy of increasingly centralized places via successively more complex marketing processes, and specialized urban products were traded down the hierarchy along similar routes, some of them reaching village people in local markets. From the point of view of villagers, the most significant unit of economic activity was the 'standard marketing area', consisting of a small 'standard market town' and its surrounding villages. Standard marketing areas were linked into wider systems of trade through larger and more specialized markets located in higher-level places: intermediate and central market towns, local, greater and regional cities above them, and regional and central metropolises at the peak of the hierarchy. Skinner (1964) argued that the standard marketing area was also a relatively demarcated social world, with the town and its associated villages providing a focus for religious and cultural pursuits, an area within which a high proportion of marriages would be arranged, a community with a distinct dialect variation and culinary tradition, and hence an area with which its inhabitants could identify. Skinner (1971) further suggested that the degree to which the lives of villagers were socially confined within this area was historically variable. In times of relative civil peace, links beyond the village and the marketing area would flourish and villagers would be open to external social influences, while in times of unrest, banditry and even warfare, these local social systems would close in on themselves for protection and security, and the social structure would present an increasingly fragmented or cellular aspect. Skinner's original fieldwork was carried out in the central plain of Sichuan Province, and later research has also suggested regional and local variation in the extent to which villagers were linked into wider systems.[5] This complicates the picture, but does not negate the basic theme of urban–rural interlinkage in late imperial Chinese society.

The beginnings of modern urbanization

Greater differentiation between urban and rural society came about from the later nineteenth century. Under the impact of foreign incursion, economic and technical developments, and a shifting balance between central authority and local urban power, forms of urban social life and structure emerged which separated the cities increasingly from their rural contexts. By the time the Chinese Communist Party had begun to take state power, the opposition between city and countryside that was a central plank in the social analysis of orthodox Marxism had become more of a reality in China than it had ever been before.

China's defeat in a series of wars with European powers resulted in the establishment of a string of 'treaty ports' along the eastern seaboard and on the navigable rivers. Hong Kong became a British colony, but the remainder of these cities were not ceded fully to the victorious foreigners. The latter exacted the right to trade through these ports, and in many cases took over rights of legal and commercial administration in sectors of the cities known as 'concessions'. Foreigners also controlled the customs and excise administrations in some ports. They set up trading companies and gradually invested in manufacturing, banking, transport and communications. The result was a concentration of commerce in these cities, especially Shanghai, and in the network of transport and communication between them, and an increasing separateness between the 'two worlds' (Murphey 1974) of the treaty ports and the rest of China. The foreign concessions also provided a new model of urban administration and self-government which complemented indigenous Chinese moves in this direction. Cities began to develop organs of local self-government in such areas as police, fire control and poor relief which coexisted with the official rule of the appointed magistrate (Elvin 1974b; Rowe 1984). The fact that the central state found it necessary to call on the support of locally raised and controlled militias to suppress major revolts such as the Taiping Rebellion also added to the growth of local urban consciousness and autonomy (Kuhn 1975). The treaty ports added to these tendencies by demonstrating the advantages of a well-run city council in terms of public order, safety and cleanliness. Cities were officially recognized as administrative units with their own councils under regulations issued in 1909. This urban modernization involved a 'restructuring process', a 'concentration of modern communications, capital and mechanized industry in a handful of coastal cities, foremost among them Shanghai. This concentration, the result of these cities' close contact with the international economy, meant that the quality of life enjoyed by their citizens soon became very different from that experienced elsewhere' (Elvin 1974a: 9).

Alongside this change in the material quality of urban life came a cultural change, the formation of specifically urban social milieus with urban ways of life often modelled on foreign patterns, with foreign clothes, hairstyles, consumption habits and leisure pursuits, and an urban disparagement of things rural. Modernizing urban elites introduced the western concept of 'peasant', translated by the neologism *nongmin*, with implications of backwardness, tradition and superstition (M. L. Cohen 1993). The Republican period in particular saw an urban attack on many aspects of traditional rural culture in the name of modernization, part of the new civilizing mission of the new ruling groups which changed the 'cultural nexus of power' (Duara 1988) in rural China. Previously, rural communities had been governed by a varying and complex network of local leaders, drawing their legitimacy from their roles in local lineage and religious organizations reinforced by the symbolism of the imperial state. At the end of the empire and under Nationalist rule during the Republic, this network was displaced and even actively destroyed by modern administrative agencies, police bureaux and modern-style schools, supposedly at first run by local councils but actually directed by central agencies. Taxation on rural inhabitants increased to pay for these new state institutions, often engendering violent resistance, and local leaders, no longer able to 'broker' relationships between 'their' village and the state and threatened by social disorder, in many cases left the rural areas to lead a new life in the modern sector of the towns and cities. The increasing separation of state and society[6] also signified an increasing separation of urban and rural society.

A further aspect of the changing social significance of cities was the beginnings of modern industrialization. In China, this occurred mainly under foreign influence and foreign initiative. In the field of textiles, which has always been of great importance in the early phase of industrialization, cotton production remained a handicraft industry located within peasant households well into the twentieth century. China did not see the growth of small towns based on textile manufacturing typical of European industrialization. Instead, in the final decade of the nineteenth century and the early decades of the twentieth, large-scale textile and steel-based industries were introduced into China mainly under foreign ownership and control, and located in fast-growing cities of the eastern seaboard such as Shanghai and Tianjin. Modern industry employed only a minute proportion of the Chinese labour force, even into the 1930s. These cities did indeed see the beginnings of the typical institutions of urban industrialism, such as employers' associations and trade unions and the conflicts between them, but much of rural China remained relatively untouched by such developments. In some rural areas, however, the influence was more marked, as the labour requirements of modern industry began to affect the structure of opportunities for the population, especially for unmarried women (Honig 1986).

The big difference: urban and rural in Chinese communism

The relation between urban and rural society has played a major role in Chinese communist theory and practice. Classical Marxism identi-

fied the opposition and conflict between town and country as central
to the historical dialectic. The city represented the march of progress,
and the opposition between urban and rural was to be overcome
through the urbanization of the countryside. Urban classes were the
progressive classes, most notably the bourgeoisie which overthrew the
landed aristocracy of feudalism and carried the dynamism of capitalist
expansion throughout the world, and the industrial proletariat whose
historical mission was to transcend class divisions and build socialism
and then communism. The first experience of a revolution made in the
name of Marxism, the Bolshevik Revolution in Russia, corresponded
to this theoretical dominance of the urban, as an urban-based movement attempting to direct social change in the countryside.

The conditions in China encouraged a different relationship
between urban and rural aspects of the Communist revolution (Kao
1974). The initial development of the CCP was indeed predominantly
located in the cities, among radical intellectuals and industrial workers. But the industrial proletariat was very small, and there was a rural
dimension to the communist movement from early on, as communist
activists such as Mao Zedong and Peng Pai worked among rebellious
peasants and explored the roots of peasant discontent. The Nationalist abandonment of the United Front in 1927 resulted in most of the
surviving communists fleeing to the countryside where the policy of
building rural base areas, eventually identified with the Maoist tendency in the party, gained the upper hand, although there remained
those who pressed for the strategy of urban insurrection. From then
on the dominant history of the Chinese revolution, in the Jiangxi
Soviet and the base areas in northern China such as Yan'an, was one
of organization among the peasants, experiments with land and
marriage reforms, the recruitment of a peasant army to fight the
Nationalists and the Japanese, and eventually the conquest of the
Nationalist-held cities by military force (Selden 1971).

This enforced exclusion from the cities encouraged an interpretation of the relationship between city and countryside which diverged
from classical Marxism. Most strikingly represented in the writings of
Mao Zedong, this interpretation reversed the terms of the urban–rural
opposition. The cities were identified with foreign imperialism and the
comprador Chinese bourgeoisie who merged their interests with the
imperialists, while the essential roots of Chinese nationhood and a
specifically Chinese communism were claimed to lie with the peasantry. Mao rejected the 'progressive' nature of urban capitalism and
envisaged a way of overcoming the opposition between town and
country (one of the 'three great differences' derived from classical

Marxism, the others being those between mental and manual labour and between workers and peasants) which would give full play to the revolutionary potential of the countryside. However, once the cities had been captured and the People's Republic established in the whole territory of the mainland, the centre of gravity of the revolution moved to the cities, which became the location for the centralized political and economic bureaucracies of the regime and of the basic industries which were the focus of the First Five-Year Plan. Resources for industrialization were extracted from agriculture, reinforcing the conflict of urban and rural material interests. There was thus a tension within communist strategy and ideology between, on the one hand, the peasant-army basis of the state, the suspicion of cities and faith in the rural masses and, on the other, the urban-based organizational hierarchy of party and state bureaucracies, the career interests of the cadres who staffed them, together with the drive for urban industrialization and the interests of urban industrial workers. This tension has resulted in several paradoxical twists and turns in the relationship between urban and rural society over the past half-century.

Transforming urban–rural differences: the first phase

The first few years of the Communist regime witnessed a period of recovery from long years of war and civil strife, as well as the beginnings of the establishment of new social forms in agriculture and industry. In the cities, the new government aimed to stabilize urban management and to start a drive to planned industrialization on the Soviet model (Kirkby 1985). Industrialization required workers, and the early 1950s saw considerable movement of rural residents into the cities to escape rural poverty and dislocation and to work in growing state industries. But these incomers also added to the need for food, housing, medical and other social services in the expanding cities. The movement to the cities stimulated by the difference in living standards exacerbated problems of planning growth in urban employment and in the provision of necessities.

The Communists' suspicion of cities was reflected most clearly in their claim that they should be 'producer', not 'consumer', cities (Kirkby 1985). Cities of the previous regimes were identified with parasitic exploiting and leisure classes, and the Communists were determined that their cities should be the location of productive industry and inhabited by the industrial working class. Cities were to be functional rather than ostentatious, consumption was to be restricted to necessities. It was also thought essential to avoid the mass movement of underemployed rural population to the cities, overburdening the infrastructure and services and generating shanty towns and slums, characteristic of so many societies at this stage of economic development. The expansion of education and medical services in the countryside and the control of urban wage rates to prevent their being too attractive to potential rural migrants were early measures taken to achieve these ends.

In the countryside, land reform and moves towards co-operative farming began to change the character of village life. The symbolic boundaries of villages were penetrated by the party teams sent in to mobilize the local people for revolutionary change and to assist with the process of registration of land holdings and their redistribution to poor peasants and landless families. Villagers were mobilized into organizational forms which differed markedly from traditional patterns. Religious and lineage associations were abolished and their property confiscated (an intensification of state-led modernization programmes begun under the Nationalist regime described earlier), and villagers were encouraged to join party and class-based mass organizations such as those of peasants, youth and women. They were also invited and later constrained to combine their families' economic activities, first into Mutual Aid Teams, then into Agricultural Producers' Co-operatives, and from 1958 into People's Communes, organizations which took the management of all agricultural, industrial, trading, cultural, educational and political work within their sphere. In the formation of these units, however, some aspects of social structure were maintained; the boundaries of teams and brigades often followed traditional divisions within and between villages, such as those based on lineage surnames, with the effect of reinforcing male solidarities in the running of village affairs (Potter and Potter 1990: 251–69).

The ossification of urban–rural difference

Despite much ideological discussion on the socialist objective of overcoming the difference of town and country, state policy from the mid-1950s actually rigidified the distinction between rural and urban society.[7] The main instrument of policy, which aimed to avoid what was seen as excessive expansion of towns and cities that might accompany industrialization and rural development, was the system of population registration known as the *hukou* system. A variant of methods of social control by household registration used for centuries by imperial regimes (Dutton 1992), and institutionalized during the 1950s by a series of measures culminating in regulations promulgated in 1958 (Zhang Qingwu 1988), the *hukou* system identified every member of the population as either 'agricultural' or 'non-agricultural' and the approved location of their residence, classified as either 'urban' or 'rural', in a specific city, town or village (Christiansen 1991, Mallee 1995). At the high point of this mechanism of social control, it was almost impossible for a person to move legally away from their registered address.

Unapproved movement was made difficult by the administrative control of access to many of the necessities of life, which came to differ fundamentally between urban and rural contexts. Goods such as grain, cooking oil and cotton clothes were rationed, and only urban dwellers with appropriate *hukou* were issued with coupons. Housing provision and the right to send one's children to school in a given town or city depended on *hukou* registration. Rural inhabitants gained access to these necessities through their membership of a particular production team, a sub-unit of a brigade which itself was a sub-unit of a commune. Production team members accumulated work-points according to the hours and type of work allocated to them over the year, and the grain available to the team was distributed to households in proportion to the work-points credited to their members.[8] Commune members who moved unauthorized to a town or city would forfeit their entitlement to work-points and hence grain, but would not be eligible for urban ration coupons. Not only would their residence be unauthorized, they would also find themselves without means of subsistence.

This system had many social consequences. It resulted in a stabilization of the spatial distribution of the population and made mobility very difficult. Apart from the programmes of sending urban residents to the countryside (see below), residential mobility was severely restricted. There were some ways in which rural residents could officially be transferred to urban registration, such as by gaining a place in a higher education institution or by joining the army, but only a small minority of the rural population could follow these routes. A more common form of mobility was that of temporary contract workers who were recruited in large numbers – 13–14 million between 1966 and 1976, according to K. W. Chan (1994: 40) – to fill urban labour shortages, but they did not gain rights to permanent urban residence and many returned to their villages. A further and more profound consequence was the establishment of almost 'caste-like' divisions within the Chinese population (S. H. Potter 1983). Urban and rural registration became hereditary, inherited from the mother, and could only be changed under very specific conditions. Membership of these 'castes' (or 'estates') affected all aspects of life. Once the systems of grain distribution were established, urban and rural personnel were identified through the source of their food: peasants ate 'their own rice', while urban workers ate 'the state's rice'. Similar divisions affected the party cadres who occupied leadership positions in the People's Communes: commune cadres appointed by the state from outside had urban registration and 'ate the state's rice', while other cadres at commune level who were locally recruited had rural registration with temporary urban residence and 'ate the commune's rice'. Leaders at brigade and team level 'ate their own rice' like any other peasant (Potter and Potter 1990: 273). After the dissolution of the communes and the introduction of markets in foodstuffs this aspect of the distinction disappeared, but many others remained. In particular, the social welfare systems have long differed fundamentally between urban and rural, with much more extensive state provision for urban residents in such fields as health care and pensions (Krieg and Schädler 1994).[9] The *hukou* regulations no longer completely correspond to the lived reality of the Chinese, but the regulations are still in force and still influence many social processes in China.

Sent down to the countryside

One of the most distinctive aspects of rural–urban experience in China was the series of policies to send sections of the urban population to the countryside. In 1958, at the time of the Great Leap Forward, thousands of urban cadres were temporarily sent to rural areas to help in programmes of rapid agricultural development and rural industrialization. In the early 1960s, the resettlement of urban teenagers began to be used as a way to relieve overcrowding and youth unemployment in the cities. In 1968, Mao announced the implementation on a much larger scale of the *shangshan–xiaxiang* (up to the mountains and down to the countryside) campaign (Bernstein 1977), under which at least 12 million educated urban youths were sent down by 1978 (Madsen 1991: 666) for the proclaimed purpose of learning true socialist values from the peasants, an extensive programme of resocialization which formed part of the Cultural Revolution.

Although such rustication policies were often officially announced as serving the goal of bridging the gap between city and countryside, in many ways the outcome was its reinforcement. For those young people whose idealism led them to go to the countryside willingly, the experience of village life often proved a rude shock; for those who were constrained to go against their will, it confirmed their stereotyped images. The dirt and poor hygiene of the villages, the low levels of education, and above all the back-breaking work, figure often in reports of the youth's experience (for example, Frolic 1980). The villagers in their turn often saw the urban youth as pampered and ignorant, a useless drain on the village's scarce resources. Many sent-down youth were not in fact integrated into village life in any meaningful way (Bernstein 1977); they were often housed in dormitories and seldom with peasant families, and tended to be put to work on special infrastructure projects such as building roads and dams or on parts of state farms separate from the resident farming inhabitants. The development of close friendships with village youth seems to have been patchy; marriage with villagers was limited by the fact that the sent-down youth were below the recommended marriage age, and became a last resort for those, especially young women, who saw themselves as permanently condemned to life away from their urban home. Vast numbers were desperate to return to the cities, and did not seek integration into village life.

The very fact that rustication was also used as a punishment for those deemed to be opponents of the Communist regime tended to reconfirm the sense of superiority of urban life. Urban youth and their families would use every means to avoid rustication, such as mobilizing connections with influential officials, and took every opportunity to return to their city homes. In late 1978 sent-down youth in Shanghai took the signs of political change as an opportunity to demonstrate against the rustication programme and to demand the right to return to the city (Gold 1980), and the policy was shortly afterwards brought to an end, although many were not allowed to leave the countryside and regain urban *hukou* status until the later 1980s. By this time many had married and had children, and a law of 1988 permitted such children also to gain urban *hukou*.

However, despite much evidence of opposition to the rustication policies and of the reinforcement of urban–rural antagonisms, there were also some other outcomes.[10] The idealistic dedication of many young people bore fruit in their contributions to rural education, health care and technological advancement. Even after the return of sent-down youth to the city, the commitment of some of them to their former village hosts lived on: for example, in the occasional supply of medicines not easily available in the village. Long periods of communal living in the village also resulted in ties, between villagers and educated youth and between the educated youth themselves, which later formed the basis of networks of *guanxi* mobilizable by all participants. Former sent-down youth have also set up associations for mutual assistance which have sometimes gained public prominence.

Low level of urbanization

The most significant overall outcome for urban–rural relations of the first three decades of the Communist regime was a notably low level of urbanization in the country as a whole. At the time of Mao's death in 1976 fewer than 20 per cent of the entire Chinese population lived in urban areas as defined by the Chinese authorities (K. W. Chan 1994: 24). Most of the growth of the urban population since 1949 had taken place in the 1950s, since when there had been stagnation in urban growth or even reversals. As Chan (1994) argues, the segmentation of Chinese society into urban and rural sectors had become even greater than is typical of developing societies in general, and the policies of the Chinese authorities had been tantamount to the erecting of 'invisible walls' around the cities to replace the real walls which in many cases had been demolished. From certain points of view, Chinese society by the end of the Cultural Revolution could be seen as 'under-urbanized'.

The reform period: the real transformation of urban–rural difference

The new course on which the post-Mao government embarked from the late 1970s has had profound consequences for the division of urban and rural society, which are continuing and extending in the present day. The return to family farming in the form of various kinds of 'household responsibility systems' and the eventual dissolution of the People's Communes transformed rural society and gave millions of villagers (who came to be described as 'surplus rural labour') an incentive to seek work elsewhere, whatever their *hukou* registration. The opening of the Chinese economy to world markets and sources of investment has had its most direct influence on the cities of the eastern seaboard, just as in the period of industrialization earlier in the

century. Between village and city have grown up many new forms of
society which occupy intermediate positions on the 'urban-rural continuum'. This chapter concludes with an examination of four aspects
of these changes: 'small town'; 'supervillage'; 'extended metropolis';
and 'floating population'. The overall social significance of these
trends will then be summarized.

'Small towns, big issues'

As was noted earlier in this chapter, in pre-communist times two
dimensions of an urban–rural continuum could be identified: the
administrative hierarchy, from the capital down to the county town
and its subordinate settlements; and the economic or marketing hierarchy, from the central metropolis down to the standard market town
and its associated villages. The Communist administrative and planning systems intensified the former hierarchy, clarifying and periodically changing the administrative capacities of agencies located at
various levels. But the development of the central planning and
state-controlled distribution systems removed many of the marketing
functions of towns of various kinds. At the high point of the Cultural
Revolution, markets were closed altogether and all distribution was
monopolized by state agencies. The policy of self-sufficiency of communes did result in the development of some rural industry, for
example in food processing and machine repair, and some communes
made great strides in the setting up of factories, but otherwise the
economic role of towns lower in the economic hierarchy stagnated
before the late 1970s.

This situation has changed drastically in the last twenty years. In a
policy shift which has sometimes been attributed at least in part to the
researches of a team led by Fei Xiaotong (Fei Hsiao Tung 1986), small
towns became the cornerstone of the reform government's development strategy (Kirkby and Bradbury 1996). There is a certain continuity from earlier urban policy, in that the government hopes
(perhaps vainly) to be able to control the expansion of cities which
economic growth would be expected to stimulate. Small towns have
been identified as the location for providing work, and to some extent
also residence, for the millions of the rural population to whom a
'leaner, fitter' agriculture can no longer give employment. Small towns
have thus seen the growth of industrial and commercial enterprises of
various types, some owned and administered by town governments,
some private enterprises, some of mixed and uncertain ownership.[11]

Well over 100 million rural residents now make their living in small towns.

However, they do not necessarily live in those towns, nor does the government expect them to. A government promoted slogan much used in the 1980s was '*li tu bu li xiang*' ('to leave the land but not to leave the rural areas'). This has been a controversial matter (Taylor 1988; K. W. Chan 1994: 127), as has the whole question of rural-urban migration. Yok-shui Lee (1992) argues that different planners interpreted this slogan in different ways, reflecting conflicts of interest generated by the movement of labour to small towns. Small town authorities effectively prevented rural residents from leaving farm areas and becoming urban residents. Instead, 'peasant-workers' (*mingong*) commute by bicycle to their jobs in nearby towns, often leaving other family members behind to work their contracted farmland. Such peasant-workers are not counted as part of the formally registered population of the small towns, nor do they gain urban *hukou*, even though they make up an increasingly important part of the non-agricultural work-force and in that sense at least part of the pattern of daytime urban social interaction. The towns become centres of economic activity, but not bases of residential expansion, a pattern which Lee describes as 'decentralized urban growth'.

The extent to which the small towns have thus contributed to the urbanization of China is a complicated and technical issue, which cannot be fully discussed here. The problem is made up of two parts: the definition of a 'town' and the residential location and *hukou* status of people who work in them. After the dissolution of the communes, the administrative centres of brigades became designated as *xiang* (usually translated as townships). The residents of *xiang* have rural *hukou* and are not counted as part of the urban population. Nor are *xiang* accorded the administrative status and rights of towns ('*zhen*'). However, the governments of *xiang* are entitled to apply for their place to be designated as *zhen*, and this has happened on a very large scale since 1984, with many thousands of former *xiang* becoming *zhen*. The extent of urbanization thus depends on many factors, including whether one takes official statistics on the numbers and population of *zhen* as the measure, whether one also includes *xiang* which are often larger in population than some *zhen*, and how one deals with the large numbers of commuters who have rural *hukou* but who work in towns (Goldstein 1990). What is certain is that small towns have transformed the dualistic nature of urban–rural divisions in China.

Village and 'supervillage'

Skinner's account of the marketing hierarchy in pre-revolutionary China, rising from the villages and their standard marketing towns to increasingly 'central places', was outlined earlier, together with the question of the degree of 'openness' of the village to the outside world, the degree of integration of villages into marketing and other social systems. Central place theory, as is implied in its name, is a view from the centre. It assumes that metropolitan cities are the most central places and villages are the most peripheral. This is not necessarily how social space was seen by villagers, however. From the point of view of villagers who were born and spent their lives in the village (mostly men rather than women, as will be seen in chapter 5), the village itself was the centre of their social world and everywhere else was 'outside' or 'beyond'. And the very fact that so many of those living in cities at any time were sojourners, expecting to return to their native place when the purpose of their sojourn was complete or abandoned, also points to the centrality of the village for most of the people of China.

But what was a village, and how are villages changing? Feuchtwang (1998) usefully distinguishes between three senses of the village as a 'second-order place', beyond the household in which people reside: the traditional place, the administrative place, and the collective. The most important of these senses in late imperial China was the first, the traditional, although it could only be conceived of as 'traditional' when under attack from 'modern' institutions. The administrative hierarchy of the state did not yet reach down as far as the village, and there were few aspects of collective activity in which villagers might engage. The 'traditional' village was a cultural entity of which one was either a member or not, an insider or an outsider. The most basic aspect of this membership consisted of rights of settlement, which were traced and transferred by heredity in the male line. A man was entitled to live in the village, to own land or to rent it on a more or less permanent basis, to build a house, and to take part as a full member in village rituals, if he could trace his ancestry sufficiently far back along a line of established villagers. Especially in villages occupying land reclaimed from river delta or uncultivated hillside, settlement rights were most forcefully claimed by those tracing ancestry back to founding settlers, hence the particular significance of lineage as a way of asserting such rights (Faure 1986). Descendants from later immigrants could for generations remain outsiders with more restricted rights of membership; conflicts between groups, especially between those with different surnames, were pursued by the manipulation of genealogy to assert claims to settlement.

Beyond this, as Feuchtwang (1998) argues, the members of a traditional village shared a sense of living in a physical as well as a social environment imbued with cosmic and spiritual meaning. Human impressions on the landscape, the siting of houses, paths and graves, had to conform to the *fengshui* of the place, the cosmic forces inhabiting the mountains, valleys and streams, the shape of the ecological setting of the village. The *fengshui* of each village was a unique configuration, demarcated from others by boundaries across which gods are invited in and demons expelled by ritual activity. *Fengshui* set the terms of harmony and dispute within the village, of collective as well as individual destiny for good or ill.

But the boundaries of the village in terms of descent and *fengshui* are not necessarily the same as the boundaries defined by state administration, by collective organization, or by economic activity. Typically, in imperial times, the boundaries defined by state administration and by economic activity and land ownership cut across the traditional sense of place. The Republican revolution imposed administrative procedures which aimed to cut the ground from under the lineage and ritual processes of the 'natural' village, though property ownership (in the shape, for example, of absentee landlords) and marketing networks continued to cross-cut administrative boundaries. The Communist regime later brought all of these aspects of rural life into congruence with each other, with the administrative units of communes, brigades and teams defining units of collective land ownership also made responsible for economic processes and subject to a single hierarchy of central places. The various boundaries of the village therefore overlapped and were scarcely distinguishable from each other. The traditional sense of place was often submerged, but also often lived on in the villagers' use of 'traditional' place-names rather than the new Communist ones.

With the dissolution of the commune system, and the emergence of patterns of property ownership, economic organization and trading networks which escape the bounds of administrative units, there is once again a divergence of administrative, marketing, property and ritual definitions of villages (Feuchtwang 1998) or, as Zhe Xiaoye (1995) puts it, a 'pluralization of village boundaries'. Zhe illustrates this through the case of what she calls 'supervillages', villages which have successfully responded to the opportunities offered by the economic reforms. Such villages, predominantly in the Yangzi and Pearl River deltas, have built up collectively owned or shareholding co-operative enterprises, some in various branches of manufacturing, some trading agricultural products. The more successful of these enterprises have a scale of operations which goes far beyond the boundaries of the village,[12] extending into the surrounding region, the country as a whole or even, in the case of those with joint-venture partnerships with foreign companies, into the international economy. Supervillages operate like large-scale companies in the market economy, diversifying activities if they see an opportunity, even relocating the more labour-intensive parts of their manufacturing activities to less developed areas of China where labour costs are lower. The definition of the village in terms of its economic activities no longer has any clear boundary. Nor can the village be clearly defined in terms of its land boundaries. In these supervillages, land has become scarce and the village has resorted to various means to extend the land available to it, leasing land from neighbouring poorer villages or even 'annexing' another village by mutually agreed merger ratified by the township authorities. Supervillages also experience influx and outflow of various sectors of the work-force; workers, technicians and managerial personnel are attracted into the village (mostly on a temporary basis) and skilled or entrepreneurial villagers whose labour is displaced by cheaper migrant workers seek opportunities elsewhere.

One might expect that, in the face of all these breaches in the boundaries of the village, the sense of a traditional place with a long-established membership would dissolve. According to Zhe, however, the very success of the village has strengthened the sense of a core membership of villagers. The very collective and co-operative nature of the economic success of the village has put a premium on the social basis for co-operation. Traditional bases for social interaction, especially kinship, once again come to the fore. In such villages there are clear divisions between the established and the outsiders. Zhe shows how in many villages this division has been formalized into an explicit system of 'villagership', according to which the rights and responsibilities of full members of the village are specified, and the conditions in which villagership may be gained by incomers or lost by outgoers are laid down. Village membership becomes a crucial component of the stratification of the local community, as existing members preserve their advantage by regulating their relationship with others.

There are important differences in the ways villages are responding to the economic reforms of the 1980s and 1990s. The supervillages described by Zhe and others are only one type. Even among economically successful villages, not all have thriving collective sectors which maintain a sense of collective identity among the privileged insiders, but rather, strong private enterprise sectors with little collective organization. Other villagers have remained poor or become even poorer. It is impossible, given the current state of knowledge, to chart the dimensions of variation in the nature of village boundaries and relations within the wider society.[13] Once again, though, it is certain that significant changes are taking place in the relation of rural and urban society.

The 'extended metropolis'

Another way of capturing the changes under way in rural–urban society in China is provided by the concepts of the 'extended metropolis' and the '*desakota* region'.[14] *Desakota*, a term coined by McGee from the Indonesian words for town (*kota*) and village (*desa*), refers to densely populated areas between major cities where small town and village industrialization linked to urban markets and sources of expertise and finance is taking place. The extended metropolis refers to the economic and social systems made up of the complex interactions between a group of cities and major towns and their associated *desakota* regions. This framework of ideas from economic geography is designed to highlight the interpenetration of urban and rural economies in certain parts of the world, especially those where the rural economy was formerly based on rice agriculture.

Extended metropolitan areas have been identified in various parts of China, mostly along the eastern seaboard. The most obvious cases are those of the Pearl River delta and of the lower Yangzi River, where there has been a considerable growth of industrial and commercial development in the formerly rural areas of Guangdong Province and of metropolitan Shanghai and Jiangsu Province. In both cases it no longer makes much sense to think of these areas as rural hinterlands of large cities. Employment patterns are changing in these areas so that a high proportion of the rural population is now engaged in non-agricultural pursuits. Despite tensions between agricultural and non-agricultural sectors of local economies, for example over access to scarce resources, new forms of accommodation between them are also developing which are expected to be long-lasting rather than just transitional.

The ideas of *desakota* and extended metropolis, although originally formulated by economic geographers, can be useful to sociological and anthropological study of these new areas which span both urban and rural. For example, Zhou and Zhang (1995–6) show how the process of 'rural urbanization' (a similar concept to '*desakota*') in the Pearl River delta is also having important social consequences. The organizational form of enterprises in both agriculture and industry is changing and diversifying. The lifestyle of the people in formerly rural areas is now little different from those in the cities, in such matters as dress, housing and interior design, eating habits and transport. Throughout the Pearl River delta new mass media have reached both 'rural' and 'urban' populations alike, promoting 'cultural integration' in the region. Zhou and Zhang also claim that rural and urban people no longer differ markedly in their thinking on a range of issues related to family, achievement, customs and authority. The evidence appears to be building up that, at least in these economically most advanced regions, 'the big difference' between town and country is being eroded far more by the consequences of economic reforms than was ever the case under the Communist policies ostensibly designed to bridge that gap in the social structure.

Mobility, migration and the 'floating population'

The final aspect of urban–rural change that will be mentioned here is the enormously increased mobility of the Chinese people, and especially of rural inhabitants. This takes at least two main forms. On the one hand, the growth of markets, the shift of production to cash crops, and the development of rural industries have all involved villagers in travelling about the country as part of their normal economic life. On the other hand, the shift towards family farming and the incentives on farmers to meet criteria of short-term microeconomic efficiency have driven millions of peasants off the land, from which they migrate in large numbers.

Since the beginning of the economic reforms, the rigidity of the social control system based on *hukou* regulations has weakened. The *hukou* system itself is still in force, but state authorities no longer have the power to prevent movement away from the designated residence, even if they wanted to. The *hukou* system specifies an official procedure for applying to change one's registered residence, and registration statistics published by the Ministry of Public Security, together with other censuses and surveys, reveal the scale and nature of approved migration. Migrants who go through the official channels to change their *hukou* have numbered approximately 17–20 million persons per year since the early 1980s, and are more likely to be highly educated and employed in technical and specialized occupations;

many of them are also, however, likely to be moving for reasons other than for employment, such as for marriage or to be reunited with other family members (K. W. Chan 1999).

But these 'hukou migrants' are markedly fewer than those who move without transferring their official place of residence. Since these movements are not so well documented, estimates of the scale of unregistered migration are uncertain and varied, but researchers agree that numbers have risen since the early 1980s and reached approximately 80–100 million in the mid-1990s. Most of these migrants come from rural areas where their labour is no longer economically required; many of them travel to other rural areas where they can find work, often on a short-term or seasonal basis. But the migration which is perhaps of greater social significance is rural to urban migration. Certainly it is this form which attracts most attention from the authorities, the media and the researchers. The response of the authorities is somewhat contradictory. On the one hand, public security authorities talk of 'waves' of 'blindly floating' migrants, 'flooding' into the cities and causing problems of overcrowding and crime, a negative view of migrants which is often reinforced in the mass media (Davin 1998). On the other hand, those responsible for economic development in the cities recognize that these armies of relatively unskilled and low-paid workers, both men and women, are indispensable for the economic transformation that Chinese cities have undergone in recent years, especially in such sectors as infrastructure, construction and light industry. Chinese researchers themselves are beginning to build up a considerable stock of empirical data on population mobility and to challenge the negative stereotypes contained in these hydraulic metaphors (Mallee 1995/6).

Researchers have begun to study many social aspects of this migration, of which only some will be emphasized here. First, there are the social consequences of the migration for the sending areas. While from the point of view of 'human capital' these areas might be seen to be losing some of their most energetic and enterprising people, the return flows to rural areas help to bind them into wider networks of social relations. Such flows include the remitting of money and commodities back to home areas, which can maintain or raise living standards there as well as finance new styles of life; the bringing back to rural areas of new ideas and new possibilities; and the return of the migrants themselves after a period of time away, many of whom start businesses in their native villages (Murphy 2000). Such 'circulation' of people, money and social conceptions can all contribute to the breakdown of internal borders within the society.

The second set of consequences which has been attracting attention from sociologists is the role of migration in creating spaces within society which are relatively autonomous from state control. Solinger (1993) speaks of migration as a form of 'civil society', while Xiang Biao (1999) refers to the 'non-state space' which is forged by migrant communities, such as the famous Zhejiang village, which formed on the outskirts of Beijing. Whether these are informal networks of relationships, based on a commoditized transformation of traditional networks in the native place, or whether they also attempt to set up formal organizations to represent the interests of migrant groups in their dealings with authorities or other economic actors (B. Goodman 1995; Yuan and Wong 1999), migration can contribute to the increasing density of the social structure in a way which is not easy for authorities to control.

Another aspect of this increased mobility which has been stressed concerns gender (Davin 1996, 1998). Many of the forms of employment available to rural migrants to cities are related to the boom in construction and attract mainly male migrants, who leave female members of the family to take care of the farm, a process resulting in a feminization of agriculture (Jacka 1997: 128–39). There are, however, particular forms of employment which attract women migrants, such as domestic service. Many thousands of young woman have moved to towns and cities over the past fifteen years to take up employment as maids and nannies, and thus gained experience of urban life (Jacka 1997: 171–5). A further gender-specific component of mobility is marriage migration. It is customary for a woman to move on marriage to her husband's family home or home area.[15] With the growing mobility of the Chinese population, this custom is compounding the scale and intensity of the movement of woman. Although in general the distance over which such marriage migration takes place has been relatively small, and marriage across provincial boundaries relatively uncommon (Davin 1996), Chinese researchers have found a rapidly growing scale of interprovincial rural–rural marriage, for example into Zhejiang Province (Wang 1994). Once again, this movement is contributing to social change. Although the women come from poorer provinces, and marry men who are themselves poor for their area, the women themselves tend to have a higher level of education than their husbands and achieve a higher status within their new family. They are able to stand up to their husbands and are developing somewhat more egalitarian marriages. Against this one has to set reports of an increasing return of the practice of kidnapping or abducting women and selling them to men who require wives. This was not the normal channel for forging marriage alliances found in the Zhejiang study, however. Most such marriages were based on introductions, and the fact that the introductions were between partners located in widely distant provinces points to a growing intensity of networks of interaction spanning the whole of China.

A final aspect of mobility which should be stressed lies in the potential for generating social conflict. Despite the softening of researchers' negative evaluation of increased population mobility, the basis for tension between migrants and the established residents of the cities remains (Solinger 1995). Mutual stereotyping and antagonistic economic and social interests can provide sources for conflict. Up to the post-Mao reforms the inhabitants of cities were relatively advantaged by comparison with rural residents, in subsidized access to material necessities and in protected niches within their work-units, even if some of them were also exposed to the political risk of expulsion from this advantaged position. What proponents of economic reforms see as a freer labour market, city residents may well see as a dismantling of the protective walls which hitherto upheld their privilege. The relatively little research evidence available suggests considerable diversity in the degree to which city residents are prepared to tolerate this intrusion (Ding and Stockman 1999).

Conclusion

This chapter has suggested that in many ways urban–rural differences are being eroded more by the economic reforms of the last twenty years than was the case in the previous thirty years of state-directed social change. However, it has also been stressed that there remain huge variations in the enormous country that China is. Subsequent chapters will therefore return continually to the question of urban–rural differences, even if for reasons of lack of research evidence and lack of space it will be impossible fully to chart the dimensions of those differences. In the next chapter, one theme will be urban–rural differences in conceptions of social relationships, while in chapter 5 differences between town and country will be one topic in the discussion of family patterns and processes. In chapter 6, the different locations of city and village populations in the structure of social power in China will also be one theme, as will differences between town and country in relation to cultural transformation in chapter 7 and urban–rural dimensions of social inequality in chapter 8. In a country where 'urban' or 'rural', 'agricultural' or 'non-agricultural', still form part of a person's official identity, and where even on the most liberal definitions approximately half the population will still live in rural areas well into the twenty-first century, the relation of urban to rural components of the society will continue to provide an inescapable issue for sociologists.

Further Reading

Skinner (1977) contains important articles on urban–rural relations in pre-revolutionary China, including versions of Skinner's own theories of urban hierarchies. Kam Wing Chan (1994) provides a thorough study of urbanization under Chinese communism. Parish and Whyte (1978) and Whyte and Parish (1984) are standard works on (respectively) the sociology of rural and urban China in the Mao era. Potter and Potter (1990) is a study of peasant society in one village at different stages of the revolution, including their analysis of the social divisions created by the household registration (*hukou*) system. Davin (1998) is an up-to-date survey of migration in China, while the papers in Pieke and Mallee (1999) give a variety of perspectives on migration.

4

Individual and Society in China

Introduction

Throughout the past century, the basic character of social relationships has been at issue in China. People have had to decide how to relate to each other in new and changing circumstances. Sometimes these changes have come about unplanned as a result of forces under no one's control. Often, however, the new situations in which people have tried to find their way have been the consequence of deliberate policies of reformers and revolutionaries, determined to reconstruct the ways in which people act in relation to each other. Faced with what they saw as China's weakness and backwardness, reformers and revolutionaries have believed that it was necessary to transform traditional social morality and social psychology, to create new Chinese citizens and new forms of social relationships better suited to the modern world.

There has been little consensus over the diagnosis of social ills or the prescription of remedies. Liberals, Marxists, nationalists, conservatives and others debated and fought over the interpretation of society and the role of individuals, families, groups, organizations and classes within it. This internal cultural debate often also had external reference points; literate elites such as politicians and intellectuals made explicit comparisons between China and other societies. Contrasts between 'western' and 'eastern' cultures, such as those mentioned briefly in chapter 2, had been current in China since at least the mid-nineteenth century, and remained so throughout the twentieth. Such contrasts fuelled a variety of strategies of social transformation, from outright 'westernization', through the partial appropriation of western culture,[1] to the reconstruction and purification of Chinese traditions. The adaptation of Marxism to Chinese circumstances also involved this kind of 'reflexive modernization'.[2]

Sociologists who have studied social relationships and social inter-action in China have also, implicitly or explicitly, adopted a compara-tive viewpoint. Both Chinese and non-Chinese sociologists have often tended to contrast Chinese orientations and values (sometimes gener-alized to 'Asian' or 'Eastern' cultures) with those of the 'West', usually stressing the individualism of western culture and the universalism of western law and morality. Proponents of the 'sinification of soci-ology', mentioned in chapter 1, incorporate and reflect on such dis-tinctions to argue that western sociology must be modified or reconstructed if it is to explain the specific character of Chinese society. More recently, however, the criticism has emerged that these contrastive discourses merely reinforce an orientalist (or 'occidental-ist') tendency, on the part of both westerners and orientals, to essen-tialize both 'western' and 'Chinese' culture.[3]

This chapter introduces the controversies over the relationships between individual, groups and society that have taken place in twen-tieth-century China, the campaigns to transform and regulate these relationships, and the consequences of these campaigns for the lives of Chinese people and their social organization.

Confucianism

It is difficult to go far into discussions of social relationships in China without encountering the term 'Confucianism'. The term is often used as synonymous with traditional Chinese culture. Throughout the twentieth century, Confucianism has been the object of radical criti-cism from social reformers and revolutionaries, who have blamed this cultural heritage for China's backwardness. Asian and western scho-lars have studied the long and complex history of Confucianism as philosophy, as political, moral and social theory, and as religion, and have debated its fate in the modern world. Sociologists and anthro-pologists have often seen Confucian writings as intellectual elabora-tions on basic cultural traits of the Chinese people, whose everyday life can be seen as governed by Confucian morality. Confucianism was analysed by Max Weber (1968 [1916]) as the key obstacle to the development of capitalism in China, while in the 1980s it was re-evaluated as conducive to a distinct form of capitalism and the root of the economic success of the 'Asian tigers'.[4] In recent years political leaders have appealed to Confucianism as the core of distinct 'Asian values' which justify forms of government and social engineering that both internal opponents and external critics condemn as authoritarian and undemocratic. The term is now used in such a wide variety of contexts that it is in danger of meaning anything to anyone (Dirlik 1995).

To get to grips with this diversity of interpretation of Confucianism, it is necessary to sketch its main elements as a theory of society and the place of individuals and groups within it. From the early history of Chinese social thought, the intrinsically social nature of humankind has been emphasized. Social organization, according to this philosophy, involved a structure of hierarchical relationships between distinct categories of people, who were expected to follow their sense of duty and behave towards each other in ways appropriate to their relationship. If everyone held to the expectations associated with their status, social stability and harmony would be maintained, and the order of the cosmos would prevail. The central social relationships were defined by the doctrine of *wu lun*, or five cardinal relations, as laid out by Mencius (D. C. Lau 1970: 102): those between father and son, ruler and subject, husband and wife, older and younger brother, and between friends. Each of these relationships was associated with a specific quality or character, respectively love (or affection), righteousness (or duty), distinction, precedence, and sincerity (or trust). Most of these relationships were familial ones, based on hierarchies of generation, age and gender. The relationship between the ruler and the ruled was also conceived on the model of father and son, while women's social roles were seen as predominantly internal to the domestic sphere.[5]

A basic Confucian concept was that of *li*, translated variously as 'ritual', 'propriety' or 'etiquette' (Dawson 1981: 26ff). Correct behaviour within a social relationship should be performed with the appropriate demeanour, including dress, the bearing of the body and the expression of the face. For the 'gentlemen' who were part of the emperor's court or who acted on his behalf as magistrates and ministers, and for all those who had pretensions to emulate this refined way of life, ritual and etiquette were elaborately codified according to precise relationship and situation. The correct observance of *li* was seen as essential to the preservation of social order and an expression of human distinctiveness. The *Book of Rites*, one of the ancient classics attributed to Confucius, provided elaborate rules for behaviour at key life-cycle events, especially for mourning dead relatives of various degrees of closeness, and also specified in detail correct forms of daily interaction between members of households so that the proprieties were upheld and human distinctions maintained. *Li* was contrasted with *fa*, meaning law; in the Confucian tradition, law was the enforcement of correct behaviour by the threat of harsh punishment (a doctrine initially associated with a rival social philosophy called Legalism), and was appropriate only for 'mean people' who, unlike gentlemen, did not have a sense of honour and duty and could not be relied upon to act according to *li*.

Only by acting correctly in social relationships could a person realize the virtues of humanity. The most basic of these virtues Confucius called *ren*, the Chinese written character for which is made of the root for human and the number two. The good person cultivates *ren* by learning how to relate to fellow human beings. This requires consideration for others, by not doing to them what you would not want them to do to you. Other social virtues stressed in the Confucian writings include good faith, loyalty, sincerity and a sense of duty, as well as filial piety. Finally, another important basis for social relationships within the Confucian framework is that of *bao*, which may be glossed as a principle of reciprocity (Yang Lien-sheng 1957). The idea that one kindness or favour should be repaid by another and that the social order is held together by a continual exchange of services is repeatedly encountered both in written reflections on social life and in everyday situations.

Confucianism and sociology

In the twentieth century, a number of Chinese sociologists have argued that a Chinese sociology should build on these Confucian concepts. The central idea is the primacy of social relationships. Sociologists often refer to Liang Shuming, a Confucian social reformer of the 1920s and 1930s, who stated that Chinese society is neither individual-based nor society-based but rather relationship-based (King 1985: 63; King 1991: 65; Alitto 1986). Both poles of Liang's contrast are important. On the one hand, he claimed, China had only a weakly developed concept of the individual self, of individual rights, individual self-development and individual freedom from interference by others. On the other hand, he argued that China had only a weakly developed notion of the group, the organization, and of society as a whole, that might enable mobilization for the pursuit of collective societal goals. What is central to Chinese society is the quality of human relationships.

Fei Xiaotong (1992 [1947]) distinguished Chinese social structure from western forms in a similar way. He called the western form the 'organizational mode of association'. In western societies, individuals make up organizations as members. The boundaries of organizations, the definitions of who is and who is not a member, are clear; the members form a group, and their relationship to the organization is basically the same, in that they are bound by the rules of the organization. The morality of organizational life is universalistic; one's obligations to others are regulated by norms which apply equally to all members of a category of persons, such as the members of an organization or of a nation. By contrast Fei described Chinese society as constructed according to a 'differential mode of association'. There are no fixed groups with defined memberships, but rather, myriads of overlapping networks of relationships. Each network of relationships appears different depending on which person is the focus of the network; each person has a different web of social relationships. The pattern of these networks 'is like the circles that appear on the surface of a lake when a rock is thrown into it. Everyone stands at the centre of the circles produced by his or her own social influence. Everyone's circles are interrelated. One touches different circles at different times and places' (Fei 1992: 62–3). The morality of differential relationships is particularistic: one's obligations to others depend on the specific nature of the relationship and the network in which it is embedded. Fei referred explicitly to the Confucian concept of *lun*, or order based on differential classifications. Obligations based on particularistic relationships, especially to kin, override wider group affiliations.

Fei contrasted modern western society ruled by law with traditional Chinese rural society ruled by ritual. Rituals are 'publicly recognized behavioral norms' (Fei 1992: 96) which govern the action of people bound by particularistic relationships. He perceived a direct continuity between the Confucian term *li* (and its contrast term *fa*) and the anthropological sense of ritual. Whereas law is enforced by the state, ritual norms are upheld by the sense of tradition maintained by the local community, by the power of public opinion concerning correct behaviour in particular situations between people in particular relationships, behaviour that becomes ingrained habit shared by the members of the community. Fei also drew on the ceremonial aspect of *li*, both in the sense of conventional forms of action and in the sense of the attitude of respect, even reverence, with which correct behaviour should be performed.

Closely related to the concept of ritual is that of 'face'. In an almost literal sense, this idea can be seen in the Confucian injunction that a gentleman should act according to the principles of *li* with an appropriate demeanour, bodily bearing and facial expression. In everyday Chinese speech, however, words which can be translated as 'face' occur in a wide range of colloquial expressions to refer to the moral quality of individuals or their families. These expressions and their sociological significance have been documented extensively by the Chinese anthropologist Hu (1944), who distinguished two different concepts of 'face'. One of these (*mianzi*) refers to the reputation or prestige attached to worldly success, wealth and power: thus, one can 'gain face' by ostentatiously holding a large wedding banquet, 'borrow face' by associating with prominent successful men, or 'give face' by going out of one's way to show respect for the wealth or power of a potential benefactor. One can also lose *mianzi* by appearing as less competent than one has claimed, explicitly or implicitly, to be. The other concept (*lian*) has greater moral significance, and refers 'to the respect of the group for a man with a good moral reputation: the man who would fulfil his obligations regardless of the hardships involved, who under all circumstances shows himself a decent human being. It represents the confidence of society in the integrity of ego's moral character, the loss of which makes it impossible for him to function properly within the community' (Hu 1944: 45). *Lian* can be lost by some major moral transgression against the norms of the community, and is made even worse if the transgressor shows no regret; such a person 'does not know *lian*', which means that they have no moral character left. According to the anthropologist Watson (1991: 374), the Confucian content of this idea appears in a synonymous expression used by Cantonese villagers he lived with, among whom someone who was oblivious to proper behaviour was said to be 'without *li* '.

One aspect of the ritual of everyday life in which the concept of *li* is encountered is in the giving and receiving of gifts. The very word for 'gift' in Chinese is *liwu*, or ritual object (Yan Yunxiang 1996: 44). Gifts are given on a wide variety of ceremonial occasions, including the major life-cycle events of childbirth, engagements, marriages, birthdays and funerals, as well as community celebrations over the course of the year. Gift-giving is subject to the principle of *bao*, or reciprocity, and face can be gained or lost by particularly appropriate or inappropriate gifting. Gift behaviour is seen as an occasion for the display of social competence, and participation in cycles of gift-giving is remarked on as essential to the maintenance of social relationships.

This considerable emphasis on the primacy of social relationships leads also to consideration of the nature of the human personality in Chinese society. Some Chinese sociologists have suggested that whereas western societies develop notions of autonomous selves seeking independence from the constraints of social ties, whether this be the increasing autonomy of the maturing adult from the child-hood ties to parents or the striving for freedom of subjects from rulers, slaves from masters, serfs from lords or employees from employers, Chinese society sees the self as immersed in and defined by its social relationships. Hsu (1985), for example, advances the concept of the 'relational self', with relational identities more deeply embedded in the personality than is the case with westerners, and the boundary between self and external world less sharply defined. The self is often seen as seeking harmony with its social environment through con-formity with its demands, rather than striving for independence and mastery over the environment. This thesis also underlies Max Weber's (1968) interpretation of Confucianism and its lack of the world-transforming orientation found in adherents of the Protestant sects.

However, even sociologists strongly influenced by the Confucian tradition have suggested that this view of the Chinese individual completely integrated into the social environment is an exaggeration, an 'over-Confucianized view of Chinese society' (King 1985: 60). Confucian scholars have modified this interpretation through studies of literature and texts relating to the lives of imperial civil servants and courtiers; they show that the Confucian is often portrayed as a person striving for self-perfection by development beyond mere conformity, as a person driven by the demands of conscience to challenge the policies of emperors even at the cost of their livelihoods or lives, and even as a critic of the constraints of stultifying social convention (Tu Wei-ming 1985; Elvin 1985). Metzger (1977) extended this reinter-pretation of Confucianism into a critique of Weber's thesis, arguing that Confucianism could indeed generate a sense of tension between the self and the world, with transformative possibilities.

Confucianism and Chinese distinctiveness

Before proceeding to examine revolutionary and reformist challenges to Confucianism, and the more recent re-evaluation of Confucian values, it is worthwhile making a preliminary assessment of these claims to distinctiveness for Chinese culture and society, which contrast the relational nature of Chinese society with the individualistic or organizational nature of western society. A full examination of these claims would involve extensive comparative studies, for which there is no room here. None the less, three main lines of criticism can be sketched.

First, this Confucian-influenced sociology can easily overestimate the homogeneity of the Chinese cultural heritage and the dominance of Confucian social assumptions. While Confucianism was the dominant form of social and philosophical thought in imperial China, the 'heterodox' currents of Daoism and Buddhism were also important and influenced Confucian thinkers in various ways. Weber described Daoism as the mystical pursuit of sainthood through withdrawal from the world of affairs into a world of contemplation, a private or even solitary life particularly attractive to elderly officials who had retired from imperial service. It was a view of life that disdained the ritual and ceremony of social relationships in favour of simplicity and inactivity. As such it was not necessarily a challenge to the ruling elite. Only if Daoism, and Buddhism too, developed sectarian aspects and a recognition of sources of authority other than the emperor were these world-views deemed to be heterodox and subjected to persecution. Daoist or Buddhist tendencies could challenge the harmony of the social order as sectarian movements, which encouraged the pursuit of virtue outside the framework of approved social relationships. An alternative model of society was thus made available to large masses of people, and took the form of the secret societies which existed in the interstices of the state and which often formed the basis for widespread peasant rebellions (Chesneaux 1973). According to Fei-ling Davis (1977: 83), the significance of secret societies lay in 'their destructive potentialities with regard to the Confucian society, and in their revolutionary affirmation of the development of the voluntary association in opposition to the ascriptive association of birth'. Confucian-influenced sociology may have a tendency to neglect such indigenous alternatives and misleadingly treat Confucianism as the essence of Chinese culture.

Second, there is a tendency for both western and Chinese sociologists to exaggerate the individualistic and non-relational aspects of western social thought and common-sense assumptions. The individualism of liberal democratic political thought and of market economics rose to dominance from the seventeenth to the nineteenth centuries in Britain and America, paralleling the rise of the urban capitalist class in the social structure. But earlier forms of social thought continued to have resonance with some sectors of society and could form the basis of alternatives to individualism. While this critique of individualism was often framed in terms of self-consciously progressive forms of social thought, such as socialism, it could also look back to pre-modern social thought with its conception of an integrated, often hierarchical society. The tradition of Aristotle, especially in its medieval Catholic guise, saw an ideal society as a set of interrelated statuses each performing a function in a stable society, with everyone accepting traditional authority and knowing their place. The individualism often thought so characteristic of 'the West', in contrast with China, never entirely displaced this organic hierarchical view of society, which reappeared in full force in the corporatist social theory of fascism in the early twentieth century. More egalitarian visions of an integrated society often also share a nostalgia for small-scale community bound together by shared morality and shared memories, and modern Catholic and Christian Democratic social philosophy also resists the march of what is seen as socially corrosive individualism. In constructing his contrast between Chinese and western society, Fei Xiaotong did recognize this complexity in western models of society, and drew on contrasts developed within western sociological theory, such as Tönnies's *Gemeinschaft* and *Gesellschaft*, Durkheim's mechanical and organic solidarity, or Redfield's continuum from village (folk society) to city. The consistent use of these ideal types would not involve the Confucian sociologist in making a sharp distinction between Chinese and western societies, since each type could be manifested in different parts or different phases of development of any society. Yet this typological approach coexists, even in Fei's writings, with an essentialization of cultural difference, a view which can easily be exaggerated into a thesis of the non-comparability of cultures (Nathan 1993).

Third, western sociology itself is part of the critique of individualism as ideology (Hughes et al. 1995: 7), and in the course of this critique has developed social theories which often bear remarkable similarity to Confucianism. Four aspects of these theories may be stressed here. In the first place, western sociology shares with Confucianism a conception of the intrinsically social nature of humanity, and hence of a realm of the social which cannot be reduced to features of individuals. Second, western sociologists have developed theories of the ritual character of social interaction, most notably in the sociology of Erving Goffman in his development of the theories of Durkheim and Simmel. In his account of 'interaction ritual', Goffman (1967) shows the necessity for each participant to exhibit respect for the social situation and for the other participants, if the interaction is to proceed smoothly and interactive harmony is to be maintained. This respect is shown by the appropriate level and type of involvement, by deference and demeanour. Most strikingly, Goffman explicitly draws on the concept of 'face' to elaborate Simmel's view of the sacred quality of the person, which may be protected or infringed by interaction with others. It becomes clear that 'face' is by no means peculiar to Chinese social morality but has characteristics which may well be universal (D. Y. Ho 1976). Third, the social nature of the personality is stressed in many traditions of sociological theory, especially that of George Herbert Mead and symbolic interactionism (Mead 1934; A. M. Rose 1962), for whom self–other interaction, role-playing and role-taking are indispensable to the development of the human person. Fourth, the stress on impersonal universalism in western social life is often exposed by sociological analysis as ideological distortion. While equality before the law and impersonal procedure in bureaucratic administration are held up as ideals, the reality often reveals considerable departure from the ideal, and much sociological work has been concerned with uncovering covert discrimination and the workings of supposedly illegitimate particularism in a wide variety of social settings.

The difference from China seems to be not so much in the real character of social relationships and social interaction as in the extent to which this is explicitly acknowledged and consciously reflected on. As Hughes et al. (1995) argue, the theses of western sociology often appear as counter-intuitive in a culture so deeply imbued with individualistic ideologies. There is much work for sociology to do, and much resistance to its proposals. If Chinese culture is different, it is perhaps in its ready common-sense acceptance of what western sociologists have to fight so hard to have recognized. Chinese sociologists have in everyday Confucianism something like a ready-made indigenous sociology, a built-in cultural recognition of the demands and constraints as well as the opportunities provided by social organization.

Modern attacks on Confucianism

Liang Shuming remained to the end of his life committed to a reconstruction of Chinese society through the development of Confucian traditional values and morality. Many other intellectuals and political activists, however, came to believe from the late nineteenth century on that a more fundamental transformation of China's cultural orientations and social institutions was required. Confucianism was identified as the problem rather than part of the solution to the need for modernization.

Reformers attacked the hierarchical structure of social relationships. Kang Youwei, one of the leaders of the 1898 reform movement, moving from practical reform proposals to Utopian speculation, rejected the Confucian doctrine that individuals should always act in accordance with their distinct statuses in hierarchical relationships (which Fei later termed the differential mode of association) and proposed the abolition of all social categories, especially those of the family, to free the energies of individuals to act according to reason and emotion (Hsiao 1975). Liang Qichao, one of Kang's followers, argued that a modern society required that the allegiance of individuals be widened from an overriding commitment to kinship obligations, the sphere of private morality, to a concern for civic virtue and public morality: this was the predominant burden of his concept of the 'New Citizen', which was also the title of the journal of ideas which he edited in exile in Japan. The new citizen of a modern state would cultivate a capacity for forming civic associations with fellow citizens beyond the realm of kinship and locality, a dynamic engagement in competitive struggle rather than a concern for harmonious ritualized relationships, an active, adventurous and enterprising spirit rather than obedience to convention (H. Chang 1971). During and after the First World War the New Youth and New Culture movements placed the emphasis on breaking down the hierarchies of age and gender and the power of the elderly; only thus would it be possible to throw off the yoke of tradition and enable the younger generation to construct new forms of social organization. Feminist movements at that time attacked the gender hierarchy and the subordination of women and their confinement to the domestic sphere (Croll 1978). Many young men and women, mostly from the educated elite, staged their own personal revolutions by breaking free of the control of their parents and making their own decisions about education, careers, and sexual and marital relationships. They took encouragement from writers such as Lu Xun and Ba Jin, who wrote in scathing terms about the stifling and irrational traditions of a backward society. The period is often known as the May Fourth period, deriving from the date of the outbreak of a widespread movement of student protest at the terms of the Versailles settlement (1919) granting former German

territorial concessions in China to Japan. The protest became a movement which continued the attack of New Youth on Confucian
morality and the constraints of traditional institutions, especially the
family (Chow Tse-tsung 1960).

In the Republican period of the 1920s and 1930s, reformers continued to bemoan what they saw as the backwardness of traditional
social relationships. Sun Yat-sen, the leader of the Nationalist
Party and the first President of the Republic of China, criticized
the Chinese people as a 'sheet of loose sand', exclusively attached to
family and clan and incapable of combining for national goals, and
his successor Chiang Kai-shek continued to use this metaphor. The
writer Lin Yutang drew a distinction between 'government by face'
and 'government by laws', arguing that China would become a true
modern republic only when government officials were subject to the
same laws as ordinary citizens rather than able to use the prestige
of office and their personal connections to gain privileges. Associates
of Liang Shuming, who led the Confucian-inspired Rural Reconstruction Movement in Shandong Province in the 1930s, believed that
the personalism of social relations prevented the Chinese from building stable collective organizations, such as political parties and
religious associations, and looked to village schools, combining the
functions of adult education, local administration and community
initiative, to transform the social structure of China from the
bottom up (Thøgersen 1998). But there was no sustained nation-
wide attempt to transform the nature of social relationships, and
sociological research of the 1930s and 1940s suggested considerable
continuity of familistic relationships at the heart of business enterprises and bureaucratic organizations, even in urban centres which
were most directly affected by the growth of the commercial economy and by the modern legal reforms of the Republican government.
Lang (1968: 181–4) found evidence in the 1930s of 'nepotistic ties'
influencing social processes such as employment in government
offices and factories, the availability of free public transportation
and access to public utilities, and the distribution of student
scholarships. Levy (1963: 350–65) also stressed the strength of
particularistic obligations in Chinese cities in the 1940s and interpreted them as an obstacle to the development of modern industrialism. Fei Xiaotong's writings of the 1940s, discussed earlier, aimed
to present western organizational forms, universalistic morality and
impersonal law as a model for social reform in China, as advocated by
the Democratic League, the political party of which he was a leading
figure.

Social relations under Communism

It was not until the establishment of the Communist regime that a sustained attempt could be made to remould the values and orientations of the Chinese people. The Communist Party intensified the attack on Confucianism, interpreting it as a feudal conception of society which had to be exposed to criticism if a new socialist society was to be constructed. Unlike previous intellectual criticism of traditional social relationships, and unlike previous reform movements, the Communists were in a position to attempt a radical transformation of the relationships between individuals and groups in society, through new forms of propaganda and social control. The Communist Party itself was a model of an organization based on a universalistic ethic, in which commitment to the cause of socialism was to override all particularistic obligations. Through a variety of techniques and campaigns, the party attempted to mobilize the entire population in the pursuit of collective goals, and to reorientate their commitments and ambitions away from the particular interests of family and locality towards the development of the whole society. As Vogel (1965) put it in a classic paper, comradeship was to replace friendship. Whereas friendship, and the even closer relationships of kinship, implied particular relationships based on mutual trust and reciprocal support, comradeship was to be universal and egalitarian. Every citizen was to be a fellow comrade, engaged in the common task of building a new social order, sharing the same 'will' or 'ambition' (this was the root meaning of *tongzhi*, the word for 'comrade') to combine their efforts in the common cause.

One of the main techniques developed by the new government was the enrolment of the population in a new form of organizational structure. Building on a method used in the Communist base areas for maintaining party control and establishing relationships with the local population, the leadership laid down guidelines for incorporating (in principle) every member of the population into small groups (*xiaozu*) for political study and mutual criticism (Whyte 1974). The aim was to unify and mobilize the Chinese people, to make them aware of party policy and goals, and to encourage and enforce commitment to those goals. Members of the group, numbering from eight to fifteen people, were to meet regularly to study official documents and statements, and to exercise mutual criticism and self-criticism in an atmosphere of unity and solidarity. The outcome was supposed to be a heightened understanding and enthusiasm for the collective goals of the society, which were to take precedence over the immediate personal preferences and interests of individuals and their families. Small groups and their activities (Whyte calls them 'political rituals') were to draw individuals out of the particularism of their primary social groups into a universalistic organizational framework under the control and supervision of higher authorities.

Mobilization through small groups was better suited to urban conditions of life than to rural, and Whyte suggests that small group organization among peasants was still relatively unsystematic by the late 1960s. The challenge to peasants' traditional conceptions of social relationships came in a series of campaigns that brought new social and moral vocabularies from the outside world. The land reform of the 1940s and 1950s introduced the language of class struggle and the idea that class interests were wider than those of family, lineage or locality, and this was continued through processes of collectivization and the formation of communes. The Socialist Education Movement of the early 1960s involved work teams of cadres and students going to villages to impress on peasants the Maoist moral discourse of self-sacrifice and 'serving the people' through open political debate and struggle. Both the universalism of Maoist morality and the techniques of public confrontation were direct challenges to peasants' traditional values, which Madsen (1984) describes as 'Confucian'.

The outcomes of these attempts to transform social relationships were complex and varied. Many people were won over to Communist ideals, if they were not already activists, and enthusiastically committed themselves to the building of socialism, even against the narrower interests of their families. Whyte (1974) argues that small group study sessions often had the immediate effect of mobilizing support and voluntary exertion, even though this might wear off as the rituals became routinized. Having interviewed middle-aged and elderly people in the 1980s, Mayfair Yang (1994: 153) portrays their recollection of the 1950s as a time of simple and straightforward social relations, fuelled partly by a collective idealism for the creation of a new socialist society and partly by the fear of punishment for attempts to use particularistic ties to gain special advantages for one's family or local group. It was seen also as a continuation of the revolutionary spirit of Yan'an[6] and of the People's Liberation Army, which had contributed so much to the Communist victory over the corrupt and inefficient forces of the Nationalists.

At the same time, however, the succession of small group meetings and campaigns created an atmosphere of uncertainty full of risk and danger. In order to gain state power and to transform the society, the

regime had broken down the walls which had previously enclosed
people's private lives. In a revolutionary situation, which had only
recently also been one of outright civil war, the authorities were
continually on the lookout for potential opposition to their rule and
to their programmes for social transformation. It was important, as
Mao Zedong put it, to know who were 'friends' and who were
'enemies' of the Communist Party which claimed to represent the
aspirations of the vast masses of peasants and workers. Enemies
were potential counter-revolutionaries, and the authorities needed
information about them, their thoughts and their organizations. Anyone might be called on to provide information about themselves or,
even more significantly, about the people they lived and worked with,
in private interrogations, in small group discussions or in large meetings. Under these conditions of actual or potential surveillance, no one
could ever be certain that private conversation would remain private.
Vogel shows how this uncertainty broke down the trust that is
required for friendship, and made it risky to confide in friends.
Thus, unlike in liberal societies where there is a relatively clear
demarcation between public spheres of association governed by
universalistic norms of impersonality and private spheres of intimacy
governed by particularistic norms of commitment and trust, in
the early years of Communist rule in China there was only a universal,
public realm of comradeship. Publicly identified 'enemies',
including the 'sinister elements' of landlords, rich farmers and
counter-revolutionaries, and later 'Rightists', were clearly not 'comrades' and occupied a no man's land of continual social marginalization and persecution, which provided others with negative role models
and a spur to conformity.

During the Cultural Revolution which began in 1966, the penetration of the private sphere and the collective mutual mistrust Vogel
described were carried to new extremes. Even the most intimate
relationships were politicized, as children were called upon to report
their parents to the revolutionary committees for failing to abandon
old customs and beliefs, and as husbands and wives or old friends
found themselves in opposite political factions and forced to condemn
each other. The years 1966–8 were ones of considerable instability
and upheaval, and when the radical Maoist wing of the Communist
Party finally reimposed order with the aid of the PLA, it did so by re-
establishing the dominance of the state over society which had been
one of the main targets of the Cultural Revolution in the first
place (Meisner 1977: 354ff). The party-state aimed to administer all
aspects of economic and social life, with the hierarchy of communes,

brigades and production teams in the countryside and the work-units in the towns and cities maintaining control, surveillance and discipline over the entire population. It might appear as if there were no social space available for the operation of particularistic social relationships.

Phases of suspicion, vigilance and heightened campaigning were, however, interspersed with those of laxer political atmosphere. Whyte (1974) argues that it was impossible for the regime's technique of small group political rituals to eliminate the private sphere completely. Small groups within organizations could not become individuals' primary groups, fully substituting for family, kin and friends. Individuals would continue to seek support from close circles of intimates, and attempt to shield themselves from the intrusive effects of study sessions and mutual criticism. An appearance of uniformity and conformity with political demands might often be maintained, but many people were merely going through the motions. Traditional bases for particularistic mutual obligation continued to exist, and people in all walks of life depended on them as a defence against the risk and uncertainty of political campaigns and as a method for improving their life chances in various ways.

The clash between traditional particularistic 'Confucian' morality and the new universalistic ethic of the Communist Party is analysed in detail by Madsen (1984) in his study of the twists and turns of relationships between leaders and other villagers in a village in southern China. Different leaders appealed to different forms of moral authority, some closer to the expectations of members of the local community, others to the demands of superiors in the party apparatus. The former tended to represent the village as structured by long-standing kinship obligations, which could be the basis for patterns of patronage, or as a big egalitarian family with shared localized interests. The latter attempted to break down such local particularism and to implement national party policy, which itself oscillated between the revolutionary purity associated with Mao Zedong and the technocratic pragmatism associated with Liu Shaoqi and Deng Xiaoping.[7] Leaders and their supporters disputed alternative visions of a good society and of appropriate social relationships, in complex and shifting alliances and combinations. Writing in the early 1980s, Madsen suggested that the collapse of revolutionary Maoism following the Cultural Revolution led to the growth of a utilitarian moral discourse in which people were encouraged to seek their own self-interest in an atmosphere of calmer pragmatism. The result, according to Madsen and many other commentators, has been an increasing emphasis on the strategic aspects of social relationships, summed up in the term *guanxixue*.

The emergence of *guanxixue*

The 1980s and 1990s have seen an explosion in academic discussions of the phenomenon known as *guanxi*. The word also appears constantly in everyday conversation among Chinese people. *Guanxi* means 'relationships' or 'connections', and can be used to refer to relationships between people and groups (social relationships, international relations) as well as between processes and ideas. Recently, it has increasingly been used to refer to the networks of personal connections (*guanxiwang*) which people cultivate and utilize to gain access to resources which may bring them some advantage, and which they might not be able to acquire without such connections. If everyday talk, journalistic commentary and academic analysis are to be believed, the use of *guanxi* has become all-pervasive in Chinese society. In fact, the word *guanxixue* has been coined to refer to the awareness of this social trend; the suffix *xue*, meaning 'study', implies that *guanxi* has become an art or a science, and the term *guanxixue* has been glossed as 'the art of social relationships' (M. M. Yang 1994) or even 'connectology' (Huang 1989: 143). Measured against the proclaimed attempt of the state to stabilize legal and administrative procedures after the 'chaos' of the Cultural Revolution, the use of *guanxi* can extend into the realm of bribery and corruption, the prevalence of which provides another focus for attention to *guanxi*. This section provides an introduction to some of the sociological and anthropological interpretations of this aspect of social relationships in China.

A useful starting-point is provided by Thomas Gold (1985) in his reconsideration after twenty years of Vogel's analysis of the replacement of 'friendship' by 'comradeship'. Some years after the end of the Cultural Revolution and the beginning of the post-Mao economic reforms, Gold saw Chinese society as thoroughly imbued with instrumentalism and commoditization. The growth of market exchange and the dismantling of collective agriculture had removed the economic basis for comradeship and had atomized society. People were concerned to gain advantage for themselves and their social group, and were prepared to go to great lengths to cultivate relationships (*la guanxi*, literally 'pull' *guanxi*) with anyone who might be able to help gain access to some valued good or service. These networks of relationships, which extended both vertically and horizontally, were built on any particularistic connection which could be mobilized for the purpose, and were maintained by a plethora of banquets and giving of gifts to establish good will. Those with the power to grant favours by pulling strings were in much demand and needed to be 'given face' as an inducement to assist. Within the various levels of Chinese bureaucracy, such inducements could easily border on, or cross the border of, outright corruption, and Gold referred to accounts in the official press which suggested that corruption was rampant in the ranks of the cadres. *Guanxi* appears to be ubiquitous in business relationships, and its use is often interpreted as unethical or corrupt by those, such as foreign business people, who find themselves excluded from advantageous networks, or by government spokespersons who wish to give their international counterparts the impression that corruption is being dealt with (R. P. L. Lee 1986; G. White 1996; A. Johnson 1997).

Gold interpreted the rise of *guanxi* instrumentalism as the reassertion of traditional cultural patterns of interaction stimulated by specific social conditions. The particularism of kinship and group solidarities had not been displaced by the universalistic ethic of comradeship, and the use of particularistic connections as a basis for reciprocal exchange of favours had not been displaced by the impersonal procedures of formal bureaucracy. In particular, the Cultural Revolution period was seen as the origin of *guanxixue*. The penetration of the state into all aspects of personal and private life and the control by the state over the allocation of all scarce resources had resulted in the continual search for irregular channels, especially contacts with cadres who might be prepared to bend the rules. It was a risky business, and the balance of trust and mistrust in such relationships had to be finely judged. The policy of sending urban youth down to the countryside[8] was a marked occasion for the use of *guanxi*, as those with contacts to appropriate cadres attempted to evade the harsher consequences of the policy and to return earlier to the cities. The excesses of the Cultural Revolution, as they were seen, had delegitimized the communist ethic of comradeship in the collective building of a new socialist society and had left people bereft of a moral framework that went beyond the advantage of themselves and their family. Gold saw this resurgence of traditionalism under new conditions as a Chinese variant on a typical crisis in state-socialist regimes which others have referred to as 'neotraditionalism' (Jowitt 1983).

Walder (1986) developed this idea of neotraditionalism a stage further in his study of social relations in Chinese industrial work-units. He showed how networks of *guanxi* developed between work-ers and supervisors, through which workers sought to gain favours by cultivating particular supervisors, for example by giving them gifts and inviting them to banquets, and how, on the other hand, managers strengthened their positions within the work-units by building up networks of followers who would support them in factional conflicts. However, Walder argued that this was not simply a resurgence of traditional particularism. Rather, these *guanxi* networks operated within a specific ideological context, in which commitment to com-munist ideology separated the ideologically pure from the ideolog-ically suspect. This commitment must be continually demonstrated in practice by showing the appropriate attitude (*biaoxian*). *Guanxi* ties were overlaid on top of this commitment to communist principles, hence Walder referred to them as 'principled particularism'. Further-more, he argued that principled particularism is just one example of a specific form of communist modernization, which the Parsonian pat-tern-variables are unable to encompass. Particularism of this kind and the reciprocal relations of dependency between workers and foremen, he suggests, are deeply rooted in the structure of the modern Chinese enterprise and are unlikely to be eradicated in the further course of modernization.

The most detailed discussion of *guanxi* to date is provided by Mayfair Yang (1994). A number of her arguments may be mentioned here. First, she sees the instrumental use of *guanxi* as a form of resistance to the increased surveillance power of the communist state during the Cultural Revolution. With the increasing politicization of all aspects of everyday life, people felt the need to construct a kind of buffer zone between themselves and the state, made up of kinship, friendship and *guanxi* networks. Cultivating particular personal rela-tionships was not merely a way to get things done which could not have been done by the normal channels, it was also an end in itself, the construction of a sphere of morality and human feeling within a chaotic and inhuman political environment. Second, Yang claims that as a means of gaining access to valued goods and services *guanxi* is inefficient and time-consuming, and with the increasing commodi-fication of goods and services of the 1980s people would prefer simply to pay money in the open market rather than go through the back doors opened by connections. However, the marketization of the economy has not displaced *guanxi*. Rather, *guanxi* has occupied new territories created by the market economy, as connections are used to widen opportunities for making or saving money. Third, Yang sees *guanxi* networks as forming the basis for a 'second society', similar to that which has been identified in eastern Europe (Hankiss 1990), emerging in the interstices of the state. Rather than referring to this second society as a kind of 'civil society',[9] Yang prefers to use the Chinese term *minjian*, or popular sphere. Explicitly referring back to the ideas of relation-centredness advanced by Liang Shuming, Fei Xiaotong and others, Yang interprets the growth of *guanxi* as a non-governmental sphere of informal social relationships, which might partly crystallize into a sphere of voluntary associations such as exists in western societies, but which is likely to remain predominantly unorganized and fluid.

Yang's research was conducted in urban settings. At the end of her book, she draws a distinction between social relations in rural and urban China, suggesting that the 'urban art of guanxi' can be seen as 'a particular instrumentalized and politicized form of a more traditional body of renqing principles and rural gift economy' (Yang 1994: 320).[10] According to Yang, the rise of *guanxixue* is often seen as a coarsening of social relations, characterized by aggressive tactics and instrumental aims. She also indicates a gendered aspect to this view, and suggests that women tend to be more critical of this instrumentalization of social relations, believing themselves to be more in tune with the obligations, debts, warmth and reciprocities involved in interpersonal relationships.

This distinction can be usefully explored by casting a glance at research conducted in a village setting by a Chinese anthropologist, Yan Yunxiang (1996). According to Yan, villagers see their *guanxi* networks as 'society', the local moral world in which they live. Within this world, their pursuit of personal interests is intermingled with the fulfilment of moral obligations, such as the exchange of appropriate gifts on a wide variety of ritual occasions, or mutual aid to provide social support when it is needed. Yan calls this the 'primary form' of *guanxi*, made up of known fellow villagers with whom one has those primary social relationships which define who one is and how one should act. Beyond this world, villagers also pragmatically cultivate an 'extended form' of *guanxi*, relationships with strangers which are developed instrumentally to pursue one's interests. One can be clever at 'pulling' such *guanxi*, but they do not carry the same moral force as those in the primary world. Also, to act towards one's fellow villagers in ways more appropriate to dealings with outsiders is seen as immoral, showing a lack of 'human feeling' (*renqing*), and thus causes loss of face. An example would be to pay money to a neighbour who had provided help with the farm or the house; more appropriate would be to give gifts, or to remain in debt until the neighbour asks for a favour in return.

Yan sees this distinction between primary and extended *guanxi* as helping to reconcile the normative and instrumental conceptions of *guanxi* in the earlier literature, and also to provide a better interpretation of the difference between urban and rural settings of *guanxi*. Urban dwellers, too, have primary social worlds in which instrumental and expressive aspects of relationships are intertwined, but they are also more likely than villagers to have to deal with strangers and to cultivate 'single-stranded' relationships with them to get favours done.

Yan's distinction between primary and extended *guanxi* is an example of the well-known sociological distinction between primary and secondary groups, or between 'insiders' and 'outsiders'. However, insiderness and outsiderness are themselves socially structured and depend on features of the wider social structure. Kipnis (1997) points to a number of features of contemporary Chinese society which provide the context for *guanxi* formation. For example, as seen in chapter 3, from the late 1950s to the mid-1980s there were strict restrictions on migration which enforced a high level of residential stability on villagers. As a consequence, on the assumption that villagers would share the same social world for perhaps their whole life, the maintenance of good *guanxi* was particularly important, and the distinction between insiders and outsiders was a sharp one (Kipnis 1997: 145). Similarly, in urban work-units such as those studied by Walder (1986), lifelong membership together with the fact that work-units were responsible for almost all aspects of members' lives meant that networks of *guanxi* were significantly restricted to insiders to the work-unit (Kipnis 1997: 151; Ruan 1993). Kipnis concludes that the emphasis on particularistic relationships described as *guanxi* should not be seen as if it were an essence of Chinese culture (as is often done by Confucian sociology), but rather as a set of practices of Chinese people responding to the varying social and political situations in which they find themselves.

A similar conclusion can be drawn from the research of Guthrie (1998) on attitudes to *guanxi* among enterprise managers. Guthrie discovered a diversity of views both on the importance of personal connections in business and on *guanxixue*, the use of *guanxi* to evade or oil the wheels of official procedures. Managers in branches of the economy where competition had become open and depersonalized were less likely to see *guanxi* as relevant to their business, and emphasized impersonal aspects such as price and quality instead. Managers

in more oligopolistic branches, especially those dominated by joint
ventures with foreign firms, were more likely to stress the value of
good personal relations, but also to believe that personal relations in
business were universal and not a specifically Chinese characteristic.
Managers in enterprises ranking higher in the administrative
hierarchy[11] more often denied that *guanxixue* was effective in relation
to official procedures. They believed that the legal framework introduced by government discouraged *guanxixue* and provided impersonal rules for everyone to follow. Managers in lower-ranking
enterprises, who thus had less close relationships with central government ministries, were more likely to claim that personal connections
could override legal procedures. Guthrie suggests that, in the sphere of
economic transactions, the extension of a legal–rational order will
gradually make *guanxi* less significant. However, one could suggest
that situationally specific variations, such as those found by Guthrie
himself, will continue to lead the weak to use *guanxi* to counter the
guanxi of the powerful. As Yang (1994) argues, there is no intrinsic
opposition between markets and *guanxi*.

Confucianism, authority and democracy

The growth of research and analysis of *guanxi* outlined in the previous
section casts further doubt on the essentialist approach to Chinese
culture and its distinctiveness, referred to earlier in this chapter. The
same conclusion can be drawn from debates over the final aspect of
Confucian social theory to be discussed here, which concerns Chinese
conceptions of authority in social relations. As we have seen, Confucian doctrine placed great weight on hierarchy in all social relationships as the bedrock of social order and stability. Starting from the
core relationships of the family, in which the obedience of the junior to
the will of the senior was seen as a fundamental principle, Confucian
social theory claimed that harmony and order depended on the incul-
cation and maintenance of belief in the legitimate authority of all
social superiors, and especially that of the emperor and his local
representatives, the county magistrates. There could be no institutionalized opposition to the rule of the imperial authorities, just as
there could be no legitimate opposition to the rule of the patriarch in
the family.

Some social scientists have constructed on this Confucian base an
account of the distinctive Chinese approach to authority. For example,
Hsu (1969) extrapolated an unquestioning acceptance of authority

from the centrality of the father–son relationship within the Chinese kinship system. Sons grow up in families knowing that they will remain under the influence of the father for the whole of their life, even after the death of the father who then becomes a worshipped ancestor, and this is supposed to generate a conformist personality type which naturally accepts the authority of superiors. Hsu drew far-reaching consequences for Chinese political culture, and a number of political scientists have developed a culturalist approach to Chinese politics based on similar assumptions. Pye (1968) and Solomon (1971) are the leading contributors to this line of analysis, portraying Chinese political culture as based on a deep-rooted craving for authority which the Communist revolution merely perpetuated in the person of Mao himself. Other sociologists and political scientists are highly sceptical about this perspective, arguing that the culturalist attempt to see continuity between Confucianism and Chinese communism is based on extreme over-generalization and conceals considerable complexity and variation within Chinese culture (Christiansen and Rai 1996: 22).

However, it is not just social scientists who have adopted the culturalist interpretation of Chinese conceptions of authority. Political leaders in China and in other parts of Asia have in recent years appealed to Confucianism, or more generally 'Asian values', to legitimate forms of government that critics see as authoritarian and un-democratic. Lee Kuan Yew, the former Prime Minister of Singapore, has been the leading spokesman for this conservative utilization of Chinese cultural heritage, but the general line of thought is wide-spread. The regimes of Deng Xiaoping and Jiang Zemin have reversed the Cultural Revolution critique of Confucianism, which can be traced back at least to the May Fourth period, and have rehabilitated it as the essence of Chinese society and culture. Confucian values are supposed, in this interpretation, to include a willingness of individuals to merge their interests with those of the wider community. Confucian 'communitarianism' is contrasted with western individualism, and provides a rationale for a view of human rights at considerable variance from that urged on China by western governments and non-governmental human rights pressure groups.[12] Western individualism is criticized for setting the interests of individuals above those of the community, allowing license, deviance, immorality and social break-down. Western individualism prevents the collective solution of social problems, solutions that would necessitate constraints over individual desires. A prime example is the official justification of the one-child family policy.[13] According to this, a level of state control over fertility

that 'western individualists' would see as an infringement of basic
human rights is necessary if population growth is to be contained
for the benefit of the whole community (Milwertz 1997).

Conclusion

The wheel appears to have turned full circle. Modernizing elites early
in the twentieth century mainly saw Chinese cultural predispositions,
summed up in the short-hand term 'Confucian', as rigid and hierarchical, preventing the release of youthful energy and initiative from the
shackles of tradition and the older generations. Both the Nationalist
and the Communist parties initially embodied the spirit of the New
Youth and New Culture movements and the replacement of imperial
authoritarianism with democracy. By the end of the century, the
regimes in both Communist PRC and Nationalist Taiwan[14] had
come to draw on an essentialized interpretation of traditional Chinese
culture, again using the term 'Confucian', to legitimate authoritarian
government through recourse to nationalist symbols and rhetoric.

Sociologists do best to be sceptical of such claims that there are
essential differences, in their conceptions of individual, group and
society, between Chinese and western cultures. It is just as important
to challenge simplified generalizations about Chinese 'relationism' as
it is to question western 'individualism', and in particular to unmask
the ideological use of such claims for the purpose of legitimating
forms of political domination. The sociological study of social relations in China needs to be no less complex and analytical than it is
anywhere else. As everywhere, this will require continued further
research into the various patterns of linkage between people, as they
work out the moral and practical basis of their relationships with
others under changing and uncertain conditions.

Further reading

Fei Xiaotong (1992), first published in 1947, is an early exercise by
China's greatest sociologist to relate western sociological theory to
indigenous Chinese, especially Confucian, categories for a general
readership. Nathan (1993) discusses the weaknesses of culturalist
interpretations of Chinese distinctiveness. Madsen (1984) provides a
provocative analysis of the clash of interpersonal moralities and conceptions of authority in different phases of the revolution. From the
growing literature on *guanxi*, Yang (1994) on urban contexts and Yan

(1996) on village ones may be particularly recommended for their ethnographic detail and subtle interpretations. De Bary and Tu (1998) contains a great diversity of interpretations of questions of human rights in the Chinese and wider Asian context.

5

Chinese Family: Continuity and Change

Introduction

China has often been seen as a peculiarly familial society, and Confucian social theory placed special emphasis on family relationships as the core of a stable and harmonious society. Yet in modern times the structures and functions of the Chinese family have come under vigorous criticism. From the earliest days of the reform movement in the late nineteenth century, the Chinese family was seen as an obstacle to the modernization of Chinese society, a backward-looking brake on the energies of the young, holding them in patterns of behaviour which had led China into decline and defeat. Since then, the reform of the family has been a central focus of modern state policy; republican regimes, both bourgeois and socialist, established programmes to transform family life by legislation, compulsion and incentive, programmes to which masses of ordinary Chinese people have had somehow to respond. At the same time, economic and cultural developments have led people to reconstruct their family life. Many women have attempted to redefine their family relationships with men and many young people have sought to recast their relationships with their elders.

This chapter explores changes in the institution of the family and its place in the Chinese social framework. A number of theoretical perspectives are relevant here. *Functionalist* theories emphasize the role that institutions of family and kinship play in the reproduction, not only of the population, but also of patterns of culture and social structure. In carrying out the primary socialization of young children, the family maintains a society's culture, transmitting basic cultural elements, value-orientations and personality characteristics from parents to children. By socially placing children within the structure of kinship and stratification, the family maintains a society's structure (K. Davis 1948; Goode 1982). In a stratified society, socialization and placement are interrelated; children are socialized into those cultural patterns which will enable them to hold their position within the structure. It follows that, if the culture and structure of a society were to be radically changed, these family mechanisms of socialization and placement would have to be transformed. The theme of radical change is taken up by *critical* perspectives on the family, including Marxist and feminist ones.[1] In these views, family processes help to maintain structures of social domination, of propertied classes over propertyless, of men over women, of older generations over younger. The family is a site of power and of the reproduction of power. Family revolution is therefore an important component of social revolution. A third perspective derives from theories of *modernization* advanced by sociologists such as Kerr (1973), according to which traditional family patterns were incompatible with economic development, and would have to change in the course of modernization. This perspective corresponds closely to the views of many Chinese reformers and to western interpretations of Chinese society put forward by, for example, Weber (1968) and M. J. Levy (1963).[2] Elements of all of these perspectives will appear in the following discussion.

Family and kinship in pre-revolutionary China

Chinese family life was traditionally structured as a series of hierarchical and reciprocal relationships, according to principles of generation, age and sex (Baker 1979). Confucian social doctrine placed great emphasis on the cultural ideal of a large, extended family household, with several generations living under one roof. The man in the oldest generation was the head of the family household, holding authority within the family, promoting its well-being, and representing the family to the outside world. Younger generations were taught to respect and obey their elders. Within a group of men of the same generation, for example the sons of the head of the household, there was a hierarchy of age, with the sons identified by their birth order and referred to by their parents as 'eldest son', 'second son', and so on.

Daughters were similarly numbered. A younger brother would refer to his elder brother as 'elder brother' rather than by his given name and would be expected to accept his authority and leadership, likewise with sisters; elder siblings were expected to take care of younger. Finally there was the hierarchy of sex. Women were theoretically subordinate to men in all family relationships, normatively expressed in the doctrine of 'three obediences': as a daughter a woman should obey her father, as a wife she should obey her husband, as a widow she should obey her son who succeeded his father as head of the family. It was also physically expressed in the practice of foot-binding, which crippled women and restricted their mobility, and which also supposedly made them more attractive and marriageable into higher status families (Levy 1966).

Families and their members were closely identified with their surnames, which designated descent in the male line. The members of a family household were seen as the living representatives of a line of descent stretching from the earliest remembered ancestors down to the present descendants and onwards to the future generations who would continue the family line (Hsu 1971). Households maintained ancestral tablets representing the genealogy of the household head; these were placed on family altars, the focus for the worship of ancestors, and symbolized the continuity of the hierarchical and reciprocal relationship of the generations after death. Ancestors watched over the living members of the family to whom they had given life, and in return living members would provide ancestors with the food and money they needed in the spirit world. Filial piety extended to obligations to the ancestors, notably to provide the ancestors with descendants, hence the overriding necessity for a man to marry and have a son. Sons were much preferred to daughters, and the birth of a succession of daughters was no cause for rejoicing.

The primary purpose of marriage was to continue the family patriline. Marriage was considered to be a family rather than an individual matter and hence was arranged by parents, sometimes when the prospective spouses were in their infancy, using go-betweens and fortune-tellers to check the suitability of the potential bride and groom and to negotiate terms and conditions of the alliance. Central to this arrangement was the injunction of exogamy, meaning that the bride's and groom's families should not share the same surname or even come from the same village. The bride moved on marriage away from the village where she was raised to the village of her husband's family, to take her place in their household; this pattern is referred to as 'patrilocal' or 'virilocal' marriage.[3] The responsibilities of the new bride included service to her mother-in-law, who determined her duties within the household. The new member of the household had a very low status, which improved only when she had fulfilled her primary function of producing a male successor.

Children were socialized and educated within the family household, where they learned the implicit elements of 'Confucian' social theory in the maintenance of harmonious family relationships, and the practical meaning of filial piety, humanity and reciprocity in everyday activities. They would learn their place within a network of relationships, identified by a complex kinship terminology referring to a wide variety of relatives, and their obligations to others within the network (M. Wolf 1970). They would learn the essential differences between the social roles of males and females. Those who learned to read would do so using primers imbued with Confucian ideas. Boys who showed scholarly aptitude, mainly from wealthier families, would be schooled to the civil service examination curriculum, dominated by Confucian texts. Most sons, however, were prepared from an early age to take over the roles of related adults in the rural economy, and daughters were socialized to accept that their fate was to leave home and marry into a family of strangers. By these methods of socialization, it appears that 'Confucian patriarchy succeeded in legitimating itself as a system among most Chinese women as well as men' (Stacey 1983: 50).

Patrilineal descent also involved patrilineal inheritance. The vast majority of family households in pre-revolutionary China were engaged in agriculture and many owned the land they worked. The custom was for all sons to inherit the family's property in roughly equal shares. Daughters did not inherit, but did customarily receive dowries, a form of premortem inheritance by which daughters were allocated an appropriate share of the family patrimony (Ebrey 1991b). The division of a family's property, especially of land, between a number of sons tended to be associated with the division of the household, although ideally this would not happen until after the death of the older generation. The process of family division (*fenjia*) had a tendency to break up accumulations of land holdings and perpetuate small family farms as the basic unit of the rural economy (Lavely and Wong 1992).

The principles of patrilineal descent also encouraged the formation of groupings of kin larger than the extended family household. The attention to genealogy implied by ancestor worship made it likely that households sharing the same surname and living in the same area would be aware of the kinship relationships between them, institutionalized in many families by a sequence of generation names, such that all males of the same generation would share the first syllable of their given names, identifying the generation to which they belonged. This awareness legitimated the formation of 'lineages', organizations comprising the households of all male descendants of a common ancestor. A lineage would have a form of government made up of elders led by the head of the lineage, in principle the oldest man of the oldest generation (the generation nearest to the common ancestor), who would govern the lineage according to written rules laid down at some time in the past (Liu Hui-chen Wang 1959). Depending on the wealth of the area and of the component households, the lineage could possess material expressions of their kin relationships, such as an ancestral hall in which ancestral tablets were kept and in which collective worship of ancestors was conducted. It could also own land, subscribed by members of the lineage in honour of a prominent ancestor; the land would be rented out to individual households (members of the lineage or not) and the rental income used for purposes advantageous to the lineage, such as meeting the expenses of a school for the (usually male) children of lineage families. In parts of China, especially the south-east, where single-surname villages were common, the lineage organization overlapped with the government of the village. In multi-surname villages, relationships between the dominant and subordinate lineages formed an important part of the village power structure.

The elements of the Chinese family system mentioned so far, which may be summed up in the shorthand phrase 'patrilineal, patriarchal and patrilocal', have been represented as the enduring or primordial nature of the 'traditional' family in China (A. Wong 1979). An alternative view is that these are the core features of an ideological discourse of the family sustained by and for the powerful elements of imperial Chinese society, comprising in particular the central imperial state, powerful and wealthy families in given localities, and men in general. Ebrey (1991a), for example, argues that the 'Confucianization' of the Chinese family took place over a very long period of time and was heavily influenced by imperial policies. The centrality of the surname in identifying patrilineal descent, the small family household as a unit of production and consumption governed by a patriarchal family head, the tendency for small family farms to predominate in agriculture, and the stress on Confucian education as the dominant channel of social mobility, can all be traced back to governmental interests in social harmony and stability, in surveillance and taxation, and were actively encouraged by state policy. These elite patterns were propagated down the class structure, and deliberately inculcated among the general population by the dissemination of texts, the issuing of edicts, the establishment of lecture series and the incorporation of such values into legal codes.

Conformity to Confucianized 'rules' of family life was therefore greater in the upper classes than in the lower. Wealthy men had larger families with more sons, either by their wife or by concubines. Poorer families were more likely to divide, and divide earlier, than wealthy families. The 'normal' pattern of patrilocal marriage was less common among the poorer classes, although it was still normatively highly valued. Some marriages were in fact uxorilocal, where the groom moved to the household of a man who had daughters but no sons, and allowed at least one son to take the surname of his wife's father, thus enabling the latter to fulfil his duty of continuing the family line (Wolf and Huang 1980). Only a poor man, or possibly a disabled man, who had no prospects of concluding a patrilocal marriage, would accept such an arrangement. The formation of lineages too was the result of deliberate strategies among the upper classes of late imperial Chinese society to extend their power and influence, rather than a primordial aspect of kinship.[4]

Generally speaking, marriage can be seen as one mechanism for preserving the structure of inequality in pre-revolutionary Chinese society. As in other patriarchal and patrilineal societies (Goody 1990), marriage was a form of social placement. The choice of a spouse creates a relationship to that person's kin group and affiliates a person to the life chances of the kin group. Where, as typically is the case, there are considerable social inequalities of life chances, this affiliation is fateful indeed; if you marry into a wealthy family, you yourself are likely to become or remain wealthy, while if you marry into a poor family, you yourself are likely to remain or become poor. The relatively small amount of research which focuses on the relationship between marriage and inequality in China, summarized by Ebrey (1991b), confirms the tendency, at all levels of society, for marriage to take place, by arrangement of senior kin, between relatively equally situated families. Affinal links, therefore, were more important than might appear in the Confucianized model of patrilineal kinship.

The Confucian model is also a male model which obscures women's conceptions of family relationships. Although patrilocal marriage entailed the departure of the bride from her natal family, much research has discovered the significance of continued relations between married daughters and their parental home (*niangjia*). Not only did daughters maintain such relations to provide fall-back support for themselves in case of problems arising in their new conjugal family (Judd 1989), they were also responsible for maintaining the strength of affinal ties which could be mobilized for mutual support, business ventures, and local political alliances (R. S. Watson 1985). Furthermore, the wife's dowry provided her with some economic resources of her own, and in some cases a widow could take over the management of her late husband's estate (Dennerline 1986). In fact, without denying the general social subordination of women in Chinese society, researchers have in many ways demonstrated the active role of women in their families and kinship networks.

A more thorough challenge to the conventional Confucian view of the patrilineal and patriarchal family has been provided by the work of Margery Wolf (1972, 1987). Based on research in Taiwan and reinforced by further research in the People's Republic, Wolf argues that the entire discourse of patrilineality is a male-orientated one which speaks to the interests of men. She shows how women in rural Taiwan had quite a different view of the family, for which she coined the term 'uterine family'.[5] Women, she argues, are less concerned with the agnatic relationships of their menfolk, and more concerned with their own immediate relationships within the family household. As incomers into a family of strangers, it is important for them to build relationships that will provide them with support, especially relationships with their own children. Child-rearing in China has typically been warm and affectionate (Sidel 1972), and children are encouraged by this to be devoted and indebted to their mothers (Stafford 1995). In the event of family frictions and disputes, a mother may receive the support of her children, especially sons, and this mitigates the generally subordinate position of women in family and society.

In many ways, then, the Confucian conception of the family must be seen as an ideological framework, deliberately disseminated to maintain the harmony of a hierarchical and unequal society. Its emphasis on patrilineal descent, on patriarchal rule and on patrilocal marriage arrangements provided the context in which various groups could pursue their interests and in which the privileged could preserve their advantages. It was an ideological framework which concealed from view alternative conceptions of family life and of the relations between old and young and male and female. Explicit criticism of it was rare until the twentieth century, but throughout that century the family and kinship have been central areas of conflict, social engineering and social change.

Pre-communist criticism of the Confucian family

Criticism of many aspects of late imperial Chinese society grew towards the end of the nineteenth century as China's weakness in the international arena became apparent through defeat in wars and the loss of control over treaty ports. Elements of the educated classes became convinced that major social and political change was necessary if China was to be successful in its search for wealth and power, and sought knowledge of the institutions of other societies (Schwartz 1969). The traditional family system came under particular attack from younger reformers and revolutionaries. Its emphasis on continuity and the dominance of the older generations over the younger was seen as an obstacle to change and to the assimilation of new ideas and practices. Educated young people sought freedom from their families and wanted to make their own decisions about marriage, education and careers. Modern schools were started by missionaries and other agencies[6] and propagated alternative views of family life, of the relationship of individuals to the family and of the position of women in society. Feminist organizations were set up and campaigns mounted for such goals as the abolition of foot-binding (Croll 1978); physical freedom was seen by many as fundamental to social emancipation (Hong 1997). The magazine *New Youth* was established in Shanghai as a vehicle for the radical critique of old institutions including the family. Ba Jin's novel *The Family*, set at the time of the May Fourth movement and published in the 1930s, represented the struggle of the younger generation to free itself from the shackles of the Confucian family system and was a clarion call for change. Sociologists working in China in the 1930s documented change especially among those segments of society exposed to new ideas (Lang 1968).

This cultural critique of the traditional family was primarily an urban phenomenon. Stacey (1983) argues that it also had a rural counterpart, brought on by the consequences of changes in the agricultural economy. Peasant families whose livelihood was threatened by population growth, landlord exploitation, rising taxes, foreign competition and other forces found it difficult to realize the values of Confucian familism. Marriage rates declined, household structure became simpler, family ceremonials could no longer be afforded. There is also evidence of resistance to patriarchal domination among young men and to some extent women, encouraged perhaps by teachers and campaigners bringing new ideas to the village from the cities. It is difficult to know how extensive and widespread these developments were, but Stacey feels they justify the judgement that the peasant family was in crisis.

The Guomindang government introduced reforms in family law which modified Confucian patriarchy with elements of modern values. The Civil Code of 1931 established the principle of free-choice marriage and granted women rights in matters of divorce, inheritance and property more equal to those of men, though it maintained patriarchal authority in other respects (Meijer 1971). The law expressed family values that had already influenced the practice of the urban middle classes, but had very little impact on family life in rural areas. In other respects the Guomindang abandoned its earlier revolutionary ethos and attempted to reinforce a conservative moral order based on a mixture of Confucian and Christian virtues.

Communist transformation: the new democratic family

The rule of the Guomindang was always contested and its credentials as a revolutionary party were not borne out by its capacity to trans-form society. The Communist Party, by contrast, was able to experi-ment with a variety of policies of social change in the mainly rural areas where it gained control in the 1930s and 1940s, and then to embark on a radical course of social transformation backed by state power from 1949. The Communist approach to the family was in many ways radical, but it was always a part of a wider programme of social change, the underlying philosophy of which did not accord very much significance to the institution of the family as such; Marxist theory allocated it to the superstructure, dependent on changes in the material base. The government was primarily concerned to develop the economy, and to this end the hierarchically structured family could at times be a useful means. The concern here is to understand not just the explicit family policy of the Communist regime, but also continu-ities as well as transformations of the place of the family in the wider social structure, some aspects of which may have been intended, others not.

The explicit family policy for the PRC was expressed in the Mar-riage Law of 1950, which aimed to replace the 'feudal' patriarchal marriage system of the old society with the 'new democratic' marriage system, 'based on the free choice of partners, monogamy, equal rights for both sexes and protection of the lawful interests of women and children' (Meijer 1971). This law prohibited bigamy, concubinage, child betrothal, interference in the remarriage of widows, and the exaction of money or gifts in connection with marriages. Husbands and wives had equal status, equal rights in family property, and the right to inherit each other's property. Divorce by mutual consent was made available by registration with the local government office; otherwise, both parties had equal right to sue for divorce. Appropriate relationships between husband and wife and between parents and children were specified, stressing equality, mutual respect, love and support, and the reciprocal obligations of each member for the welfare of the family as a whole. The law envisaged a 'family revolution', the main elements of which were the curtailment of patriarchal rights over women (Stacey 1983). The power of the state was to be used to shift the basis of family relationships away from the hierarchies of generation, age and sex to a more egalitarian model. The conjugal family of husband, wife and children was to be extracted from its embeddedness in patrilineal and patriarchal structures and made the basis for a new form of harmonious family life; the husband–wife relationship was to replace the father–son relationship as the core dyad of the kinship system (Hsu 1969). Apart from a desire to reduce the power of patriarchs, the aim of the Communist leadership was to lay the foundation for a stable and happy family life which would enable family members to devote their efforts to the construction of a new socialist society.

However, the family policy of the Marriage Law has to be seen in the context of the wider dynamic of social change. Stacey (1983) argues that, when family policy is seen in conjunction with other elements of the Communist programme, especially land reform, it appears that the actual consequence was to create the conditions in rural China for a new, democratized form of patriarchy. Land reform[7] transferred vast areas of land from landlords and rich farmers to poor peasants. This land, nominally allocated to all adults individually but in fact consolidated into family holdings, provided the material conditions in which poor peasant men who had hitherto been unable to marry and have children were now able to become the head of a family household. The 'rural family crisis' was thus solved, and the traditional family was rescued at the same time as it was being transformed. This is essentially what poor farmers had wanted when they gave their support to the Communist Party and fought for the Red Army, to gain the material basis necessary for living a proper family life as a respected family head.

The need to retain the support of the rural population, especially the poor peasantry, also led the party to back-pedal or go slow in the implementation of some provisions of the Marriage Law (Davin 1976; Stacey 1983). Divorce was a sensitive issue, as peasant men did not want to relinquish their hold over 'their' women. After a spate of divorces in the first two years of the law's existence, it became increasingly difficult for a woman to gain a divorce and the emphasis shifted towards conciliation procedures and pressures on couples to stay together. The rights of women over land were also curtailed in practice, with married women's names seldom appearing on title deeds and divorced women prevented from retaining rights over their share of the family's land. After 1953 the party deemed the law to have done the necessary work in constructing the new democratic family, and implementation of its provisions ceased to be a major priority of government agencies (K. A. Johnson 1983).

Another combination of continuity and change can be seen in the role of lineage in rural China. The early phase of the land reform process distributed land to large numbers of family farms. The subsequent phases aimed to increase the degree of co-operation and co-ordination between farming families, at first through the formation of Mutual Aid Teams, then of Agricultural Producers' Co-operatives, and eventually of the People's Communes. The family which was a property-owning unit in the MATs and APCs became an organizational, income-earning and consuming unit in the communes. In all of these larger levels of organization, kinship links between the men of these families took on new functions. Land redistribution had ostensibly removed the material basis for lineage organization, since lineage corporations had been dispossessed of their land-holdings. But the men who had organized lineage activities remained in the hamlets, neighbourhoods and villages around which mutual aid teams, agricultural co-operatives and eventually production teams within communes were formed, and their kinship networks played a central role in the power structure of these organizations. Agnatic kinship ties thus re-formed around the new collectivized institutions in the countryside (Diamond 1975; Parish and Whyte 1978; Potter and Potter 1990). Kinship, however, was not the only social principle maintaining ties between groups of men resident in the same village; as we saw earlier, the stress on patrilineal kinship could at least in part be seen as an ideological framework legitimating a range of aspects of male domination of village life, which has led some writers, such as Judd (1992), to use the term 'androcentry' for the structure of social relationships preserved by patrilocal marriage customs.

It is striking therefore that the Communist authorities never mounted any campaign against the system of patrilocal marriage[8] which, together with its counterpart of *de facto* (if no longer *de jure*) patrilineal inheritance, remained the basis for women's relative exclusion from control over economic and political affairs in rural China (K. A. Johnson 1983; Stacey 1983), and which remained a powerful principle for decades after the revolution (Whyte 1979). The stabilization of residence by the household registration regulations discussed in chapter 3 intensified the consequences of patrilocal marriage. Until the growth of mobility stimulated by the economic reforms of the 1980s, the vast majority of rural men remained in the village in which they were born, thus cementing the networks of relationships between them. Men also inherited the most important component of family property remaining in private hands after collectivization, namely housing, and this gave parents continuing influence over their sons and their marital plans (Parish and Whyte 1978).

Stacey (1983) refers to the new family system in the countryside produced by this combination of factors for continuity and change as 'patriarchal-socialism'. The elements of this system – patrilocal marriage and residential stability of men, aspects of patrilineal inheritance and patriarchal authority, male networks in local power structures, and a continued sexual division of labour – made up a new and unique system of family and kinship, but one which resembled the pre-revolutionary system more than had perhaps been intended by the radical revolutionaries who led the CCP. Peasant men, and many older women too, saw the new society as one in which they could attempt to realize traditional family values rather than those propagated by urban reformers, and they had a degree of power and leverage to mould the 'new democratic family' to their own ends.

The situation in the cities developed quite differently (Whyte and Parish 1984). Family life among young educated urbanites had been moving towards a 'new democratic' conjugal pattern since the May Fourth period (Lang 1968). Furthermore, unlike in rural areas, there was no structural or material basis for a reconstruction of patriarchal power. Most families ceased to be units of production; most urban inhabitants became income earners in state or collective work-units, and housing was provided either by the work-unit or by local government housing departments. Such factors weakened the power that parents had over their children. Parents' influence over their children's marriages was considerably reduced, though by no means eliminated (Whyte 1992). Nor could parents directly influence the placement of their offspring in jobs, once the system of state assignment of school-leavers to work-units had become established (Bian 1994). Increasingly, young married couples were able to live in accommodation allocated through their own work-units rather than with the parents of either bride or groom, although stem families of both kinds remained common (patrilineal ones more so) in the early years of married life. From the late 1950s it became normal for married women to work full-time in state or collective work-units (proportionally more in the less privileged collective sector than men), thus contributing to the family budget and raising their status and influence within the family. Correspondingly, urban husbands found it necessary to contribute more to the domestic tasks of housework and child care, though women still did most (Stockman et al. 1995).

There were also major changes in the nature of urban kinship. Lineage organization in cities had already been much weakened before 1949. In the early decades of the PRC, pressures for the elimination or simplification of life-cycle or calendrical rituals resulted in the attenuation of kinship ties, the need for support from kin was lessened by the extension of welfare services made available through work-units, and shortage of time together with poor urban transport made it difficult to visit kin. Extended kinship ceased to be an important basis for social organization. Kinship on a narrower scale shifted from a patrilineal to a bilineal emphasis, as parental preference for sons declined and daughters became just as important as a source of support or of a home in old age (Davis-Friedmann 1983). Young women were not separated from their parental homes by patrilocal marriage.

As in the countryside, there were also elements of continuity in urban family life, especially the high degree of co-operation and mutual support between the generations, whether or not they resided together. Younger adults retained a sense of obligation to care for and support elderly parents. So long as they were capable, the older generation expended great efforts for the welfare of the family as a whole, for example by doing the shopping or the cooking, or looking after grandchildren while their parents were at work.

In general, the family reforms of the Communist regime were more acceptable in urban areas. The model of the 'new democratic family' had long corresponded more closely to the values and practical constraints of urban dwellers than those of peasants, and family life would have moved in that direction with or without the 1950 Marriage Law. The model must not, however, be confused with the 'structurally isolated nuclear family' of modernization theory; the intergenerational links and even shared households mentioned above, together with the operation of the urban work-unit (of which more below), generated considerable differences in the context of family life from that supposedly common in European or American cities.

Despite the changes mentioned so far, in both rural and urban areas the family continued to be an institution central to people's lives. The Communist party-state had no intention of destroying the family as an institution or even of removing its core functions. Rather, it attempted to gain some control over the way those functions were performed and to co-opt family activities and family loyalties in the service of the revolution. Membership of a family continued to define who a person was and to place them in society, but in terms increasingly supervised by the state; family membership allocated people not only their name, residence and property, but also their *hukou* classification, their class label,[9] their share of collective income and their ration coupons. The family continued to be the only legitimate location for sexual activity, and any extra-marital or pre-marital sexual experience was seen as a threat to social order (Evans 1997).[10] Families continued to socialize their own children, and although child care facilities were increasingly provided by urban work-units and neighbourhood organizations as younger married women were encouraged into the social labour force, parents interviewed by Whyte and Parish (1984: 169) in the early 1970s did not believe that collective child care was subverting children or turning them against their families.

Only in relatively short periods of intensely radical campaigns, such as during the Great Leap Forward and the Cultural Revolution, did the Communist party-state take major steps to remove basic social functions from the family. During the Great Leap Forward rural and urban communes were encouraged to take over almost all the functions of the family, including child-raising and the provision of domestic services, in order to achieve economies of scale and to intensify time and work discipline. This generated considerable resistance from both men, who saw their patriarchal power being further eroded, and older women, who found themselves loaded with additional burdens just at the stage of life when they would normally have daughters-in-law to help them (Stacey 1983: 213ff). The experiment was quickly brought to an end. The Cultural Revolution campaign to encourage children to resist their parents and their 'feudal' upbringing had consequences deemed by the party to be anarchic, requiring the reimposition of control by the army. Thereafter, the authorities once more stressed the role of parents in helping to educate new generations of socialist citizens and in maintaining discipline.

None the less, the boundaries around the private family were to some extent penetrated by the party-state, partly to mobilize family members for the building of a socialist society, but also to limit some aspects of patriarchal domination. This was especially the case in urban work-units, which created a markedly new context for those family activities (Stockman et al. 1995: 26ff). Urban work-units (*gongzuo danwei*) in the 1960s and 1970s were multifunctional organizations that, as well as undertaking a range of productive and political functions, also shared with families many reproductive activities which in capitalist societies are left to the preserve of the private family.[11] They were heavily involved in the education of members and their children, in providing for the welfare and social security needs of members and their families from cradle to grave, in family planning and birth control, brokering marriages, mediation in marital discord, and cultural provision for free time. This interpenetration of productive and reproductive spheres was one of the key conditions for the relative reduction in urban gender inequalities, for example in education and incomes, which was achieved in the Maoist period (Stockman 1994).

Family, state and society in the post-Mao era

A number of elements of state policy in the post-Mao era have drastically altered the conditions of family life. Three aspects in particular will be the subject of the last part of this chapter: first, the state's explicit family policy as expressed in law; second, the state's attempt to control one of the most basic functions of the family, that of biological reproduction, through what is usually referred to as the 'one-child family policy'; third, the restoration to many families of economic functions removed by state planning.

Family law

State policy in the post-Mao period has begun to operate more through the medium of codified laws than in previous decades, including in the sphere of family policy. There has been a proliferation of laws governing or affecting family relationships (Palmer 1995), beginning in 1980 when a considerably revised Marriage Law was introduced. The family has officially been designated the basic institution of Chinese society and is seen to be functional for social stability and harmony. The family is the only legitimate sphere for sexual relationships and childbearing. Parents are legally required to protect their children and socialize them appropriately into social values and behaviour, to educate them and to ensure that their right to attend school is respected. Parents are required to discipline their children and are responsible for disturbance or damage they cause; no longer are children to be taught that 'to rebel is justified'. The family is responsible for the care of dependants, including the elderly; children have reciprocal obligations to their parents, to support them and care for them if needed in later life. Family ownership of property, including the means of production, is legally guaranteed, and the Inheritance Law of 1985 regulates the disposition of such property.

Palmer (1995) identifies a number of points of tension between law and social practice. The state attempts to enforce clear procedures for the registration of marriage, which have run into conflict with customary weddings and with attempts to avoid registration, for example in order to marry below legal ages or to evade birth control regulations. Access to divorce has been eased, with 'freedom to divorce' under the condition of 'breakdown of mutual affection' written into the 1980 Marriage Law, while there is considerable official apprehension about the rising, though still low, divorce rate. The state's attempt to enforce a one-child family policy conflicts, especially in rural areas, with the desire of parents to have sons and the need of farming families for an adequate family labour force. As in many other areas of state activity, the ambition of the state to mould family life through law has run ahead of its capacity to enforce that law.

The anti-patriarchal claims of the earlier communist movement have not been eliminated from the overt formulation of law and policy, and the state remains explicitly committed to the curtailment of patriarchal rights over women and children. For example, the state has become increasingly involved in questions of family abuse and sexual violence, attempting to provide legal protection for wives and children, and has expressed much concern over the rise in 'trafficking in women' and prostitution (Keith 1997). In 1980 the PRC signed the UN Convention on the Elimination of All Forms of Discrimination Against Women, and the 1992 Law for the Protection of Women's Rights and Interests consolidated and built on earlier legislation (Palmer 1995). There is much discussion over the significance of the language of 'rights and interests' in newer Chinese legislation and doubts as to the existence of adequate procedures available to women to enforce their lawful rights. There remains a tension between the state's attempt to use the family as a mechanism of social control and the commitment to extending rights.

Family and state in fertility control

One of the most profound ways in which the Chinese state has attempted to penetrate and police families is in the sphere of fertility. Prior to the Communist regime there had been no state intervention in this aspect of family life, except in so far as Confucian orthodoxy reinforced popular belief in the importance of having children, especially sons. Families would want to have 'many sons (to bring) much happiness' (*duozi duofu*), and surveys of older women suggest that the idea of a preferred family size did not have much meaning to them (Greenhalgh and Li 1993: 17). Educated urbanites began to discover modern ideas of family planning and methods of contraception in the 1930s, but this had little impact in the society as a whole. It was when the communist idea of planning began to be applied to the sphere of population that the state really became involved.

Small-scale campaigns to encourage birth planning were launched in 1956–8 and the early 1960s, but these were cut short by the Great Leap Forward and the Cultural Revolution. More significant were Zhou Enlai's 1965 call for a reduction of China's annual population growth rate to one per cent by the end of the century and the subsequent incorporation of population targets into the draft of the Fourth Five-Year Plan. From then on population issues were treated officially as questions of physical planning under the slogan of 'jointly grasp two kinds of production' (T. White 1994). The 1971 policy of 'later (marriage), longer (birth spacing), fewer (children)', with its recommendation of two children as the ideal number for urban families and three for rural ones, was finally superseded in 1979 by the call for all couples to limit themselves to one child. In 1982 the revised constitution of the PRC stated that 'both husband and wife have the duty to implement fertility planning' (Lieberthal 1995: 365). To enforce these policies, cadres were appointed in every work-unit, neighbourhood and village as the lowest level of a system of administration to educate in family planning, provide contraception and abortion, oversee birth plans, collect fertility statistics, issue single-child certificates, and punish couples who had children outside the plan. Routine implementation was supplemented by periodic campaigns during which cadres were required to meet targets of birth planning, contraception use and sterilization (Croll et al. 1985).

The state has had very mixed success in implementing the one-child family policy. It is difficult to generalize as there never was a single policy, but rather a framework within which different provinces laid down different regulations specifying, for example, the conditions in which a second child would be licensed. Resistance to the policy was widespread (Wasserstrom 1984), and enforcement made difficult by the cadres' own actual or reputed evasion (Bianco and Hua 1988). The impact of the policy on fertility is also questionable: the birth rate in China, especially but not only in the cities, had already fallen considerably before the policy came into effect, for a wide variety of reasons (Banister 1987; Peng 1989). In rural areas, the policy came into direct conflict with the labour requirements of peasant house-holds, a contradiction exacerbated by the knowledge that the more prosperous households were also the ones with more available labour (Croll 1983). However, even though the policy was modified in some areas, especially those populated by minority nationalities, it has never been abandoned. The implications of the policy for the gender balance of the population have also been much debated, and while Greenhalgh and Li (1993) have shown that it is much too simple merely to identify a resurgence of 'traditional' preference for sons, it is also clear that the abandonment of infant daughters is a consider-able problem (K. Johnson 1996). It seems that a complex process of policy bargaining and policy adjustment goes on in different parts of China, as local cadres and authorities respond to the pressures and the fertility behaviour of families, especially in relation to the family's preferred gender composition (Greenhalgh 1993).

Fertility has become a major battle-ground in Chinese society, with women caught in the cross-fire of the private patriarchy of their husband's families and the 'public patriarchy' of the state. Women's sexual and reproductive behaviour has become subjected to scrutiny and control of a historically and culturally most unusual intensity. The authorities have sought women's active acceptance of this supervision, with varying degrees of success (Milwertz 1997). Fertility control is just one of many examples of the extended 'reach of the state', an issue taken up further in the next chapter.

In response to this combination of state policy and economic and social conditions, family size in urban areas has fallen considerably, and the vast majority of newly formed families now have only one child. This has given rise to extensive reflection on the social signific-ance of the one-child family. If it continues, the trend will result in the further attenuation of kinship linkages, as fewer people will have cousins, aunts and uncles. The only child will eventually become responsible for producing the wealth to support two parents and four grandparents (often referred to as the 4-2-1 pattern) and even for their personal care in old age. In the meantime, there is evidence that the one-child family is becoming increasingly child-centred (Bian 1989; Davin 1990). Parents of only children spend more of their spare time with their child than other parents do, and spend more of their income on their child. There is much discussion in the media and elsewhere, attaining according to Davin the status of a 'moral panic', of the alleged problems of social competence and discipline of these pampered 'little emperors' (less is heard of little empresses), and of the supposedly necessary remedial moral education in schools (S. Rosen 1993). From another point of view, this child-centredness appears as a determination on the part of parents to invest heavily in their child's future, to transfer to their child whatever cultural capital they have and purchase more if possible, and thus to maintain or improve their family's social position in a more unequal and competitive society.[12] This orientation to child-rearing chimes in well with the state's continually expressed emphasis on 'raising the quality' of the nation's population as part of the strategy of modernization (Wu 1992; Anagnost 1997: 116–37).

Family farm and family business

By 1978, the economic activities of the vast majority of Chinese families had for twenty years or more been incorporated into larger forms of social organization, production teams in the case of rural families, work-units in the case of urban ones. Families and their members had few choices as to how they were to make a living. The economic reforms brought in from 1978 had the effect of reallocating many economic functions to family households. In rural areas the dissolution of the commune structure led to family households once again becoming units of production. To a lesser extent urban families have also regained some control over their economic activities, in particular where they have established private family businesses, but also where the growth of new employment opportunities has enabled families to pursue more diversified household work strategies. The implications of this shift of economic decision-making to families for the structures of power and inequality in the society will be taken up in chapters 6 and 8. Here the emphasis will be on the consequences of the economic reforms for patterns of family relationships and family authority.

The restructuring of the rural economy prompted considerable diversification between peasant households (Croll 1987). Relatively few households are now completely reliant on crop agriculture. Many have diversified into various combinations of cropping and domestic sidelines or into branches of specialized production; alternatively, some members of a family household take the main responsibility for the family's contracted land while others find employment in local industry, start a small business, or seek work in larger towns and cities. Some families even sub-let their land to others and withdraw from agricultural work. Each of these patterns, and the differential involvement of different family members in them, have different consequences for the structure of family relationships.

Families remain entirely dependent on agriculture only where no alternative economic opportunities are available. These families tend to revert most clearly to traditional patriarchal forms. Where both husband and wife work in the fields, the economic contribution of the wife, even if it is considerable, tends to be less apparent than when she was earning her own work-points under the commune system, with a consequent loss of authority in the family (Davin 1988). In other families, the traditional pattern of the men working the land ('outside') while the women take care of domestic duties ('inside') is reproduced (Jacka 1997). However, both of these types are uncommon. Far more widespread is the situation often referred to as the 'feminization of agriculture'. Across much of rural China, agricultural work in the fields is taken over for most of the year by women, as well as by children and the elderly, while men work in local industry or in cities. The consequences of this for family relationships are varied. Agricultural work may be seen as backward and less profitable, relegated to women as lower status 'inside' activity while men go 'out' to work in higher status, modern industrial branches. Alternatively, women may prefer to locate their activities within the household economy because it gives them greater autonomy and control over their lives. Judd (1994) argues that the household economy gives many women the best chance of escaping from the wider patriarchy of male-dominated structures beyond the household.

In rural households that have developed profitable sidelines or have become fully specialized in a particular branch of production, authority in the family depends on which family member has managerial control of the business (Entwisle et al. 1995; Jacka 1997). If both husband and wife are involved in the business, it tends to be the man who takes major decisions and represents the business externally. Where the business is the woman's responsibility, especially when her husband is working away from home, relationships within the family are likely to be more egalitarian, although it is also possible for the wife to be subject to the authority of her husband's male relatives in his absence.

Wives who are employed in township and village enterprises are also seen to be making an identifiable contribution to the family finances and gain corresponding authority within the family. However, such women are more likely to be employed in low-level, routine manual occupations with relatively lower wages and to be excluded from leadership positions (Judd 1994). In these families, as in all others, women are assumed to have the main responsibility for domestic duties of housework and child care, and the weight of these responsibilities can be heavy, especially where there are sick or elderly members of the household whose care falls increasingly on the family (Riley 1997). These rural women are thus faced with a particularly intense form of the double burden.

The post-Mao economic policies have also had consequences for relationships between the generations. In some respects these resemble pre-revolutionary patriarchal forms. Children have in some circumstances become important to the household economy although, because employment of children is illegal, the extent of child labour is uncertain. Some children, especially girls, are removed from school in order to do farm work while their parents concentrate on earning money elsewhere, or even to be put to work in village enterprises (Riley 1997). In some cases, sons remain under the authority of their parents after marriage, since profitable family businesses provide fathers with the resources to hold their sons within the enterprise and give the sons a reason to stay. The great investment in rural housing that was financed by rapid economic growth from the early 1980s was in part the construction or extension of houses intended to keep sons within stem or even joint family households, and a rise in the number of such households has been noted among the most prosperous entrepreneurial families (Selden 1993). In some areas parents attempt to influence the marriage decisions of their children to fit in with what they see as the corporate interests of the family, and pay high bride-prices to prevent their children moving away (Siu 1993). However, many researchers stress that these phenomena should not be seen merely as the restoration of traditional patterns. The younger generation has far greater autonomy than in pre-revolutionary times, the younger couple has greater control over its own finances, and is likely to bring pressure for earlier rather than later division of the family. If the older generation wish to maintain the multi-generation family business, they have to handle relationships carefully and go some way to satisfy the demands of the younger generation (M. L.

Cohen 1992). When the younger people have alternative economic opportunities outside the family, they tend to form separate nuclear family households even before the birth of children (Selden 1993).

However, to maintain family economic co-operation it is not necessary for the various conjugal units to live together in one household. Croll (1994: 172–7) has investigated a form of rural family that she calls the 'aggregate family'. This is an aggregation of ostensibly separate households who merge their economic activities to take advantage of income-generating opportunities. This could simply be the continuation of a joint venture operated by father and sons before the division of the family. However, it could also be formed by related families joining an already successful family enterprise. The participating households often live in close proximity, but sometimes more distant kin living in towns are brought into the operation, for example to handle the marketing of the produce of the village-based families. Such aggregate families can also become politically powerful groupings, able to bargain with local officials and to protect their component households from fees and other exactions. The concept of the aggregate family points to the need to study interrelationships between family households and not just the structure of relationships within them.[13]

In the cities, the economic reforms started later in the 1980s and made less impact on the basic economic structures from which families derived their living. Most urban residents remain employees of state-owned and collective work-units, though some have found work in joint ventures and foreign companies, and a small proportion have started small businesses. Many urban families have experienced a significant improvement in housing and living standards and an increasing opportunity for younger people to find their own employment in a widening labour market. One might have expected these conditions to be conducive to a continuing loosening of patriarchal domination in family relationships, but such expectations would only partially be borne out.

In the vast majority of urban couples of working age, both husband and wife are economically active. Conjugal relationships are relatively egalitarian, both compared with the past and with other urban societies (Stockman et al. 1995). They tend to share family decision-making and control over family finances, and husbands make a significant contribution to domestic labour and child care, although the main responsibility for these still falls on the woman. The marked equality of incomes in urban areas prior to the reforms[14] meant that differences between husbands' and wives' economic contributions to the household were relatively small. In the 1990s this began to change. Income differentials have widened, and the greater autonomy given to enterprise managements has enabled them to put into practice their general prejudice against employing and promoting women (Riley 1997). In some cities, such as Shanghai, hundreds of thousands of women have lost their jobs or have been put on to a low basic pay. One must expect that this will lower the authority of such women within their families, although little systematic evidence is yet available.

This reduction in the relative economic standing of women reinforces the tendency for the older generation to seek the support of sons rather than daughters. Despite a general trend towards a higher proportion of nuclear family households in urban populations, there is still a large minority of stem family households, and of these most are virilocal rather than uxorilocal (Davis 1993; Unger 1993; Ikels 1996). Newly married couples, if they cannot find or afford housing of their own, are far more likely to move in with the groom's parents than the bride's. And when elderly couples decide that they need to reside with one of their married children, they are more likely to live with a son than a daughter, although even then women often prefer daughters as sources of emotional support (Milwertz 1997). Parents with one child do not have this choice, and are almost as likely to live with a daughter as a son, and this may become more the norm as one-child families reach that stage of the life cycle. However, as in rural areas, these stem family households do not simply reproduce traditional patriarchal hierarchies. The younger couples have their own incomes and their own concerns, and even newly-wed brides do not accept the unbridled authority of mothers-in-law. The relationship between the generations is more in the nature of mutual aid and reciprocal support, or what Ikels (1993) calls an 'intergenerational contract', with the older generation taking over as much of the child care and domestic work as they are able, in the expectation that the younger couple will care for them as they become more dependent. It is in fact a relationship of mutual dependence, as the younger generation recognizes; Whyte (1997), in a survey of parents and their adult children carried out in the northern city of Baoding in 1994, found that adult children had at least as strong a sense of filial piety and family obligation as their parents had, although in other respects the younger generation had more liberal views and cultural tastes. Whyte argues that adult children remain bound to their parents in many ways, for housing, jobs and other social resources, and that they therefore tend to see the relationship between the generations as one of mutual obligation and support.

Finally, brief mention may be made of family relationships in urban small private enterprises (*getihu*), still a small minority of households in the cities. Many such businesses are established and run by unmarried women, or by married women without the participation of their husbands, and this provides women with a sphere of autonomy and financial control that did not exist either in the pre-industrial urban economy or in the more recent era of large state organizations (Riley 1997). Women who make a substantial entrepreneurial contribution to the family business also have greater control over their fertility since they can argue, employing commercial reasoning, that their time is more profitably spent in the enterprise than in raising children (Gates 1993). However, an ethnographic study of private business households in Chengdu, Sichuan Province (Bruun 1993), points in a different direction. In such households there is little distinction between work and spare time, between business and family life. There are strains towards a unified authority structure of these households-as-enterprises, with a reversion to patriarchal control. Men like to exert their authority as head of the household, and the running of the business reflects this, with women allocated more menial and subordinate tasks, and men taking every opportunity to avoid the manual labour associated with the business. Pressure is also brought on children to remain in the business to fulfil their filial obligations. The male head monopolizes external representation of the business. Disputes can arise where there is a mismatch between household and enterprise, as when a shop run by the wife makes higher profits than the wage of the husband who has retained state employment. If such findings are typical of the situation of urban private business, it may foreshadow a return to patriarchal structures characteristic of the pre-communist period.

Conclusion

An apparent overlap was noted in this chapter between the arguments of radical Chinese reformers early in the twentieth century and those of mid-century sociologists of modernization. Both argued that the Confucian family structure, with its patriarchal hierarchies of generation, age and sex, was an obstacle to China's modernization and at the heart of its backwardness. After the somewhat feeble attempts of the Nationalist government to reform the family through the civil law, and the endeavours of younger members of urban elites to adopt what they saw as modern western family patterns, the Communist regime seemed determined to rid China of a patriarchal heritage that weighed like a nightmare on the minds of the living. It turned out that for many supporters of the new regime, especially men of the older generation, patriarchy was a dream and not a nightmare. For this and other reasons, family revolution has had ambiguous consequences. Certainly, younger generations and women have achieved a degree of liberation from the domination of old men, many of them have a measure of economic autonomy from family control, and legal statements of the rights of women and children have become more explicit. But the family as an institution has not only retained its functions of socializing the younger generation and placing them in the social structure; it has also regained many of the economic and control functions that have underpinned patriarchal authority.

What, then, of the arguments of the modernizers? It is striking that in the last few years the Confucian family has been the object of a significant reinterpretation. Chinese sociologists and politicians speak of the family as the bedrock of the society and see any disturbances in its proper functioning, such as rising divorce rates or filial impiety, as pathological symptoms of social disorder. Likewise, many western social scientists, confronted with the rapid economic growth of the PRC and the 'four little dragons' (Vogel 1991), have taken to finding great potential for economic development and modernization in Confucian family values.[15] The arguments are complicated, and the reader must be referred elsewhere for a more thorough discussion of the debates (Berger and Hsiao 1988; Greenhalgh 1990; Whyte 1995, 1996). As a thesis in social explanation, Whyte is surely right in his assessment that Chinese family structure and values can only have played a partial and probably minor role in the economic take-off of east Asian societies, and even then only in conjunction with other social structural conditions. However, in line with earlier comments on the ideological significance of Confucian patriarchal doctrine, ideological components in this re-evaluation of the Chinese family have also been uncovered. Greenhalgh (1994b) refers to a discourse of 'Orientalist economics' that supports a flexible form of capital accumulation based on the exploitation of gender inequalities. Duara (1995) points to the identification of the Chinese nation with family morality as a central feature of nationalist discourse. As with all ideologies, an appropriate sociological attitude is suspicion.

Further reading

Baker (1979) is a useful introduction to family and kinship before the revolution and the early revolutionary changes. Stacey (1983) provides a challenging analysis of Chinese patriarchy and its socialist forms, while C. K. Yang (1959b) gives a more conventional sociological interpretation of family change. Davis and Harrell (1993) is an important collection of papers on developments in family life in the post-Mao period. Stockman et al. (1995) analyse the family and work experience of Chinese urban women in comparative context. Judd (1994) gives a sophisticated perspective on changes in gendered power relations in rural north China.

6

Power and Revolution: Economic and Political

Introduction

Power in China has been reshaped almost continually throughout the last century. Different groups, classes, and parties have come to the fore or been destroyed. The constitutional and legal framework, which in many other societies represents a relatively stable configuration of power, has in China been undermined and transformed several times. War and civil war have been crucial ingredients in these restructurings of power. Periods of revolutionary upheaval can be identified: the revolution of 1911 which brought the empire to an end and introduced the subsequent attempt to construct a republic; the Communist revolution which grew throughout the 1920s to 1940s and resulted in the establishment of the People's Republic in 1949; the Great Proletarian Cultural Revolution launched in 1966. But these periods of revolution are only the more identifiable phases in a long-term instability in the structure of power, a de-institutionalization of an old power structure and a 'failure' to reinstitutionalize a new one. This chapter and the next review the transformations of power in China from pre-revolutionary times to the present.

The concept of power relates to the fact that in all societies some people and groups are more capable of pursuing their objectives and overriding the desires or interests of others.[1] These capabilities rest on the possession of different kinds of resources. Many sociologists[2] distinguish three forms of social power, on the basis of three kinds of resources: *economic* power, based on the possession of goods enabling the owner to influence other people's actions, especially their labour; *political* power, resting ultimately on the possession of means of coercion or violence, but very often institutionalized in relatively stable forms of government or state rule, through which rulers or officials influence people's actions by laying down and enforcing laws or regulations; and *cultural* or *ideological* power, the ability to influence people's actions through control over the content of social ideas, such as norms and values, beliefs or what counts as knowledge. While these three forms may be analytically distinguished, they also interrelate; in particular, there may be rivalry or conflict between the possessors of the different resources, resulting in varying degrees of autonomy of different sectors of society from each other, or varying degrees of hegemonic control by one sector. Shifting relationships between different forms of power have been especially apparent in twentieth-century China. This chapter will concentrate primarily on economic and political sources of power; the main themes will be the changing balance of class forces, the nature of the state and of internal and external challenges to it, and the fate of the revolutionary attempts to 'put politics in command' of the economy. Chapter 7 will deal with the topic of ideological or cultural power. The consequences of these revolutionary transformations of power for the patterns of social inequality between individuals and groups will be the subject of chapter 8.

Power in pre-revolutionary China

By the beginning of the twentieth century the power structure of imperial China had become highly unstable. The main elements of that power structure had been the centralized imperial state, the only legitimate holder of political power, and the 'gentry' class of landowners, who exercised limited economic power over tenants, farmworkers and debtors, as well as within their own families and lineages, and who also played important political roles at the local level. As a result of both internal social and economic developments and the changing external environment impinging on China, both of these traditional wielders of power faced increasing challenges, which brought about the conditions for revolutionary upheaval.[3]

The reach of the imperial state had always been limited (Shue 1988). It had never managed to extract sufficient resources to pay a large enough staff to exercise detailed administration of the huge

territory. The lowest level of administration was the county magistrate, of which there were approximately 1500, governing an average
population of 250,000, at the end of the empire. The magistrate was
responsible for the basic political functions of tax collection, maintenance of law and order, and ensuring adherence to the state cult of
Confucian orthodoxy. Even to fulfil these basic functions of rule, he
needed the informal co-operation of leaders of the locally powerful
families and lineages, often referred to as the lower gentry. Beyond
this, the lack of financial and organizational capacity meant that the
state could not penetrate far into the everyday life of the population,
who were mainly left to live according to their local customs. The
local power of the gentry was relatively unconstrained, and might be
used to resist the encroachment of the state in the interests of the
gentry themselves or their local clientele. However, gentry families
were also incorporated into the state through their links with state
officials and their aspiration that their sons might enter the state elite
(the upper gentry) via the civil service examinations.

The state's control over the means of coercion was also limited, and
was often threatened from within and without. Internal challenge was
frequently mounted from peasant rebellions against excessive taxes or
rents, 'bad gentry' (*lieshen*) who usurped the appointed magistrate
and became local petty rulers, banditry, and uprisings of subject ethnic
or religious groups. External challenge traditionally came mainly
through incursion from the north, against which the state built the
defences called the Great Wall with only partial success, but also from
piracy on the China seas. At a local level, and in the absence of state-
funded police forces, villagers mounted armed protection against predation, and this could escalate to feuding between lineages or villages.
At many times in Chinese history, internal disorder and external threat
combined, resulting in conquest and the establishment of alien dynasties, such as that of the Mongols (*Yuan*) and the Manchu (*Qing*).

Economic power was relatively diffuse in late imperial China. There
was no large landowning aristocracy, partly because the state resisted
the concentration of landownership and promoted a smallholder
economy, partly because of the repeated division of estates between
all of a man's sons. In local areas, especially in the south, lineage trusts
could be large landowners and wield considerable economic power,
but many small landlords owned little more land than well-to-do
peasants.[4] The extent of large-scale managerial agriculture varied
regionally, but was generally not common (P. C. C. Huang 1985); in
most areas there were far more smallholder peasants than farm
labourers. Infrastructure work did sometimes require large-scale

organization and considerable economic power over many workers, though by no means as often as suggested by the theory of 'oriental despotism'.[5] Industries such as tea production, cotton and silk textiles, iron-smelting and ceramics frequently operated at a higher level of organizational complexity, and many urban trades were regulated by guilds exercising power over their members. Trading, money-lending and pawn-broking became lucrative activities, drawing investments away from agriculture in the nineteenth and early twentieth centuries, but the scale of firms seems to have been small, even if they were locked into complex market relationships. Conflicts over economic power therefore remained mainly localized and without extensive social significance, as was typical of most agrarian civilizations.

The potential tensions in this imperial structure of power were exacerbated by developments in the second half of the nineteenth century. Among these, changes in China's external environment were especially significant. Faced with imperialist expansion from Europe, America and Japan, which revealed China's military weakness, China was drawn into wider international processes of economic and political power on very unfavourable terms (Lippit 1978). Defeats in war resulted in loss of territory (Hong Kong), loss of jurisdiction over urban districts called 'concessions', and loss of control over customs administration, over foreign trading companies operating through Treaty Ports, and over foreign inward investment in crucial modern industries such as textiles and railways. This went far to damage the prestige and legitimacy of the imperial regime, encouraging opposition movements and stimulating conflicts within the state elite over how to reform the Chinese state, the better to cope with external challenges and internal divisions.

New sources of political power enabled various groups in Chinese society to challenge the authority of the imperial state. In order to quell a series of rebellions, most notably the Taiping rebellion of the 1850s, provincial armies and local militias were raised, and control of the means of coercion partly shifted from the central state to provincial governments and local leaders. From then on, armed forces played more independent roles in political conflicts than previously. New social forces, including overseas students and other *émigrés*, merchants and industrialists, women, and urban workers, as well as disaffected sections of the traditional gentry, formed the basis for organized political movements. Some of these, with links to secret societies, became revolutionary organizations aiming to overthrow the Manchu regime; others became the germs of political parties and factions which could seek representation in the elected councils and provincial assemblies established in the early years of the twentieth century.

New sources of economic power were predominantly linked to foreign interests. Foreign investment capital poured into China, investing in mining, heavy industry and communications, especially railways. Foreign companies controlled high proportions of industries such as textiles and shipping. Foreign traders also saw in China an inexhaustible market for a wide variety of commodities. Much economic power was thus concentrated in the hands of foreigners, both the market power of investors and traders and the direct managerial power of foreign managements over their Chinese work-forces. For Chinese, the most obvious route to participation in these new forms of economic power was through alliance with foreigners, through collaborative ventures, or as managerial employees or intermediaries. Marxists later identified these groups as the 'comprador bourgeoisie', agents on behalf of imperialism, and distinguished them from the Chinese capitalist class; but the latter, operating companies in a range of consumer industries, commerce and banking, remained small, weak and only loosely organized (Bergère 1983). New economic interests clashed with old ones and generated new conflicts: conflicts between foreign and Chinese interests in railway rights were particularly intense, as were industrial conflicts on the railways, but there were many other economic sources of instability.

The first revolution and its aftermath

The tensions created by these shifts in political and economic power came to a head in October 1911, when a mutiny among army units that had been infiltrated by a revolutionary organization escalated out of control. The Manchu court came under challenge from alternative power bases: the provisional national assembly which elected the military leader Yuan Shikai 'Premier of China', joint meetings of provincial assemblies which elected Sun Yat-sen 'Provisional President of the Chinese Republic', and senior commanders of the northern army. On 12 February 1912 the court announced the abdication of the boy emperor Puyi and the Qing dynasty came to an end.

From then until the establishment in 1949 of the People's Republic of China and its subsequent consolidation, China was the site of almost continuous and often violent struggles for power. All forms of power, economic, political and ideological, were actively contested in recurrent situations of great instability and uncertainty. In societies with relatively stable power structures, contestation is usually held within strict limits by the knowledge of all participants as to where power lies and by varying degrees of acceptance of its legitimacy. The collapse of imperial political institutions, the sharpening of economic antagonisms, the challenge of new social beliefs and values, and the threat and reality of external aggression, especially Japanese expansionism, all rendered such knowledge uncertain and undermined legitimacy. Power could not be assumed, it had to be proved in practice, ultimately by resort to armed force. In Mao Zedong's words (1967, II: 224), 'political power grows out of the barrel of a gun'.

After the collapse of the empire, political power, the power to rule over the territory of China, dissolved. Attempts to establish coherent state institutions which could maintain control over the whole country failed. China fragmented into a large number of more or less fluid regimes dominated by military leaders, the so-called 'warlords' (Sheridan 1983). Conflict between warlords could escalate into heavy fighting, and control over territories could change hands frequently. The local dominance of a warlord depended on personalized and hierarchical relationships between himself and a followership of aides and advisors, military adjutants and civilian officials, in a pattern reminiscent of European feudalism. Warlords also needed access to funds, which they gained through support from business and finance, foreign loans, regular taxation and predation. In this way, they also exercised economic power, either directly or by coming to terms with other economic power holders.

A warlord might dominate a whole province, but none had the resources to attempt the reunification of China under consolidated state rule. Two organized political movements, each with their own armed forces and their economic and social constituencies, competed with each other to achieve this task: the Guomindang (GMD), or Nationalist Party, and the Chinese Communist Party (CCP). Both were formed as revolutionary movements committed to revolutionary transformation of Chinese society. Like any large-scale social and political movement, they were composed of a large number of groupings with diverse views on goals, strategies and tactics. Holding each of them together despite this diversity was a conception of socialism. The CCP's conception of socialism was essentially a Marxist one, as mediated through the Soviet Union and the Comintern, and adapted to specific Chinese circumstances. The Nationalists' conception of socialism was enshrined in Sun Yat-sen's 'Three Principles of the People', one of which referred to the people's livelihood, jeopardized (according to the American socialist Henry George) by the landlords' appropriation of rent, which the revolutionary state should restore to the people. In either case, revolutionary change would require the movement to wrest economic and political power from established classes and institutions. In both cases, however, their capacity to do this was restricted throughout the 1920s, 1930s and 1940s, not only by the power of those established classes, but also by the competition and military confrontation between the revolutionary movements themselves,[6] by the strength of local warlords, by the Japanese occupying forces in much of eastern and central China, and by the leverage exercised by other foreign powers in return for aid in the struggle against the Japanese. Until the Communist victory in 1949, neither movement had the power to carry out a radical restructuring of society on more than a local scale.

The GMD's power bases were in the cities. First in Nanjing (1927–37), later in Chongqing (1938–45), the Nationalists set up governmental apparatuses to administer the territories remaining under their control, to collect taxes, and to maintain the enormous armies needed to combat the Communists and to resist the Japanese. The organizational and financial problems of government were immense, and in the process of struggling with them the Guomindang's revolutionary ambitions went by the board. Chiang Kai-shek's government, having at first attempted to gain by coercion the financial support of wealthy businessmen, accommodated to the growing entrepreneurial class in the cities and attempted to maintain favourable conditions for investment. The regime was also dependent on shady alliances with secret society gangs, especially the Shanghai-based Green Gang. In the countryside the regime had little influence, and tended to support landlords rather than peasants. The government was constantly short of funds, making it difficult to pay civilian officials or military forces enough to retain their loyalty or maintain their honesty; corruption became widespread, and soldiers survived by looting and stealing. At times military leaders formed breakaway regimes in the provinces and secret societies and gangs flourished in the cities. Some warlords and foreign governments, in particular that of the United States, backed Chiang Kai-shek and the Nationalists as the only plausible counter to the Communists and to Japan, as did much of the politically conscious sections of the urban population. Gradually, the Nanjing government managed to regularize its rule in the cities and to pursue policies of economic development, but the Japanese invasion in 1937 shattered this stabilization of political and economic power. During the war with Japan, the Chongqing regime was more concerned with survival than with social change. After the surrender of the Japanese, the Nationalist government was overwhelmed by the problems of reconstruction, civil war against the Communists, inflation and a collapsing currency, from which it did not recover.

The situation facing the Communists was entirely different. Driven out of the cities and then from one mountain fastness to another by Guomindang troops, the Communists' very survival depended on their relationship with the local rural population. Military policy was directed to ensuring good relations with rural people: many full-time troops were stationed in their own home areas, backed up by part-time militias, and all Communist forces were under strictly enforced instructions not to exploit rural communities, to pay for food and supplies, and not to offend local women. Necessity coincided with ideology in favouring a strategy of mobilizing rural people in support of change. Wherever the Communists gained a foothold, they followed a policy of redistribution of tax burdens and of access to land, based on detailed study of local economic and social conditions. The details of these policies shifted over time. They developed as part of a learning process, as Communist leaders schooled in organization and agitation in the urban labour movement gained more experience of government in rural areas under war conditions. They were also forced to respond to the exigencies of the military and political situation. Land reform was a central issue over which policy was subject to twists and turns. In the early rural soviets, a radical policy of confiscation of the holdings of landlords and rich farmers was attempted, but this generated much resistance from local lineages and was quickly moderated. None the less, land redistribution continued to be the basis of the restructuring of economic power, until the 1937 united front with the Guomindang against the Japanese forced the Communists to abandon appropriation from landlords. For the next few years, the 'Yan'an way' abandoned radical class conflict and maintained existing rights to private property, using taxation policy and control over money-lending as the main weapons to counter inequalities of economic power.

Political power in the regions conquered by the Japanese was concentrated in a number of puppet regimes installed and maintained by Japanese armed forces. Apart from maintaining order and preventing resistance to Japanese occupation, the main tasks of these regimes was to contribute to the economic development of industries relevant to the Japanese war-effort. Chinese industrialists in such industries as mining, steel, power, transport and communications were forced to collaborate with Japanese companies and Japanese-controlled development corporations. Industrial workers and peasants generally accepted the inevitability of Japanese rule, though some hundreds of thousands voted with their feet to join the Nationalists in Sichuan or the Communists in Shaanxi.

The outcome of the unstable trilateral conflict between the Guomindang, the Communists, and the Japanese, and their diverse relationships with the economic power of propertied and unpropertied classes in urban and rural China, was settled by military force. The reasons for the Communist victory in the civil war (1946–9) that followed the surrender of Japan are many and complex, and cannot be discussed here.[7] Apart from the Nationalist retention of Taiwan, and the perpetuation of colonial rule in Hong Kong and Macao, the victory was total, and laid the political basis for a more thorough revolutionization of the structure of power than had been possible hitherto.

The Communist restructuring of social power

The victory of the Communist forces confirmed the military basis of its political power. The People's Liberation Army became the only legitimate and effective military force on the Chinese mainland, confining the armed forces of the rival Republic of China to Taiwan and eliminating the scattered warlord regimes which remained at the end of the civil war. The Communist Party gained a monopoly over the means of violence and re-established central political power within a unitary state. This gave the new regime the coercive backing for its revolutionary programme to transform society and in particular to restructure economic power. Consequently, armed force was available if needed in the elimination of the dominant economic classes of the old regime: the landlords and the owners of private businesses.

Land reform was intended to break the dominance of the landlord class in the countryside and to relieve rural poverty (Lippit 1974; J. Wong 1973). Once the Communist Party no longer had to moderate its policy in order to maintain the alliance with the Guomindang, it was able to confiscate the holdings of landlords and redistribute them to poor peasants and landless families. These redistributions were handled at local level by work teams of cadres and students in conjunction with newly formed Peasant Associations. The work teams had the task of collecting information about local land holdings, identifying landlords, and deciding on appropriate reallocations of their land.[8] The atmosphere surrounding land reform was deliberately confrontational, in order to mobilize poor peasants behind the revolution, to dissolve their customary attitudes of deference towards the gentry, and to accustom villagers to the idea of class struggle. People identified as landlords were pilloried at village meetings, and over the whole country about one million were killed. Landlords were not passive in the face of this onslaught, and tried every method to avoid confiscation: bribery and blackmail of cadres, transferring land holdings to other names, threats of violence, and engendering fear of a return of the Guomindang.

In the process of land reform, the rural population was classified according to class categories developed over the years in the careful study of rural conditions (Mao 1967, I: 23–59; Mao 1990; Hinton 1966: 623–6). The class categories were allocated to families, and became a fixed part of the family's status for decades to come, inherited in the male line;[9] class designation was highly consequential for the life chances of the subsequent generation, since 'bad class' families were discriminated against and scapegoated in campaigns, while 'good class' families were favoured (Kraus 1981). Later research has suggested that the confrontational method of land reform, and its implementation at village level, resulted in families being identified as landlords even though their economic conditions did not fit the prescribed definitions. The work teams with their poor peasant villagers were under great pressure to find local landlords; in many areas, however, landowners had in the preceding decades moved to the cities and become absentee landlords. In these situations, many farmers who employed a few wage-labourers but who did not live on the returns of rented out land were identified as landlords and dispossessed or even killed, with their families bearing the stigma of the 'bad class' category for the next two generations (P. C. C. Huang 1995).

Land reform destroyed the economic power of the landlord class. Along with its loss of land ownership went also the elimination of other institutions of its economic dominance: lineages (as mentioned in chapter 5), networks of relationships among the gentry, money-lending and pawn-broking businesses. In its place, at first, appeared a large self-supporting and property-owning peasantry. But this was not to last long. The elimination of the landlord and gentry class signalled the penetration of the state into rural life in a way that had never happened in China before. The peasantry owned the land only under sufferance from an increasingly powerful party-state (Friedman et al. 1991). Throughout the 1950s, the party-state brought pressure on the peasantry to develop ever more collectivistic institutions: firstly mutual aid teams involving a few households; then lower-level, and later higher-level, agricultural co-operatives; and finally the People's Communes, through which peasant families gave up their individual ownership of the land and merged ownership into the collective. This situation prevails to this day, despite the dissolution of the communes themselves in 1984. It was the state that emerged the dominant economic power in the countryside, through its increased capacity for local organization and its control over prices and purchasing of agricultural products.

The process by which the party-state restructured economic power in the cities also took several years and went through several stages. As in the case of land reform, the initial approach taken in northern cities such as Tianjin (which was occupied by Communist forces in January 1949) was confrontational, organizing workers against employers and managers (Lieberthal 1980). But it was soon realized hat this would stretch the capacity of the cadres to maintain order and revive the city's economy, and a new strategy was developed based on gaining the co-operation of private capitalists and administrators of nationalized enterprises in the more modern sectors of industry. City-wide employers' associations and labour unions in specific industries were set up and instructed to reach collective agreements over wages and conditions, under the oversight of the municipal government's Labour Bureau. Concessions were made to existing holders of economic and financial power and expertise, but provisions were also imposed that would increasingly concentrate resources and information in the hands of the party and city government; for example, 'excessive' profits had to be reinvested in the city rather than held as liquid transferable capital. Labour-capital consultative committees were formed in enterprises, with workers represented by trade union cadres; production competition campaigns were mounted in which production targets were set and through which trade union cadres gained experience and knowledge in running the factories; trade conferences were held of firms involved in production and marketing within specific trades, bringing them steadily under government supervision. Eventually the party authorities were strong enough to gain control over investment in the city through the Tianjin Investment Company. Similar processes were followed in other cities, such as Canton (Vogel 1980), and merged into nation-wide strategies.

The new regime also moved to destroy the secret societies which, in the absence of adequate trade unions or urban welfare institutions, had built up a significant power base among the poor. They combined protection rackets (competing successfully with the legal authorities in providing protection for private business) with labour contracting and welfare services in unorganized trades such as transport. The new regime used the Suppression of Counterrevolutionaries campaign of 1950 and 1951 to turn the members of such societies against their leaders, publicly executing key leaders and setting up alternative Communist-controlled organizations to provide jobs and security for ordinary workers. The same campaign was also directed against religious sects which had influence over large sections of the urban populations.

From late 1950 the new regime moved more decisively against private economic interests, firstly by freezing the assets of foreign-owned businesses and driving foreigners to sell up and leave the country.[10] In 1952, with the Five Anti (*wu fan*) campaign against bribery, tax evasion, fraud, theft of government property and stealing state economic secrets, the state extended its control over Chinese-owned private companies, the so-called national bourgeoisie (Gardner 1969). Business men were publicly criticized in struggle sessions and forced to confess to these economic crimes. Few were killed, many were fined, some were sent to labour camps. As in the case of land reform, although less systematically, class categories were imposed on the urban population. None the less, in subsequent years the private sector continued to expand along with the state sector of industry. Only with the First Five-Year Plan, 1953–7, did the state take full control of production and investment, extend joint state–private ownership, and finally eliminate the private sector of industry altogether in 1956. From then on all economic as well as political power was concentrated in the hands of party-state authorities.

Power in the Communist party-state

With alternative bases of power removed, it might appear as if the new regime would be able to set up new institutions that would stabilize the power structure and lend greater certainty to the conditions in which people led their lives. Certainly the organizational capacity of the Communist Party, together with it revolutionary ideology, enabled it to penetrate further into the everyday life of both rural and urban residents than any previous regime had done (Schurmann 1968). Power was, in outward form at least, comprehensively bureaucratized. In the state sector every work-unit was allocated a place in the bureaucratic hierarchy of its functionally specialized ministry, such as energy production, education, health or transport. The activities of every ministry were specified in successive Five-Year Plans, from which specific targets for every level below the central ministry were derived. Every urban resident was a member of a specific work-unit, and every rural resident a member of a specific production team in a specific brigade in a specific commune, and these units maintained control over their members in all aspects of their lives (Li Hanlin 1991). Every functional unit also contained within it a Communist Party committee to ensure conformity with political demands as well as with specialized commands. With the elimination of alternative sources of economic power, the Communist party-state unified political and economic power into a single hierarchical system. In principle, the power of the party-state was absolute.

This picture of a hierarchical system of absolute power became widespread in western sociology and political science at the height of the Cold War in the 1950s, and underpinned theories of totalitarianism applied to societies such as the Soviet Union and China. There were certainly elements of truth in it. However, the theory of totalitarianism has also been much criticized. While keeping in mind the real concentration of power in the hands of the Communist Party and its state apparatuses, it is also important to sketch out the main dimensions of conflict within the social fabric. Without this, it is impossible to understand such complex struggles as the Cultural Revolution and the further transformation of power after the death of Mao.

First, the image of a monolithic communist party is thoroughly misleading. Like any large organization, the Chinese Communist Party has always been characterized by a complex mixture of consensus and conflict, the analysis of which has generated complicated debates among sociologists and political scientists. One very influential model of division within the party is that of factionalism (Nathan 1973), a view of the party as riven between different groups of leaders each with their own networks of clients and constituencies bound to them by shared experience and interest, reaching out from the political centre to the provinces and localities. Even if the detail of this model is much disputed,[11] the general assumption of structured division is correct. A major feature of intra-party division concerned the general conception of socialism to which the party should be committed. As mentioned in chapter 2, Solinger and her colleagues usefully distinguish three 'visions of socialism' (Solinger 1984b): first, a centrally planned economy administered by a Leninist vanguard party organized on principles of democratic centralism; second, a more decentralized economy, with a mixture of planning and market mechanisms, still administered by the Communist Party but with greater scope for initiative, especially for private business, managers and technical experts; third, an image of continual radical revolution, aiming to destroy inequality and class privilege wherever it is found, including in the Communist Party itself, and giving wide scope to the energies of the 'masses' from whom all revolutionary virtue stems. All three visions have coexisted in the CCP at least since the formation of the PRC and underlie many of the tensions and conflicts experienced since that time. In particular, the third vision is associated with Mao Zedong and his supporters, with the mass line and with radical attacks on party bureaucracy during the Cultural Revolution, while the second vision is associated with pragmatic and technocratic economic reformers who were overruled and branded as 'Rightists' in the 1950s and who re-emerged and became dominant after Mao's death.

A second aspect of conflict was between different levels of the party and state bureaucracy. The tension between centre and periphery is an inherent one in the power structure of any large-scale territorial state, and the monopolization of power by the Communist Party does not eliminate this tension. Rather than simply serving to transmit and execute decisions from the centre of power, intermediate and lower levels of party and state operating under their specific local conditions can develop interests and a momentum of their own. The organization of the communes structured this centre–periphery tension in a specific way (Potter and Potter 1990). Communes were organized at three levels: the commune itself, its component brigades, and the production teams within each brigade. Each level operated its own economic activities and had its own financial status. However, as outlined in chapter 3, the leaders at each level had different positions within the power structure. Higher-level commune leaders were appointed by county authorities, often came from outside the commune, and were paid salaries by the state, rather like county magistrates in imperial times; lower-level commune cadres were paid by the commune. Production team leaders were elected by the team members and derived their salaries from the production of the team; they were not necessarily party members and were bound into local networks of obligation (Madsen 1984). The brigade cadres were local people paid from brigade resources, but were under the supervision of the commune party. Thus, whereas commune leaders were required to transmit commands from the centre to the peasants, and team leaders were elected to represent their members, brigade cadres had to face both ways at once, subjected simultaneously to party control and to local expectations. Whether brigade cadres had the capacity to shield 'their' peasants from excessive demands and thus limit the reach of the state (for example by manipulating statistical returns on grain harvests)

(Shue 1988), or were forced to bend to the will of higher levels of the party and state and exercise strict control over the peasants (Unger 1989), is a matter of dispute and probably also of considerable variation over time and place.

A further cleavage within the party-state was a distinction that emerged within all units between political cadres, whose role was political work, propaganda, personnel management and security, and the administrative, managerial and technical cadres who had specific expert roles. In the course of the campaigns of the 1950s political cadres, whose social origin was usually from the working class or the peasantry, gained 'good class' categories, while the technical cadres in particular, whose high level of formal education derived from their families' relative privilege, were more likely to be branded with 'bad class' labels. The power exercised by less educated but politically reliable political cadres was resented by the more highly educated but politically marginalized technical cadres. Furthermore, the children of good class political cadres tended to be favoured within the education system, and this was resented by the offspring of bad class experts as well as by the children of good class peasants and workers (A. Chan et al. 1980). The potential conflict between these groups had a major influence on the formation of warring factions during the Cultural Revolution (Wang Shaoguang 1995a).

The terms in which these and other power struggles were waged between the early 1950s and the late 1970s made frequent use of the distinction between 'redness' and 'expertise'. 'Redness' referred to revolutionary purity and virtue, a general charismatic quality that could be claimed and counter-claimed on a variety of grounds; 'expertise' referred to technical knowledge, competence and skill in specific areas. The radical attack on expertise as reproducing elitism and class privilege was a central element of the ideological struggles culminating in the Cultural Revolution.[12] However, such claims to redness were inherently contestable. As Shirk (1982) argues, standards of revolutionary virtue, like other forms of charismatic authority, are vague and conducive to continuous conflict, and a regime based on revolutionary virtue, which Shirk calls 'virtuocracy', tends to be unstable.

Such instability was certainly characteristic of power in China. Structural sources of conflict, overlaid by struggles between different 'lines' and personal antagonisms, resulted in continual shifts of policy and successive campaigns to root out deviations and rectify aberrations. The result was that, although power was concentrated in the hands of the Communist Party, and no other source of economic or political power was recognized or tolerated, that power could not always be stabilized in regularized bureaucratic procedures. In fact the rigidification of party power in bureaucratic forms was one of the main deviations attacked by radicals in the name of Mao Zedong. In such conditions of uncertainty, people would seek relative stability within a narrow circle of personal relationships, relying not on formal procedures and explicit criteria but on personal ties and networks of patronage between party officials and their clients. Despite the official rhetoric that revolutionary virtue and commitment to the party should override personal interests and private relationships, the uncertainty generated by the vagaries of revolutionary transformation reinforced traditional cultural predispositions to particularistic relationships.[13]

The high point of uncertainty was during the Cultural Revolution, which became the occasion for power struggles at various levels of Chinese society: between different elements of the top leadership, as the radical group based in Shanghai later known as the 'Gang of Four' used their association with Mao to wrest control from the established party leadership headed by Liu Shaoqi on the charge that they were restoring capitalism; between different elements in the armed forces; between local party cadres and contending organizations of industrial workers seeking a variety of economic and political goals; between groups of high school students from different class backgrounds in various cities, who organized themselves as conflicting Red Guard associations; between divergent groups in professional occupations such as teachers and doctors. Spurred on by unclear clarion calls to action from the top, but also guided by assessments of rational self-interest, millions of people in all walks of life found themselves wrenched out of the routines of everyday life and facing situations full of unpredictable consequences. As struggles escalated, many were drawn into armed conflict, and at times during 1967 and 1968 China was close to anarchy or civil war. The army restored order, but the radical clique retained control at the higher levels of the party, and further campaigns were mounted in the following years to preserve their dominance and to maintain the momentum of the Cultural Revolution. Repeatedly, millions of Chinese were brought on to the streets in violent power struggles whose outcome was unpredictable.

The years from 1966 to 1976 are now often referred to in China as the decade of disaster. Those who lived through that time, especially those who were active in radical movements, have told researchers that they were led astray into wild acts of rebellion by the wicked 'Gang of Four'. Political sociologists, following the modern tendency in studies of riot and rebellion to interpret the action of participants as based on rational consideration of advantage and risk, have preferred to look for the logic of individual involvement and group action (Wang Shaoguang 1995a). Both perspectives are right in their way. The stability of a social order, including its structure of power, rests in part on its capacity to make normal everyday activities appear rational. Revolutionary upheaval must disrupt those rationalities and, when it fails firmly to establish new ones, participation in the upheaval may well appear to have been irrational.

The Cultural Revolution, in this sense, did fail. The wild shifts in the messages reaching ordinary people from the centre did nothing to clarify their understanding of the direction of social and cultural change advocated by the party, and left many confused, exhausted and sceptical, with a longing for life to return to 'normal'. The upheaval over several years also displaced many of the top leadership, as well as cadres at lower levels, who therefore had an interest in bringing this disruption to an end. Party leaders who had been stigmatized as 'Rightists' or 'capitalist roaders' re-emerged in the last phases of the Cultural Revolution as Mao Zedong's death was clearly approaching. When Mao died in September 1976, a group of party officials led by Hua Guofeng, backed by crucially placed military commanders, took the opportunity to restore 'normality' to China. The members of the 'Gang of Four' were placed under arrest and eventually tried and imprisoned. The top leaders were still divided over basic policy, but during 1977 and 1978 Deng Xiaoping and his supporters in the party and army came increasingly to the fore, committed to a new direction for China's development, summarized in the slogans of 'Four Modernizations' and 'the Open Door'.[14] Over the next few years, these policies resulted in new sources of social power which are still being defined.

The shape of social power in post-Mao China

The main tendency of the post-Mao era has been the re-establishment of sources of social power, especially economic sources, that have some degree of independence from the political power of the Communist Party. The Communist regime continues to hold a formal monopoly of political power, backed by control over the means of coercion, which has been used to suppress popular protest and opposition. However, new developments in agriculture, in industry, and in external relations, have all resulted in bases for economic power which increasingly escape the control of the central party-state.

There has been no simple restoration of economic power to the classes that were dispossessed in the revolution, but the period of economic reform has seen the emergence of new classes whose members are capable, either individually or collectively, of some autonomy of economic action. That autonomy remains partial; economic and political power remain intertwined in various ways. Related to these shifts in economic power, lower levels of the state apparatuses have gained greater autonomy from the centre. The consequences of these changes, including new patterns of social inequality[15] and new forms of conflict, remain controversial, the subject of political debate and potentially the source of political instability.

The earliest transformations took place in agriculture. Between 1978 and 1984 agriculture was largely decollectivized. In place of the collective system of production teams fulfilling targets set by central planners and transmitted down through communes and brigades, there emerged the 'household responsibility system'. The land of the teams was divided up among households, which contracted with the collective to farm a certain amount of land and to deliver a certain quantity of crops as a fee for using the land and as tax, beyond which output could be sold on the market. Households thus once again became autonomous units of production, able to make their own decisions on land use, crops, sideline production and investment. The ownership of the land remained with the collective, though the length of time specified in contracts (usually fifteen years or longer) enabled long-term planning by households. By the middle 1980s China had seen the re-emergence of a family-farming peasantry (Saith 1987).

The decollectivization process has been interpreted as an expression of the power of the peasants (K. Zhou 1996). It was indeed prompted by spontaneous moves towards household contracting in local areas, and only later taken up as policy by central authorities. It was often resisted by local cadres who stood to lose authority as household autonomy took over from collective organization (Zweig 1997). However, individual autonomy of households is very different from collective power of peasants as a class. As Kelliher (1992) argues, the actions of the peasants who dismantled the institutions of collective farming were co-ordinated, if at all, only on a very local level, and the only pressure they could bring to bear on the centre was the pressure of numbers. Their power consisted in the unorganized rejection of an uncongenial system by millions of people forced into similar conditions of existence by the homogenizing influence of commune hierarchies, the state grain procurement system and the *hukou* registration procedures. Under these specific conditions, unorganized pursuit of their interests could have the force of collective action (X. Zhou 1993). Since then, agriculture in China has become increasingly differentiated and the peasantry has become increasingly fragmented. The fact that the land remains the property of the collective also limits the power of the farmers, and prevents the growth of a property-owning rural bourgeoisie employing an agricultural proletariat. It is however possible for larger land-holdings to be formed, either by specialized households fulfilling state contracts or by the setting up of voluntary agricultural co-operatives. Cadres and former cadres also found new roles and new sources of advantage in mediating between peasant households and their wider environment 'between plan and market' (Oi 1989).

Members of farming families now have freedom to seek alternative non-agricultural employment. The family can either work its contracted land with fewer family members, or can abandon farming altogether. Farming families have provided the labour force for the rapid expansion of rural industry, a development that has also contributed to a significant shift in power. The decollectivization of land in the 1980s was paralleled by a decollectivization of commune and brigade enterprises: they remained in public ownership, but their management was contracted out to private individuals. When the communes and brigades were dissolved and their administrative responsibilities transferred to township (*xiang*) and village (*cun*) governments, these enterprises came to be known as 'township and village enterprises' (TVEs). They continued to expand, and by the early 1990s there were more than one million such enterprises accounting for nearly one quarter of all industrial employment in China (Walder 1995).

TVEs operate in an increasingly marketized environment, buying their inputs, hiring labour, and selling their products in markets that stretch way beyond their local areas, even overseas. It has been argued that this so-called 'market transition' would shift power away from local officials towards managers and technical experts who have marketable skills and knowledge of the workings of the market economy (Nee 1989).[16] However, this is countered by an alternative theory, which suggests that local cadres play a key role in a new configuration of power which is variously called 'local state corporatism' (Oi 1992) or 'local market socialism' (Lin 1995). According to this view, local governments have property rights in TVEs,[17] and function as complex industrial firms (Walder 1995). Their relationship to the managers of enterprises is like that of employer. Local government officials co-ordinate the activities of the enterprises in their charge, bargain with higher levels of the state on their behalf, and monitor their performance closely. Cadres have been encouraged to take this role in local industrialization by fiscal changes that allow them to retain a higher proportion of various taxes collected locally so long as they are reinvested in local enterprise. Although cadres clearly stand to gain in personal and family terms from their activities as 'directors' of the local 'corporation', they also maintain their local power by bringing benefits to the local economy. Lin (1995) also argues, on the basis of a study of the 'supervillage' Daqiuzhuang, that the system of local corporatism is embedded in local kinship networks, with members of powerful families occupying key positions within the complex of companies and government agencies.

The reintroduction of private enterprise signifies another shift in control over economic resources. Large-scale private capitalist enterprise had been abolished in the 1950s. Despite considerable divergence of opinion within the party, the petty traders who had occupied the lower levels of marketing systems for centuries were also eliminated or brought under state control during the Cultural Revolution, as were local markets and fairs. The reforms beginning in 1978 reversed this process, in a series of at first hesitant and fluctuating policy shifts (Wang 1990). Initially the recognition of private enterprise was limited to petty traders and specialized individual households (*getihu*) which were allowed to take on up to seven assistants. In 1988 the state also legalized private enterprises employing eight or more workers (*siying qiye*), although it seems these had been tacitly condoned since 1983 (Christiansen 1989). By 1992 there were about seven million private enterprises registered in China, with an average of three employees per enterprise (Walder 1995: 274); the vast majority therefore were still individual household businesses; though several hundred thousand larger, some much larger, private enterprises had also come into existence.

As with farming, small private enterprise gives its owners a degree of autonomy but little collective power. Organizations of petty entrepreneurs, for example the Self Employed Labourers' Association, are more like the mass organizations used by the party for purposes of control than self-directed interest groups (Bruun 1993). Formally the same is true of the main association for larger private business, the Industrial and Commercial Federation, but the latter seems more capable of representing the interests of its entrepreneurial constituency (Nevitt 1996). The real significance of the growth of private business in this context lies in its relation to the power of local state

officials. The nature of this relationship varies according to the size
of the enterprise. Household enterprises are very much at the mercy of
the bureaucracy, but they have little interest to cadres; their interaction tends to be with the lowest levels of petty bureaucracy (Bruun
1995). Larger entrepreneurs have developed more symbiotic relationships with cadres (Solinger 1992; Wank 1995). Entrepreneurs need
to cultivate good relationships with officials, who can smooth or
obstruct the paths to permits, licenses, materials, contracts, loans
and other desirable commodities and services. But the dependence is
not all one way; cadres increasingly have an interest in the prosperity
of their local area, and this makes them dependent on local private
business rather than on their superiors in the state hierarchy. Both
cadres and entrepreneurs therefore stand to gain from entering into
patron–client relationships with each other, in which officials protect
and favour their clients who in return can offer pay-offs, employment
(to officials or their kin) or partnerships, a patterns that Wank (1995)
refers to as 'symbiotic clientelism'.[18]

The continuing interpenetration of economic and political power
is especially evident in the case of large-scale enterprise. Under the
system prevailing before 1978, the bulk of the industrial and commercial economy was concentrated in large-scale state organizations
owned and controlled by central government, provinces and pro-
vince-level cities, and counties. Control over these economic resources
was thus fully politicized, and varied in practice according to the
dominant political tendency. There was always a strand of thinking
within the Communist Party that advocated greater autonomy of
economic decision-making from political control, and the dominant
elements in the leadership since 1978 have supported this tendency.
Moves in this direction have, however, been cautious and steady.
There has been no rush to full-scale privatization of state-owned
industry as in much of the former Soviet Union and eastern Europe
(Nolan 1995). Instead, work-units, especially those owned below the
level of central government, have been gradually opened up to various
new forms of ownership and management and to various degrees of
market exposure, as part of a strategy of developing a system which,
at the 1992 Fourteenth Party Congress, was entitled the 'socialist
market economy' (White 1993). Up until the Fifteenth Party Congress
of September 1997 (at which Jiang Zemin's main speech envisaged a
wider variety of forms of ownership, including those which looked to
observers very like 'privatization') change in ownership was the least
significant element of the reform process (You 1998). Most state-
owned industry remains in public ownership. Even in the case of

enterprises in which the stock system introduced in the early 1990s has been implemented, the major part of the shares is still often held by state firms and agencies. Alternatively, shares have been issued to managers and to workers, but these are 'internal' shares which cannot be transferred. Only a small number of enterprises have been allowed to issue shares that can be traded on the stock exchanges at Shanghai and Shenzhen, and an even smaller proportion of companies can issue shares available to foreign ownership. This relatively limited shift in ownership of large-scale industry in itself signifies only a partial diffusion of power over economic resources, although the growth of capital markets is beginning to have an impact on the direction of investment (Karmel 1994). More significant have been steps to increase the autonomy of enterprises from state control and to expose them to market conditions. Under the enterprise contract responsibility system set up in 1984, managers (or work-forces) contracted to run state-owned enterprises and to meet agreed output and productivity objectives in return for considerable autonomy of decision-making and for substantial retention of profits for reinvestment in the company. At the same time pricing and marketing reforms enabled companies to buy materials and sell products at market prices, and to hire temporary or contract workers and specialists at market wages. Increasing proportions of workers in large-scale industry are therefore now able (or forced) to sell their labour power on the market, although much of the core labour force of state-owned enterprise has not been fully exposed to labour market conditions and retains membership of their work-units. Increasingly, both managements and workers have been propelled into dependence on the diffuse economic power of market relationships. The possibility of bankruptcy for state enterprises has been admitted and some major companies have indeed been forced into bankruptcy. In practice, however, the continued involvement of state organs as owners, and state officials as regulators, means that authoritative political power has not by any means fully withdrawn from the economic sphere.

Opening the door

With the admission of the PRC to the United Nations in 1971 and the visit of President Richard Nixon the following year, China began to rejoin the international political system. Opening the door to external economic forces became official government policy at the Third Plenum of the Eleventh Central Committee in December 1978. Since that time China has become increasingly incorporated into the international capitalist economy (Howell 1993; Sklair 1995). Restrictions on foreign trade were relaxed by licensing several provinces and cities to engage in foreign trade, commercializing state trading agencies, and giving enterprises certain rights to retain foreign exchange earnings. China is now becoming one of the world's most important trading economies (Ho Yin-ping 1995). Foreign direct investment was encouraged first in the form of joint ventures between foreign companies and Chinese enterprises, frequently state-owned enterprises, and then by admitting investment by wholly owned foreign companies. By mid-1996 there were over 120,000 foreign companies and joint ventures operating in China, employing 17 million workers (You 1998: 170). Perhaps the most well-known aspect of China's opening to the world economy is the establishment in 1979 of a number of Special Economic Zones (SEZ) at Shenzhen, Zhuhai, Shantou and Xiamen, with Hainan Island being added in 1987. The SEZs offered foreign companies special incentives to invest such as tax concessions and favourable labour regulations.

This reincorporation of China into the world capitalist economy has two main sets of implications for power in China. First, power over economic resources increasingly shifts outside of China. Instead of an autarchic economy controllable by internal political means, the more open Chinese economy has become enmeshed in webs of diffuse economic power constellations involving diverse external economic actors. Foreign demand for Chinese exports has an increasing impact on Chinese production and investment. Transnational corporations with investments in joint ventures or in wholly owned enterprises make decisions with effects in many parts of China. World stock and currency markets set uncontrollable parameters for the activities of Chinese economic agents in both public and private sectors. The economic and financial policies of foreign governments and transnational organizations such as the World Bank increasingly enter the calculations of Chinese participants in the global economy. All of this is familiar in other countries, but rather new to a China that, until the late 1970s, was economically closed in on itself.

Second, there are the effects on the power of individual and collective actors within China, many of whom are increasingly orientated towards external economic relationships. Despite some opposition to the 'Open Door' policy within the Communist Party, government officials and cadres at all levels have been drawn into the web of the international economy, promoting the interest of their province, county or city in attracting foreign investment or expanding export industries, regulating (or attempting to regulate) external economic relationships and their effects, participating in joint venture enterprises, managing Labour Service Corporations supplying workers for foreign companies, or in a host of other capacities. In these relationships, officials are in key locations where they can pursue a variety of goals, advancing their own official careers through successfully furthering the local economy, combining official duties with legal entrepreneurship, or exacting pay-offs for smoothing the path for Chinese or foreign concerns. Where a high proportion of international economic relationships is mediated through state agencies, public official involvement shades gradually into the private sector. In international banking and finance, international trade, and joint venture industry and commerce, segments of both Chinese officialdom and the Chinese business class have emerged whose primary engagement lies in the international sphere. At least at the higher echelons of these organizations and agencies, a Chinese component of the transnational capitalist class is forming whose interests actually or potentially transcend either their locality or the nation-state and are located in the global system itself (Van der Pijl 1989; Sklair 1995).

Class conflict in market socialism

As enterprises in China find themselves in a more competitive marketized environment, the potential for conflict in relationships between management and workers increases. There had been industrial conflicts in earlier phases of the Communist regime, for example a major strike wave in Shanghai in 1957 (Perry 1994) and considerable unrest during the Cultural Revolution (Perry and Li 1997). These were often a result of the resentments felt by more marginalized groups of workers, such as workers who lost security, pay and welfare benefits during the early socialization of private businesses in the 1950s, or temporary and contract workers in state enterprises in the late 1960s and 1970s. This resentment was directed not only at managers and party cadres, but also at more privileged permanent members of large state workunits, whose relative acquiescence was secured by greater security, better pay and welfare provisions, as well as by clientelist relationships with supervisors (Walder 1986).

In the period since 1978, by contrast, industrial conflict has been sparked by new conditions in state-owned enterprises, joint ventures and foreign companies.[19] Under the enterprise contract responsibility system, managers have an incentive to increase the productivity and profitability of their enterprises, and have brought pressure to bear on the work-force to achieve this aim. The results appear to be very variable. In the early stages of enterprise reform, managers used their new autonomy in setting wages to buy workers' co-operation, in a continuation of previous consensual patterns (Walder 1989), but as the state steadily withdrew its financial backing for loss-making companies this strategy pushed firms towards bankruptcy or to large-scale lay-offs (A. Chan 1995). In some enterprises, managements began to use the full range of methods of intensifying the labour process typical of capitalist industry at earlier phases of industrialization: lengthening the working day, speeding up the line, reducing manning levels, cutting rates of pay, and so on (Zhao and Nichols 1996). Either way, workers in state-owned industry found that they were not participating in the promised rise in living standards supposed to follow economic reforms, and many turned to protest and resistance (Walder and Gong 1993).

A characteristic feature of the conflicts generated by market pressures in state-owned enterprises and joint ventures has been the formation of independent workers' associations and autonomous trade unions. Prior to the economic reforms, the role of trade unions was defined by Leninist principles: they were to transmit party policies to urban workers and try to secure their support, and to protect the interests of workers and transmit their problems to the authorities. There was an ambiguity between these two roles, and episodes of labour unrest, even in the 1950s, led some unions to stress the latter role and to seek some autonomy from the party, which was never allowed. The economic reforms posed new problems for the official trade unions, marginalizing their position within enterprises and making it even more difficult for them to protect the interests of their members. At the same time, reformers provided some support for the unions to exercise greater autonomy and to be included in the process of industrial and social security policy formulation, but up to the mid-1990s this autonomy had not developed far, and the unions were being seen by their members as increasingly irrelevant. Grassroots union cadres, according to Chinese research, clearly recognize that the official unions face a major problem of credibility (Feng 1996). In some areas they have been increasingly challenged by unofficial workers' organizations and by left-wing labour activists. These unofficial associations were, for example, a noticeable presence in the protest movements of 1989 (Perry 1995). White (1995) concludes his survey of the position of trade unions in China by expecting that these trends towards a diverse range of workers' organizations and an increasingly volatile situation in industrial relations would continue, making it unlikely that a stable state-managed form of corporatism, which has been envisaged by some other writers (A. Chan 1993; Unger and Chan 1995), could take root.

Conclusion: the decline of state power

The trends surveyed in the last few pages all point in one direction: the power of the Communist party-state is weakening. Walder (1994) has advanced a plausible, essentially Weberian interpretation of this decline. The power of an administrative state to secure obedience to its commands depends on the capacity of superiors in the state hierarchy to monitor, discipline and reward the subordinates who must actually implement state policy in localities and organizations. In a Leninist party-state, this capacity resides primarily in the functioning of the Communist Party and of the central economic planning apparatus. Any departure from the monopolization of the party-state over the control of economic resources may weaken the dependence of subordinates in state and party on their superiors and the ability of superiors to supervise and sanction subordinates. This is exactly what has happened in the last twenty years of economic reform. Through the development of private business, the growth of township and village collective enterprise, the devolution of authority in state enterprise, the encouragement of joint ventures and foreign direct investment, and the marketization of the conditions facing these economic actors, not only has more and more economic activity escaped or been released from the reach of the central state authorities, but there have also emerged ever more sources of economic and social reward for subordinates in party and state over which their superiors have little leverage. Officials and cadres increasingly have incentives to form relationships with economic organizations at local levels, as facilitators, gate-keepers or even partners, from which they may expect to derive, legitimately or illegitimately, advantages greater than those derived from their party or state careers alone. The younger, more talented and ambitious among them may even decide to abandon their official careers and 'plunge into the sea (of business)' (*xia hai*). Through such mechanisms, the organizational capacity of the party-state, which was such a crucial feature of the rise to power of the Communist Party, has been significantly weakened.

Through a number of its cumulative effects, this weakening of state power is self-reinforcing. One of these is the declining capacity of the state to control corruption among its officials at all levels. The rise of corrupt practices has been remarked by everyone affected by it, including Chinese entrepreneurs and self-employed tradespeople, foreign corporate executives, and senior Chinese politicians. This corruption derives not only from the increased incentive and opportunity in a more commercialized society to exploit office for private gain, but also from the reduced capacity of superior authorities to monitor and punish actions that they might wish to define as illegitimate (White 1996). In fact the state is not able to impose a clear and agreed conception of corruption, which shades easily into the use of bureaucratic office to further the prosperity of communities much broader than the official's private membership groups, a process that can generate considerable public support, or simply the use of particularistic relationships to get official business done. In a society where universalistic norms have not displaced traditional particularistic assumptions, state definitions of corruption may not be entirely congruent with popular norms (R. P. L. Lee 1986).[20]

A further aspect of the weakening of central state power is the decline in its rate of extraction of financial resources (Wang Shaoguang 1995b). As a corollary of reforms in agriculture and industry and the decentralization of decision-making, there has been a significant reduction in the fiscal income available to central government. Part of what used to be channelled to the centre through taxation remains in the hands of enterprises as extrabudgetary funds, part remains at lower levels of government. The consequence is a decline in the capacity of central government to steer the economy and a corresponding rise in the power of local government.

Related in part to this reduction in state extractive capacity, but also to the general commercialization of the society, has been increased incentive and opportunity for the state's coercive apparatuses to become involved in economic activity. The People's Liberation Army has become a major entrepreneur in its own right, controlling tens of thousands of enterprises (Bickford 1994); on a smaller scale, the People's Armed Police also operates money-making undertakings (Ding 1996). There is a fine line between legitimate fund-raising to make up for limited state finance and illegitimate or unauthorized private enterprise by military units. One potential outcome of the commercialization of the military is a weakening of state control over the armed forces (Shambaugh 1996).

Finally, the state is also faced with competitors which state law defines as criminal, but which may be seen merely as alternative service-providers. There has been a significant increase in crime of all kinds in the last twenty years, and the publication of a classified report compiled by a Ministry of Public Security research unit (Dutton 1997) confirms a picture of a police force under considerable strain. Much of this is individual or small-group crime, such as murder, rape, theft, burglary, and other similarly illegal actions that concern state police forces and their wider public constituencies everywhere. A further category is economic crime, stimulated by the growing commercialization of the society. Beyond this there are many forms of organized service-provision where clients prefer (or have no choice but) to turn to alternatives to the state. There is, for example, a growing demand from businesses of all kinds for security services, demand created by the rise in theft and extortion. As in many other regions of the world, in China these services are increasingly provided by private enterprise, sometimes legal, sometimes not. In Hong Kong these and other services have for years been provided by Triad secret societies (Chu 1996), as they were in China before the Communist Party stamped them out, and there seems to be a resurgence of such organizations in China. As elsewhere, there is also a great demand for narcotics and other drugs which the state deems to be illegal, and which are provided by organized operations spanning continents. In China there is a great demand for opportunities to emigrate, but these opportunities are severely controlled by the Chinese state as well as by the potential receiving countries, so human smuggling operations find a ready market. It is naturally difficult to estimate the scale of these activities, but it seems that they are at a level at which the Chinese state is incapable of controlling them. As in the case of Mafia-style organizations in other parts of the world, Chinese secret societies might be seen as a kind of counter-state, and their existence as an indicator of the failure of the 'legal' state fully to monopolize the business of rule in the territory (Tilly 1985).

In all these respects, the power of the Communist party-state has weakened. It remains formidable, and continues to be capable of suppressing opposition. However, although the Communist Party retains a monopoly of formal political power, the limits to the use of that power are increasing.

Further reading

Shue (1988) provides an interpretation of the changes in the 'reach' of the state from pre-revolutionary times onwards. Schurmann (1968) documents the changes in power structure brought about by Communist Party organization and ideology. Hinton (1966) is a classic study of land reform by an American eye-witness. Solinger (1984b) contains analysis of ideological divisions within the Communist Party. White (1993) is a detailed study of political and economic power in the reform period, while Walder (1994) puts forward a stimulating interpretation of the decline in power of the Communist Party as a result of the economic reforms. Wasserstrom and Perry (1994) is a collection of papers on protest movements and the events of 1989.

7

Power and Revolution: Cultural

Introduction

In the previous chapter, three aspects of power were distinguished: economic, political and cultural. This chapter takes up the theme of cultural power, and explores the revolutionary transformations that cultural power has undergone in China over the last century. Cultural (or ideological) power refers to the ability of the powerful to influence people's actions through control over the content of social ideas, such as norms and values, beliefs or what counts as knowledge. Such power is embedded in a wide range of institutions, including those of the family, religion, education, and the arts, and often is not recognized by the participants as power at all, since the norms, beliefs, and the workings of institutions may be taken for granted as part of the natural order. In times of great social conflict and revolution, however, the institutions of cultural power become the location for overt struggles. This has been the case in China for the whole of the last century. Previous chapters have already considered elements of these conflicts, especially chapter 4 with its discussion of struggles to transform basic conceptions of the person and of social relationships, and chapter 5 with its emphasis on battles over the family. This chapter concentrates primarily on two other key sets of institutions in which struggles for cultural power are situated in modern and modernizing societies: on the one hand those of education, and on the other the arts and entertainments, communications and media.[1] Some consideration will also be given to the place of religious institutions in twentieth-century Chinese cultural revolution.

The theoretical framework that underlies the following discussion is derived mainly from the ideas of Bourdieu and Gramsci.[2] According to Bourdieu, cultural power (or 'symbolic violence') is both a partially autonomous form of power exercised by cultural specialists, such as educators, intellectuals, priests and artists, to uphold their social distinctiveness, and a resource used by dominant economic groups or classes to legitimate or disguise their economic power as cultural superiority. Educational and cultural institutions thus play a crucial part in the reproduction of class power; in modern societies especially, schools and universities take on central roles in transmitting and legitimating privilege, in symbiotic relation with the institutions of the state. Bourdieu stresses that cultural institutions are fields of conflict in which groups seek to maintain or usurp positions in social hierarchies. As a communist political leader as well as theorist, Gramsci further argued that the revolutionary Communist Party needed to undermine the cultural hegemony of the dominant economic class of capitalist society and its associated intellectuals, and to lay the ground for an alternative cultural hegemony of the proletariat with its own organic intellectuals. Communist revolution was not just economic and political struggle, but also cultural struggle. In their attempts to transform society, revolutionary parties would have to transform the workings of educational and cultural institutions to prevent them from reproducing the power of the dominant class. Twentieth-century China presents an instructive arena in which to see such processes in action.

Confucian hegemony and its limits

Cultural power was a fundamental component of the imperial regime. In the perspective of the ruling elites, culture in the sense of cultivation (*wen*) was the essence of Chinese civilization, and closely associated with literacy and command of the written heritage. In the eyes of later generations, one of the main achievements of the first emperor, Qin Shi Huangdi, was to have standardized the written language and made possible communication in writing across the empire. Imperial control of culture was eventually fully institutionalized in the system of competitive examinations by which civil servants were recruited for more than a thousand years. The syllabus for the examinations, the education that prepared candidates to enter for them, and the values that they enshrined, constituted the cultural cement that bound together the imperial court, the ruling elites, the local gentry, and all those scions of the lower classes who aspired to emulate their rulers or enter their ranks (Elman 1991).

The core syllabus for the examinations comprised the Confucian classical texts and the extensive scholarly commentaries that had accumulated over the centuries. Candidates were also tested on their mastery of traditional forms of literary discourse, including poetry and the so-called 'eight-legged essay', as well as on their calligraphy. Preparation for the examinations thus required disciplined study from a very early age. Competition was intense, and the stakes were high, since success in the examinations gave potential access to an official career with all the advantages in wealth and social status that accrued to the candidate and his family (C. Chang 1974). In normal times, this was sufficient to maintain the loyalty of scholars to the state, even if they themselves had not yet gained an official post. It also encouraged the sons of peasants and artisans who showed any intellectual aptitude to devote themselves to their Confucian-dominated studies, since this was the main form of social mobility available to the sons of the lower classes (P. Ho 1962).

The examinations defined the dominant cultural capital[3] in imperial society and stimulated families, clans and local communities to invest in schooling for their children. While the state effectively determined the curriculum and prescribed textbooks, most schooling was paid for privately. Tuition was given by individual tutors, by traditional, single-teacher private schools (*sishu*), at local academies (*shuyuan*) or temple-schools (*xuegong*), financed by tuition fees, clan investments, and official subsidies (Rawski 1979). Only at the highest level of scholarship did the state play a major role in funding education. Teachers were mainly recruited from the ranks of examination candidates and lower degree-holders who had failed to gain official posts. Although lack of success in the examinations might breed resentment, teachers were steeped in Confucian learning and likely to uphold official ideology.

The imperial state employed many other means to reinforce its cultural hegemony. From the late seventeenth century, lectures were to be given twice monthly in all settlements to explain the Kangxi emperor's *Sacred Edict*, a set of sixteen commandments exhorting the people to live a good life according to Confucian moral principles. The state over many centuries strove to eradicate 'superstitious' elements of popular religious belief and practice. Rulers believed that ideas of the supernatural could be harnessed to strengthen acceptance of the regime, and tried to control religious forces to this end (C. K. Yang 1961). The hierarchy of deities was patterned on the structure of imperial government, and co-operated in the maintenance of order. Government claimed a monopoly over the worship of Heaven and the interpretation of portents. The Board of Rites, one of the six boards of administration in the central government, exercised control over the administration of temples and the licensing of Buddhist and Daoist priests. These two religions had gained acceptance despite being considered heterodox,[4] and were actively patronized by some Qing emperors, but the state condemned and persecuted other religious movements and sects. In general, any religious activity seen by the ruling elite to be conducive to rebellion and disorder was forbidden.

Opportunities to discuss or publish ideas that went against the dominant ideology or were critical of the imperial regime were constrained. Literati out of office were forbidden to form societies, and no right of association was ever established under the empire. Books and popular dramas deemed to be subversive were censored or banned. There were no newspapers in the modern sense until missionaries introduced them in the early nineteenth century. Communication of opposition was institutionalized only within the hierarchical structure of the regime, for example through petition to the emperor. The imperial Censorate existed to investigate inadequacies and wrong-doing within the bureaucracy and bring them to the attention of the emperor and his ministers. Ministers themselves were charged with the responsibility of 'remonstrating' with the emperor if they thought he was acting wrongly, but they exercised this responsibility at the risk of their careers or their lives.

Despite this constraint, there were discourses that the state might rather have suppressed, if it had had the means to police all expressions of unorthodoxy. Publishing was highly commercialized from Song times on, and there was a large market among literate classes for all kinds of reading matter, most of which was politically and morally innocuous; but there also developed forms of satirical literature in which social criticism could be formulated, among which the eighteenth-century novel *The Scholars* by Wu Jingzi remains the best known. Local popular festivals, which existed everywhere in China, could express alternative visions of political authority to those proclaimed by the imperial regime (Weller 1987; Feuchtwang 1992) Similarly folk opera, the most popular form of entertainment in Chinese villages, could give mildly subversive voice to peasant doubts about the ideology of filial piety and the morality of village elites, and thus be seen as a 'weapon of the weak' (Arkush 1990). Other popular religions more explicitly departed from the hegemonic framework, such as the White Lotus sect, a millenarian conversion-orientated religion which proselytized mainly in northern China (Naquin 1985). The sect staged several rebellions in the late eighteenth and early nineteenth centuries, but was mostly suppressed by the Qing state.

Cultural revolution: the first phase

Although Chinese indigenous culture was neither static nor homogeneous, alternatives to Confucian hegemony could only appear within the interstices of the dominant institutions. The opening of Chinese cultural and intellectual life to external influences in the nineteenth and early twentieth centuries accelerated change and contributed to the break-up of the Confucian hegemony. A wide range of influences resulted in both institutional change, especially in the field of education, and in a diverse array of movements to reform Chinese culture, most notably the May Fourth movement. This whole period of cultural effervescence, in which struggles for cultural power were overt and sometimes violent, has been compared, both at the time and since, with the European Enlightenment of the eighteenth century (Schwarcz 1986).

Christian missionary activity was one such challenge. Catholic missionaries had had a presence in China since the sixteenth century, but had made few converts. In the nineteenth century, they were joined by increasing numbers of Protestant missionaries from Britain and other European countries as well as the United States, but conversion was still not the most significant aspect of their influence. In fact they generated considerable hostility which was also directed against Chinese converts (P. A. Cohen 1978). An indirect outcome of missionary work was the doctrine of the leader of the Taiping rebellion, Hong Xiuquan (Spence 1997), an amalgam of Christianity and Chinese religious ideas, but this also had little cultural impact beyond the considerable fact of the rebellion itself. More significant was the educational work of the missions. From the mid-nineteenth century Protestants established primary schools at their mission stations, preaching the Christian gospel but also teaching secular learning. Later, the larger stations added secondary classes, and eventually developed liberal arts colleges on the American model (Lutz 1971). Mission schools, which were open to the children of non-Christians as

well as converts, broke the monopoly of traditional Confucian schooling and began to introduce alternative world-views, wider knowledge,
and new teaching methods. They accepted girls, who made up about a
quarter of all enrolled pupils by 1919, thus initiating the modern
education of girls on a par with that of boys, and opposed the practice
of foot-binding. Christians also introduced western-style medical education into China as an outgrowth of their training of assistants to
medical missionaries.

Missionary schooling was also one of the ways in which Chinese
students found their way to Europe or America. Others were sent
under government-sponsored schemes to learn about western naval
and military technology. However, it proved impossible to appropriate
western technology without also importing other aspects of western
culture, and returned students brought back with them knowledge of
western social and political thought as well as information about
western educational institutions and processes.[5] Japan, too, became
a favoured destination for Chinese students. Their command of foreign languages and their experience of foreign ways of life provided
alternatives to their Chinese cultural assumptions and detached them
from those sectors of Chinese society still deeply rooted in those
assumptions. They formed the beginnings of a new intelligentsia
whose cultural resources lay outside the Confucian hegemony (Furth
1983). They also formed the readership for new forms of writing, both
literary journalism and fiction, published in the growing array of
newspapers and magazines. This new self-consciously modernist
urban intelligentsia were uncomfortably aware of their separateness
from the mass of the population, to whom their intellectual concerns
would be unintelligible (L. O. Lee 1990).[6]

In the early phases of this external cultural contact, the established
scholarly and official elite was highly suspicious of all things foreign,
and the students sent abroad were strictly controlled to bind them to
Confucian orthodoxies (Bastid 1987). However, the educated elite
came to believe that China had to learn from foreign experience,
just as the Meiji reformers had done in Japan. Members of the government decided that reform of educational practices was required and
inquired into various foreign school systems. From 1900 the imperial
government itself and the local gentry in the provinces began to
establish modern schools on foreign models, first Japanese and later
American. The abolition of the imperial examinations in 1905 signified the institutional abandonment of the Confucian hegemony
(Franke 1960), and was tantamount to a cultural revolution from
above. No longer did Confucian scholarship represent the dominant

cultural capital endorsed by the state, even though the scholars themselves retained popular respect as teachers, especially in rural areas,
and even though certain basic Confucian assumptions reappeared in
apparently more modern ideologies.

In the turbulent conditions following the 1911 revolution the government was unable or unwilling to maintain firm central control over
educational institutions. National education policy-making fluctuated
rapidly in a series of attempts to find an appropriate model of modern
elementary and secondary schooling, but had little impact on a
nation-wide scale. In urban areas, modern schools began to educate
the children of the wealthy and middle classes and to prepare them for
further education abroad or in the prestigious Christian colleges
such as Shanghai's St John's University (Yeh 1990). New urban educated classes emerged who were more interested in foreign culture
and modern professional occupations than in traditional Chinese
learning, but in rural areas parents remained attached to the traditional Confucian schooling and preferred to send their children to
the old *sishu*, even though these no longer had government recognition. Cultural divisions between urban modernity and rural traditionalism, and between urban elites and workers, were becoming
apparent, and these divisions were superimposed on older educational
hierarchies. It was this urban intelligentsia that took upon itself the
task of mounting a wide-ranging critique of all aspects of traditional
culture and of developing a 'New Culture' before and after May
Fourth.

However, this cultural and educational modernity, although embraced by the foreign-orientated intelligentsia, the bourgeoisie and
the professional classes, was not uncontested. The isolation of the
educated elite from the rest of the society came under criticism from
various quarters. Even before the collapse of the empire, for example,
attempts had been made to establish a different form of overseas
study, in which students would combine work with academic studies
and bridge the gap between education and manual labour (Bailey
1988). Work-study students in France especially, between 1910 and
the mid-1920s, were attracted to anarchism and later to communism,
and a number of later leaders of the Communist Party including Deng
Xiaoping took part in such schemes. As the empire and early republic
fragmented into warlord regimes, a wide variety of school experiments were tried in different parts of the country, including literacy
classes for urban workers and peasants. Although much energy was
put into these alternatives, they made little impact on the evolving
dominance of modern urban schooling and foreign studies, the new

path to officialdom that had replaced Confucian scholarship. This did not amount as yet to a new cultural hegemony; reformers, radicals and conservatives all had plans to 'reform the people' (Bailey 1990), to shape their behaviour through ideological domination, but they were different plans, and none of them yet had the full backing of a powerful state.

The same diversity and increasing gap between town and country were found in other spheres of culture and communication. The last years of the imperial era and the early Republican period saw an explosion of new media driven by both commercial and political interests. The press that developed in the late Qing mainly reported on trade and financial matters and was aimed at the business community, but political and propaganda journals flourished with the reform and revolutionary movements after the defeat by Japan in 1895 (Lee and Nathan 1985). All political parties and movements published newspapers to publicize their aims and points of view. The readership remained limited to the highly literate minority until the expansion of education and the urban population in the early twentieth century, when newspaper reading was also stimulated by the shift to the written form of the vernacular language which was part of the New Culture movement. The press then became increasingly commercialized and differentiated, with a range of specialist newspapers and magazines produced by new professional groups, progressive lifestyle newspapers aimed at urban middle-class youth, journals for women, and 'mosquito' tabloids relaying gossip from the worlds of politics and entertainment. Most of the press remained restricted to specific urban markets, especially Shanghai and other treaty ports, and the same was true of radio and the cinema. In all these media, attempts were made by central government and local authorities to regulate their content, as part of a general surveillance of popular culture and recreation, mainly from the point of view of decency and public morals. However, the authorities were too diverse and fragmented to allow any of them to impose a hegemonic cultural framework, and cultural competition remained relatively open.

Another element of this cultural competition came from outside China. As part of their pursuit of economic and political interests, all the main imperial powers also strove to increase their cultural and ideological influence in China. By protecting missionary endeavours, encouraging Chinese students to study in their universities, forming cultural associations and friendship organizations, promoting the study of their languages in Chinese schools, and in many other ways, the imperial powers competed with each other for cultural predominance within China (Y. C. Wang 1966; Kirby 1984; Bailey 1988). Chinese educators and intellectuals drew on their experience with different foreign countries, thus intensifying the cultural diversity in the early Republican period.

Hegemonic projects: Nationalists

The re-establishment of centralized state power in 1927, now in the hands of the Guomindang, and the formation of rural base areas by the Communists who proclaimed the Soviet Republic in southern Jiangxi in 1931, began fundamentally to alter the conditions of cultural production and reproduction. Both political movements saw a need to concentrate cultural power in their own hands. Faced, as they saw it, with diverse and predominantly private educational institutions, with relatively uncontrolled commercial media of communication, and with scholars and intellectuals responding mostly to foreign academic and aesthetic impulses, with each party confronted with the revolutionary political and military challenge of the other and with foreign imperialism on all sides, both the Nationalists and the Communists devised policies on education, publishing, broadcasting, and cultural life in general which were more in tune with the needs of the country as they defined them. Each attempted to construct a new and politicized cultural hegemony.

The Nationalist government claimed to make policy for the whole country and began to impose their political goals on schools and universities (Cleverley 1991). Regulations were laid down for all forms and levels of schooling. Curricula were prescribed, examinations required, textbooks approved. Courses in party doctrine became mandatory, and Sun Yat-sen's *Sanminzhuyi* (Three Principles of the People) became the basis of all social and political education. Teachers were required to attend courses in anti-communism. Mission schools and Christian colleges were pressured to register and their teaching of religious doctrine was forbidden or restricted. Scientific, technical and vocational education were to be strengthened so that schooling became more relevant to China's economic and military needs. Universities were regulated and students could apply to university only if they had a diploma from an accredited secondary school. Adult and part-time education were also subjected to regulations. By these means, the Nationalist government attempted to specify the cultural capital which any person would need to gain access to professional, scientific or administrative careers, and to control the political and religious content of all schooling.

The reality differed significantly from the policy stipulations. The GMD's main power base was in the cities and their educational policy had little impact in the countryside. Neither the financial resources nor the teachers were available to extend the government school system into rural areas. Attempts to control urban secondary schools and universities simply alienated both teachers and students and provoked protest from student associations. Schooling remained predominantly bound to literary traditions and irrelevant to practical concerns.

The Nationalists also made efforts to regulate other aspects of culture, especially those identified with communism. Its new police force, the Public Security Bureau, suppressed publications deemed to be communist or reactionary, and in 1931 it was made a crime to criticize the Nationalist Party in the press (Wakeman 1995). Book shops were raided and 'seditious' books confiscated. Films were censored, film scripts rejected and film studios closed down. This ideological control was part of a project to create a new national culture which combined the 'true' essence of Confucianism with militant revolutionary virtue. To this end the leadership established movements and organizations that have often been compared to European fascism (Wakeman 1997). The Blue Shirt Society and its secret core group, the Society for Vigorous Practice, set up in 1931, and the New Life movement established in 1934, were charged with promoting this revolutionary Confucianism and Sun Yat-sen's Three Principles of the People. They were to set for the people an example of moral living, which Chiang Kai-shek understood in terms of order, neatness and cleanliness, scientific precision and military exactness. They were also to combat its opposite, not just communism but also modernist decadence, in art, drama and literature, and in public behaviour such as gambling and prostitution.

It is difficult to know how this hegemonic project would have developed. Nationalist plans were disrupted by the outbreak of war with Japan in 1937, and educational and cultural policy in Sichuan and Yunnan provinces operated under war conditions. In Japanese-controlled areas, Japanese advisors were sent into schools, pro-Japanese teachers were installed, and Japanese language and political ideas taught. The Japanese replaced the Nationalists as the censors and regulators for the next eight years. The Nationalists' defeat in the subsequent civil war confined their cultural power to Taiwan, under very different circumstances.

Hegemonic projects: Communists

The Communist project for cultural hegemony, as it unfolded in the period prior to 1949, shared certain features with that of the Guomindang, but there were also differences, partly due to doctrine, partly due to the rural settings in which the Communists were constrained to build their power bases. Marxism came to China as a foreign import through the experience of Chinese students studying abroad in the last decades of the empire. Its ideas and literature were discussed in study groups, purveyed through left-wing book shops, and taught to workers by students and teachers such as Mao Zedong. From the beginning, the communist movement in China was a pedagogical one. The educators had themselves to be educated, and the fledgeling Communist Party of China set up the Self Study University in 1921 to train revolutionary cadres and to mount public lectures on Marxism. Top-level cadres went to the Soviet Union for more intensive training and became acquainted with Soviet debates on education, culture and intellectuals. Others remained in China and became increasingly involved in the role of education and of intellectuals among peasants in rural areas.

In principle, the Communist cultural project aimed to create a new, specifically proletarian culture with its own 'organic intellectuals' (Gramsci 1971). As the early Communist leader Li Dazhao declared in 1919: 'Those intellectuals who eat but do not work ought to be eliminated together with the capitalists' (Meisner 1967: 87), though much was to hang on what was defined as 'work'. In this radical view, educational and cultural policy was to be directed at the elimination of 'bourgeois' or 'feudal' ideology, at the wresting of cultural power from the hands of 'reactionary' social forces, and at making education directly relevant to the labour of the workers and peasants. It also aimed to eliminate the gap between urban and rural culture. However, in practice the Chinese Communists discovered that other considerations could conflict with these goals. Especially in rural areas, there was a great shortage of literate people who could take on tasks of education, administration and propaganda, and those that there were had been educated in the old Confucian manner or in the modern urban schools of the bourgeoisie. Conflict developed among Communist leaders as to whether these intellectuals from the old society could be employed in the service of the revolution; in these debates, Mao took the contentious line that there was no sensible alternative but to accept them, even if they stemmed from the families of landlords or capitalists, but others disagreed and identified all intellectuals with the ruling classes. In education, argument revolved around the tension between a mass education drive that would eliminate class differences and make learning relevant to productive labour, and the need (as some saw it) to concentrate scarce resources on training new cohorts of experts and administrators, leaving the mass of peasants to make do with elementary schooling.

Pepper (1996) argues that the inherent contradictions in these positions made themselves apparent in the 1920s, and echoed down the decades that followed, causing periodic swings between, on the one hand, radical egalitarianism and, on the other, a hierarchical system promoting 'quality' education for the few and elementary education for the rest. The radicalism of the Jiangxi Soviet was at first continued in the border area around Yan'an after the Long March, but very soon conventionally educated teachers who streamed away from Japanese-occupied China to the base areas began to reconstruct the regular system of schooling that they were accustomed to. Similarly, writers, artists and dramatists who were trying to adapt their literary skills in the service of Communist propaganda expressed their dissatisfaction with what they saw as the low artistic quality of what they were being asked to do. Faced with these entrenched cultural attitudes, Mao launched a rectification campaign in 1942 to bind intellectuals more tightly into the Communist hegemonic project. His talks at the Yan'an Conference on Literature and Art (Mao 1967, III) defined the appropriate stance of intellectuals: on the side of the proletariat and the masses, wearing their clothes, performing manual labour alongside them, learning from them and writing for them. They were to merge their command of elite and foreign culture with the culture of the masses. Those who refused to do so, especially those who maintained the right of autonomous intellectuals to criticize the Communist Party, and those who were committed to 'art for art's sake', had to be punished. In the aftermath of the rectification campaign, education policy also moved temporarily to the radical side, with the development of the *minban gongzhu* model of schools 'run by the people with public assistance'. Schools were to be run on the basis of local needs and local demands, uniting education with the work of the local peasantry, though the party, aiming to eradicate traditional Confucian schooling, did set limits on permissible textbooks and curricula. The model depended on the support of local cadres and teachers, and without a clear vision of an alternative tended to relapse back into a division of basic literacy for the masses and preparation for more advanced education for the most academically promising. Thus, by the time the Communists gained control over the whole country in 1949, the difficulty of constructing a new cultural hegemony was already apparent.

By 1949 the Communists had also accrued considerable experience of the hold of pre-modern cultural patterns over the mass of the peasantry. While seeking their main allies among the land-hungry and exploited peasantry, of necessity or through conviction, in other respects Communist leaders often shared the same assumptions as many Nationalist politicians and westernized intellectuals, that the 'feudal superstition' of the peasants was an obstacle to China's modernization. The mass line strategy developed in the Yan'an period called for constant dialogue and mutual learning between party leaders and the popular masses, but was also in tension with a powerful technocratic version of socialist modernization held by much of the leadership, who saw it as their task to eliminate the backward elements of popular culture, in religion, in family and gender hierarchies, in medicine, and in everyday behaviour.

Moving into the cities, the Communists came up against concentrations of institutionalized cultural power that represented further obstacles to their hegemonic project. Established schools, colleges and universities, publishers of newspapers, magazines and books, circles of writers, artists and musicians, associations of lawyers, journalists and other modern professions, may well have contained some members who supported or sympathized with the Communist Party, but also many others whose exposure to foreign writings and ways of life had convinced them that there were alternative routes for China to enter the modern world. Many had emerged from the turmoil following the May Fourth movement as pragmatic liberals with a belief in development through science and technology, and a society based on economic, political and cultural pluralism (Goldman 1981). Their key positions in educational, professional and cultural institutions were resources of cultural power, as was the need for the Communist Party leadership in the newly occupied cities to rely on their expertise. Over the following years the party mounted numerous campaigns to convert this large and diverse intelligentsia to Marxism–Leninism, but the tensions within the Communist project for cultural hegemony resulted in inconsistency and fluctuations of direction. At times the more radical tendency in the party would gain predominance and liberal intellectuals would be subjected to persecution and intense control; at other times the more technocratic tendency would come to the fore and liberal intellectuals would be accorded more freedom of expression. At all times the liberal intelligentsia, often older and western educated, potentially faced challenges from more radical intellectuals, often younger, lower in the hierarchy, with a more Marxist-orientated education and suspicious of foreign culture.

The campaign for cultural hegemony operated at various levels. As the regime consolidated its hold, all cultural institutions were brought into state or collective ownership and control. Private schools were taken over by the state, rural *sishu* closed or reorganized, and mission schools were squeezed out of existence. Foreign-run universities, along with all others, were brought under state control with the establishment of the Ministry of Higher Education in 1952. Research was organized under the Chinese Academy of Sciences. All book publishing was brought under the government's General Bureau of Publications in 1950, and all magazines and newspapers were under party control by the mid-1950s. Periodical distribution through subscriptions and kiosks was assigned exclusively to the post office. Cultural policy followed the lines laid down in Mao's 1942 Yan'an talks: artists and writers became members of state work-units under the Ministry of Culture, private art colleges and music conservatories were taken over by the state or closed, private patronage was abolished, and cultural workers were organized into party-controlled mass associations under the umbrella of the All-China Federation of Literature and Art (Clunas 1997). Film studios, radio broadcasting stations, performance troupes, orchestras and so on likewise became state-controlled work-units.

The Communist Party established direct control over all realms of culture. At the top, cultural control was exercised by the Propaganda Department of the Central Committee, which supervised the mass media, literature, art, music, education, publishing, scientific research, sports, and all other cultural activities. Every school, university, cultural or media organization included among its staff a contingent of party members and was led by its party committee. In addition, local-level media organizations were supervised by the party secretary of the relevant province or city. Specialized journals and other units of cultural production were placed under the control of the appropriate party organization. No cultural work of any significance could be done without party knowledge and approval.

Intellectuals who worked in any of these organizations were given ideological re-education to ensure conformity with party doctrine. In the early years of the PRC many teachers, scholars and writers responded with enthusiasm to the party's call for co-operation in the building of a new society and voluntarily attended courses on Marxism–Leninism and its application to their roles. Those who conformed were well treated and rewarded. Those identified as recalcitrants were publicly criticized, forced to write self-criticisms and punished harshly as a warning to others. Large numbers of intellectuals were accepted into the party in the years after 1949. However, tensions continued to grow between the 'red elite' of party cadres and the 'expert elite' of intellectuals (McDougall 1984), and the relationships between them and within the party leadership fluctuated. In 1956, the Hundred Flowers movement improved conditions for intellectuals and encouraged criticism of the party; in 1957, faced with an unexpected barrage of criticism from liberal intellectuals, the leadership mounted the Anti-Rightist campaign, in which many such intellectuals were branded as 'Rightists', a stigma many carried for the next twenty years; in 1958, the Great Leap Forward was accompanied by policies of subordinating professional artists and writers to amateurs working in native popular traditions and of sending intellectuals to the countryside to learn from peasants; in 1961, with the failure of the Great Leap recognized, a new period of relaxation and freedom for intellectual debate and cultural production began. These fluctuations clearly show the inherent tensions within the Communist project for cultural hegemony.

Yet, despite all this apparatus of control over intellectuals and their cultural activities, in many ways cultural elitism continued to be reproduced. The complex written language, for centuries past a symbol of cultural domination, was to some extent simplified, but more radical proposals for language reform were rejected and the mystique of calligraphy was retained (Kraus 1991). Following the Soviet model, the Ministry of Education decided to concentrate scarce resources placing highest priority on specialization and academic preparation for higher education (Pepper 1996). After an immediate post-Liberation expansion of elementary schools in the countryside, further development in both elementary and secondary schooling was concentrated in urban areas to contribute to the drive for industrialization. Provinces and cities were to designate 'key-point' schools as centres of excellence and give them better teachers and improved facilities. Criticism of the urban bias and elitism of this strategy surfaced during the Anti-Rightist campaign of 1957, and the Great Leap Forward of 1958 saw the stress put on half-work, half-study schools in rural areas as the only way in which enrolment in secondary schools could be extended. The maintenance of the key-point schools resulted, however, in a dualistic system with an academic stream concentrated in the cities and available disproportionately to the children of the urban intelligentsia and party cadres, and a range of agricultural and specialized vocational schools for the majority.

Despite ideological teaching on comradeship and serving the people, this hierarchical and selective system encouraged academic competition, including competition to demonstrate political correctness and revolutionary activism (Shirk 1982; Thøgersen 1990).

The Cultural Revolution

Chinese Communists of all tendencies agreed that cultural revolution (with lower-case letters) was an essential part of transforming Chinese society. For example, in a report to the Second Session of the Eighth National Congress in May 1958, Liu Shaoqi, later to be attacked as 'the number one person in authority in the party taking the capitalist road', proclaimed that 'to meet the requirements of the technical revolution, we must at the same time carry through a cultural revolution, promoting culture, education, and public health in the interest of economic construction' (Selden 1979: 392). Liu referred to the need to eradicate illiteracy and to reform the written language, to improve sanitary conditions, promote sports and eliminate diseases, to break down superstitions, reform customs and change habits, to promote recreational and cultural activities among the masses and develop socialist literature and arts, and to train new working-class intellectuals and remould old ones, predominantly technicians, but also professors, teachers, scientists, journalists, writers, artists, and Marxist theoreticians. Yet by the middle of the 1960s the more radical wing of the party viewed the result of cultural revolution to date as the creation of a new elite of experts, many of them within the Communist Party, who were more concerned with technocratic modernization of the economy than with egalitarian social revolution. This new elite, it was thought, was also open to accommodation with 'bourgeois' intellectuals from before the revolution, many of whom, after the failure of the Great Leap Forward, had been reinstated to the positions which they had lost in the Anti-Rightist campaign. In 1966 Mao and his allies launched a series of mass campaigns against this new 'ruling class' of intellectuals and technical specialists, aiming to destroy the dominance of 'expertise' in all fields and to replace its elitism with a popular radical egalitarianism. Issues of education and culture figured prominently in the build-up of these campaigns, which became known as the Great Proletarian Cultural Revolution (with upper-case letters).[7]

Whyte (1972) has identified four components in the Maoist criticism of intellectuals: first, that intellectuals had too much influence on decision-making in a range of organizations, and used their claims to expertise to protect their own status and monopolize technical decisions; second, that they tended to be armchair theorists, divorced from practice and from the masses; third, that they tended to be elitist, feeling that their expertise entitled them to special treatment and privileges; and fourth, that there were simply too many of them, and that most organizations could get by with fewer experts. The policy of the Maoists in the Cultural Revolution towards intellectuals and experts was consistent with these criticisms. Intellectuals and experts of various kinds were subjected (to varying degrees) to mass criticism and struggle, involving beatings, house searches, and arrests. Many were sent to the countryside, where they might remain for several years. Many lost their posts and were confined to forced labour camps. Many were obliged to attend study classes, often under the supervision of veteran workers or peasants, to rid them of their elitist notions. Campaigns were also carried out to reduce the numbers of experts, with those declared superfluous allocated manual labour posts within their work-units or transferred to other units.

The Cultural Revolution had far-reaching consequences for all levels of education. From 1966 to 1968 these were mainly disruptive. Schools were closed altogether for several months, in some cases longer. The university entrance examinations were first postponed and then abolished, and universities became sites of violent struggles between Red Guard factions. Teachers were accused of revisionism and capitalist restoration, paraded in dunces hats and forced to write self-criticisms. Once order was restored in late 1967 and 1968, however, a phase of consolidation began in which the critical ideals raised earlier in the revolution could be once more pursued. The main goals were to reverse the urban bias and to dismantle the narrow elitism of key-point schools. The policy was to provide state funds for a middle school in every commune and financial assistance for virtually all brigade schools. County education bureaux were made responsible for providing buildings and recruiting teachers. In this way, the aim of providing schooling for rural children on a par with urban ones was vigorously pursued, though only partially achieved. In addition, once institutions of higher education reopened, entrance procedures were to facilitate the admission of the children of workers, peasants and soldiers, with an entrance requirement of at least two years' work and the recommendation of the members of the work-unit. A considerable expansion of enrolments in secondary schooling in rural and urban areas followed, though there were still significant differences in provision between wealthier and poorer communes and provinces.

The content and methods of schooling also changed. Courses were shortened, elementary schooling usually by one year and secondary schooling by two. New curricula and textbooks were prepared, intended to reduce the impractical bookishness of regular courses and to make school more relevant for productive work, whether industrial or agricultural. Manual labour became a compulsory and expanded part of the curriculum. Teachers were put under the supervision of PLA teams, worker propaganda teams, students, mass organizations, and mass management committees, to ensure that 'redness' rather than professional expertise remained in command. Teachers varied considerably in their responses to this upheaval, some cooperating enthusiastically, others less so, and many covertly retaining a commitment to what they saw as academic standards and the procedures needed to uphold them.

The Cultural Revolution also sought to redefine all aspects of the arts and all media. The party committees that supervised publishing, broadcasting, and performance were displaced or taken over by Red Guards and subjected to factional struggle. Writers and journalists, especially those who had been branded as 'Rightists', were condemned, sent to the countryside or referred to May Seventh Cadre Schools for re-education. Broadcasting, especially transmissions to loudspeakers in public places, penetrated many parts of the countryside and conveyed doctrinally selected political messages and stirring music. All forms of literature, art, music and film deemed to be elitist or bourgeois were banned, as was the vast majority of foreign culture. They were replaced by a narrow repertoire of permitted works, such as the 'revolutionary model operas'. As well as the text and performance versions of the model operas, they were also filmed, replacing almost all feature films made before 1966, which were withdrawn from release at the beginning of the Cultural Revolution. Popular culture was homogenized, and intellectuals were prevented from 'distinguishing' themselves through their elitist artistic tastes (McDougall 1984). However, there were exceptions to the general tendency for the Cultural Revolution to reject both traditional cultural forms and western models. One of these was the classical poetry of Mao Zedong, written in his inimitable calligraphic hand and published in leading newspapers. Another was the use of western musical forms and musical instruments, incorporated into the model operas in the belief that they represented scientific modernity (Kraus 1989).

A further intensification of the Communist hegemonic project during the Cultural Revolution was the campaign against the 'Four Olds', in which Red Guards were encouraged to root out old culture, old beliefs, old customs and old habits. Primarily this was an attempt to replace local and traditional religious practices by state-centred practices. Red Guards ordered peasants to destroy their ancestral tablets, religious books, images of gods and symbols of good luck. In their place, peasant households were adorned with pictures of Mao and copies of the little red book containing quotations from Mao's writings and speeches. Traditional ritual practices were banned or discouraged, and new ones substituted; for example, burial of the dead was outlawed and cremation enforced as a more hygienic method allowing a better use of productive agricultural land. Traditional festivals held at dates marking the lunar calendar were also marginalized and new government holidays such as New Year's Day in the western calendar introduced. All of these changes represent a continuation of the urban cultural penetration of the countryside begun earlier in the century by previous regimes (Duara 1988).

In retrospect one of the most striking aspects of Communist cultural hegemony was the eradication of all aspects of consumer culture. Communist aversion to consumerism grafted Marxist opposition to bourgeois market culture on to Confucian elite prejudices against markets, with their connotations of disorder and immorality (Skinner 1985; Stockman 1992a). Policy on marketing fluctuated, reaching its extreme point during the Cultural Revolution. Rural markets were severely restricted or closed altogether. Distribution became the preserve of supply and marketing co-operatives and state trading companies. Advertising of all kinds was banned. Clothing became homogeneous and lost any basis for social distinction. Industrial investment was directed into heavy industrial development and very few consumer goods were produced. Trade with foreign countries was very limited and foreign brands and products were almost unknown. Whether as buyers or as sellers, the Chinese people were to be ideologically weaned from all aspects of commercialism.

The fragmentation of Communist cultural hegemony

The end of the Cultural Revolution rapidly led to changes in policy and in the shape of social power. Over the next twenty years, the Communist project for cultural hegemony was drastically redrawn. The Communist Party retained a monopoly over formal state power, and attempted to do whatever was necessary in the ideological arena to prevent or resist challenges to its rule. At times, this involved vigorous campaigns against ideological tendencies that were seen as threatening, such as the campaigns against 'bourgeois liberalization' and 'spiritual pollution'. The counterpart to these campaigns has been the policy of maintaining and building 'socialist spiritual civilization', which is the task of all government and party departments concerned with education and culture. The predominant tendencies in all spheres of culture to the date of writing, however, can be characterized in terms of elitism, stratification, diversification and commercialization. This shift in cultural policy is seen as necessary to support the economic growth on which the legitimacy of the Communist regime now rests.

Education

These tendencies are particularly evident in the field of education. The policy of 'Four Modernizations' involved a renewed emphasis on the contribution of education to industrial development (Bastid 1984). The egalitarian experiments of the Cultural Revolution were rejected and the system of 'key-point' schools and universities reintroduced (Thøgersen 1990; Pepper 1996). The concentration of resources in key-point schools resulted in the closure or down-grading of many secondary schools and a considerable reduction in enrolments at secondary level. In inland rural areas, senior middle schooling was concentrated in county towns and even junior middle schooling was considerably restricted, whereas coastal cities were allowed to provide universal senior secondary schooling to meet the expanded demand for college students (Pepper 1995). The competition for entry to senior middle schools put examinations back in command and increased the pressure on school students (Thøgersen 1989).

The emphasis on educational qualifications together with the cut-back in state funding led to the re-emergence of private provision in education. In areas that have experienced considerable economic growth (such as Shanghai and the Pearl River delta), there are now large concentrations of wealth among people who are prepared to finance the education of their children, and the state has been unable to resist pressures to allow private schools (Mok 1997). Private schools pose a challenge to Communist cultural hegemony; apart from their anti-egalitarian significance, they also represent values of diversity and freedom of choice, of market-orientated curricula, and of professional autonomy of teachers from state control (although this may well be replaced by subordination to market constraints). Official suspicion of private schools leads many of them to be referred to as *minban* (run by the people), which diverts attention from their elitism. Some private schools are in fact very expensive and exclusive, with extensive campuses, sports facilities and boarding opportunities. At the other extreme is the re-emergence of the traditional *sishu* school in poor rural areas, cheap elementary schooling with private tutors offering basic literacy and numeracy (Pepper 1995).

Related tendencies are also seen in tertiary education. Key-point institutions have been identified and key majors have been favoured, encouraging stratification and specialization within the system (Rai 1991). The 'marketization' of higher education (Yin and White 1993) signals a partial transition from the politicization of knowledge to its commodification. The higher education curriculum is being shifted in the direction of commercially useful knowledge, and university research is becoming increasingly subject to the demands of enterprise. Higher education reflects a hegemonic shift from the world view of a politically self-conscious revolutionary intelligentsia under the control of the Communist Party to that of a blend of technocratic officials and an entrepreneurial class. However, the Communist Party is not willing to relax its ideological hold altogether. At the same time as the curriculum is shifting towards applied science and technology, trade and finance, management and English, students still have to attend courses in Marxism–Leninism–Mao Zedong Thought (as further developed by Deng Xiaoping).

Culture and mass media

The mass media also display tensions between diversification and commercialization, on the one hand, and communist domination on the other. Since 1978 there has been an enormous expansion in all forms of media communication (A. P. L. Liu 1991). Newspapers and magazines have proliferated and aim at specialized as well as mass markets. Competition for readership is intense, and even the leading party national paper *Renmin Ribao* (*People's Daily*) has been forced to reshape its presentation to increase its attractiveness. Radio and television reception has become universal in urban areas and has increased considerably even in poorer and remote rural areas (T. Lau and Wang 1992–3). The state has lost the monopoly over broadcasting through the availability of satellite transmissions and broadcasts from Taiwan and Hong Kong. The state-controlled television channels themselves take a considerable part of their output from abroad,

including carefully vetted films and serialized classics. Sports broadcasts are particularly popular, and include live coverage of many
international football matches and athletics events. The film industry
has also expanded, and many films are co-produced with Chinese and
non-Chinese finance. The cinema has come under pressure of competition from alternative forms of leisure, especially the growth of television, and from 1988 studios were encouraged to make large
numbers of lightweight, entertaining and profit-making films (Berry
1991; Browne et al. 1994). The opening of China to the outside world
has also allowed in foreign culture in many other forms, such as video
and audio cassettes.

The Communist Party attempts to maintain surveillance and control over the mass media in all their forms, but the commercial
expansion and diversification of output has made this practically
impossible. The difficulties of controlling a more diverse and open
network of communications are compounded by the uncertainty
within the relevant bureaucracies as to what policy is being followed.
Although there remain elements within the party that would like
to maintain the predominance of Marxism–Leninism–Mao Zedong
Thought and the values of socialism, the pragmatic emphases encouraged by Deng Xiaoping, with the slogan 'seek truth from facts',
and the abandonment of political campaigns to enforce doctrinal
conformity, weakened the influence of the bureaucracies concerned
with propaganda and education. Among the groups marching in the
1989 demonstrations in Beijing were those with banners claiming to
represent the Central Committee Propaganda Department and the
People's Daily. Such divisions within the control agencies do not
indicate complete abandonment of cultural control, and unapproved
writers can still be arrested, but party control is increasingly hap-
hazard and contested. Attempts are made to control access to the
Internet, to restrict the influence of foreign and dissident ideas. With
the increased diversity and volume of mass communication, control
often takes the form of encouraging self-censorship and engendering
fear of being caught reading 'inappropriate' material.

None the less, this fragmentation of Communist hegemony means
that a greater diversity of values and interpretations has become
available to the Chinese population. A striking example of this was
the broadcasting in 1988 of the television documentary series
Heshang (variously translated as 'River Elegy', 'Deathsong of the
River', and others) (Su and Wang 1991). The series represented the
thesis that Chinese culture was inherently incompatible with modernization, and identified sacred images of China such as the Yellow

River and the Great Wall as relics of feudalism. Opposed to the 'yellow' culture of China was the 'azure' culture of the West, symbolized by the Pacific Ocean. The series was highly controversial, was much discussed in Chinese circles (including on the Internet) as well as in non-Chinese journals, and was strongly criticized by Communist Party ideologists for promoting westernization and national nihilism. Yet divisions within the party apparatus, together with competitive pressures on television channels, combined to allow the programme to be made in the first place and to be shown not once but twice on party-controlled CCTV (Ma 1996). *Heshang* gave internal Chinese legitimacy to the flood of other representations of modern western society that were reaching Chinese audiences.

The re-assertion of cultural diversity can also be seen in the form of cultural stratification. The years since 1978 have seen the re-creation of a self-conscious intellectual elite that identifies with itself and produces cultural works for itself, though often retaining a Confucian-like sense of responsibility to the society as a whole (Link 1992). In literature for example, some work is written by intellectuals for intellectuals, taking the predicament of the intellectual as its subject-matter (McDougall and Louie 1997). In cinema, the 1980s saw the emergence of a form of market-based stratification, with a clear demarcation between an intellectual art-film aesthetic and the dominant popular cinema (Browne et al. 1994). In music, there has been a resurgence of interest in western music among a cosmopolitan elite, and Chinese musicians and composers have themselves begun to join the international world of competitions, concert performances and 'classical' recordings (Kraus 1989). In the plastic arts, modernist avant gardes emerged to challenge official orthodoxies of realism as Chinese artists pursued their own interests and elite markets (Andrews and Gao 1995). The elitism in all branches of culture has been characterized as 'high culture fever' (J. Wang 1996).

As in societies with a longer and more continuous development of commercialism in the media, the counterpart to 'high culture' is a wide range of commercialized forms of 'popular culture'. With reduced state funding for many cultural enterprises, there has been more incentive for writers, directors and musicians to seek wider audiences. The most favoured form of leisure is watching television, and television networks have sought to provide new types of entertainment for the growing numbers of viewers. Soap operas have become popular, most notably the highly successful series 'Yearnings' (*Kewang*) first broadcast in 1991, representing the everyday life of two families, one of workers and the other of intellectuals, during and

after the Cultural Revolution (Zha 1995). A diverse array of popular
music genres has become accessible, from Cantopop to the harder
rock of the leading indigenous rock star Cui Jian (A. F. Jones 1992).
Tabloid newspapers, magazines on myriads of subjects, and popular
stories and novels have also flooded on to the market. As Zha (1995)
shows, much of this output is produced for commercial reasons by
intellectuals who explicitly distance themselves from the unsophist-
icated tastes of their customers, thus reinforcing a sense of cultural
stratification. The Cultural Revolution attempt to homogenize the
mass audience, to eliminate the reinforcement of social division by
cultural status distinction, has clearly been reversed.

Consumer culture

Another major departure from the cultural hegemony of Maoist communism, though not unwelcome to its successors, is the growth of
consumer culture, accompanying the return of markets as the predominant mechanism of distribution of consumption goods. Particularly
noticeable has been the growth of advertising. Advertising on bill-
boards, in newspapers and magazines, on radio and television, all re-
emerged in the late 1970s and grew rapidly thereafter, together with
the agencies which produce and place advertising (Stross 1990). Survey evidence shows high levels of interest in consumer goods and the
advertising for them, knowledge of global brand names and beliefs
as to the relative superiority of brands (Sklair 1994). Ownership of
consumer goods is increasing, and is also unequally distributed among
the population.[8] Families' concern for their own private and relative
comfort (Lu Hanlong 1997) has displaced the egalitarian ideology of
the Maoist period. Consumerism also contributes to the reconstruction of gender, with the expansion of the fashion and beauty markets
targeted especially but not exclusively at women, and the association
in advertising of femininity with domestic and decorative functions
(Hooper 1994).

The reintroduction of financial markets has also had a great impact
on urban culture. Stock market fever swept Shanghai from 1992, and
the culture of share dealing (*chao gupiao*: stir-fry shares) took hold of
the city (J. E. Gamble 1997). Several hundred thousand people have
share-dealing accounts and some spend more time dealing than they
do at their work-units. The facilities for dealing are stratified according to the size of the deal and the wealth of the dealers. There has been
an enormous growth of the insurance market in recent years, with

transnational insurance companies as well as domestic ones. The growth of life policies suggests that people are embracing commodification, placing a monetary value on their life to protect their dependants. Property insurance is also a growing market, spurred in part by the rise in crime in the major cities.

However, the commodification of everyday life remains controversial. Pieke (1995) remarks on the strength of everyday 'Maoism', especially in the moral outlook of state sector employees, who disapprove of the vulgar pursuit of money and of the monetary value now placed on various occupations, with teachers and medical doctors earning less than petty traders. They retain Maoist ideas of everyone 'eating from the big pot' and use them to resist threatening aspects of the economic reforms. Entrepreneurs themselves on the other hand, including small traders, equate the market with a morality of personal freedom, freedom from state direction and freedom to make what you want of your own life. Apart from the added tinges of Maoist radicalism, this conflict of views on the morality of the market reproduces the conflict between the entrepreneurial ideal and the collectivist ideal that has existed since the early days of industrial capitalism in the West.

Religion

The comprehensive attack on all aspects of religion that characterized the Cultural Revolution has been scaled down. Although party ideologists continue to hold an evolutionary interpretation of secularization, and believe that religion will gradually disappear along with China's socialist modernization, for a variety of reasons some aspects of religious practice are tolerated and even encouraged, while others are condemned as feudal superstition and policed as criminal behaviour. Space has opened up for what is often referred to as a 'revival' of religion, though whether what is 'revived' is the same as what went before requires careful inquiry.

The fragile and partial toleration of religion is partly motivated by economic considerations. Especially in the south-east of the country, the regime encouraged inward investment from Chinese people resident in Hong Kong, Taiwan, other parts of south-east Asia and North America. This investment was stimulated by appealing to the symbolic attachments of overseas Chinese, many of whom wanted to direct their investment capital to their native places. In many parts of Fujian and Guangdong provinces, the reuniting of emigrants with their kin and fellow villagers has been marked by the rebuilding of temples and ancestral halls and the revival of village processions and festivals, for which wealthy investors provide the finances. The fact that in many inland areas not so capable of attracting investment these religious revivals have not been permitted highlights the economic reasoning involved. Another reason for tolerating traditional religion is to attract tourists. The state has allowed the restoration of many temples and other religious sites that had been damaged during the Cultural Revolution or earlier, and these become stages in the progress of tourists, bringing foreign currency earnings into the country. The temples and monasteries are reoccupied by priests, monks and nuns who perform religious services for paying customers. As in other societies, the economic basis for the tourist industry is compounded with ideological elements, in this case the state's desire to bolster its legitimacy by appealing to a sense of national heritage. The Ministry of Culture has been charged since 1949 with the preservation of China's traditional culture, including architectural protection and archaeological excavation, and those aspects of traditional customs that are deemed to be 'healthy' in a socialist context (Feuchtwang and Wang 1991). In the post-Cultural Revolution period, this role has become more heavily imbued with nationalist content. Such practices as *wushu* (traditional martial arts) and *qigong* (exercises that mobilize the body's vital energies), for which there is considerable popular enthusiasm (Chen 1995), have been officially interpreted as acceptable customs showing quintessentially Chinese ways to health.[9]

The somewhat less threatening atmosphere of the 1980s created a space for the overt commitment to many other religious practices, some of which remained stigmatized by the authorities as 'feudal superstitions', vulnerable to repression and criminal prosecution, others recognized as valid religion, and therefore protected under provisions of the 1982 constitution. Among the latter are the institutionalized religions of Christianity, Buddhism, Daoism and Islam, all of which have seen a growth in adherents in recent years. The state exercises a certain control over these religions, primarily to resist non-Chinese influence, such as that of the Pope, over Chinese people. If Chinese are to be Christians, the authorities would prefer them to be members of officially recognized Chinese churches rather than of international ones (Chan Kim-Kwong and Hunter 1994). Tibetan Buddhism continues to be persecuted. Islam is also held in official suspicion because of its association with the wider Islamic world and with separatist movements in the far west of the country.[10] None the less, the world religions continue to attract believers, some of whom risk persecution for their beliefs.

The Cultural Revolution clearly did not eliminate all those practices that Chinese communist ideology defines as 'feudal superstition' (Anagnost 1985, 1987). In fact, whereas communist theory suggests that superstition would decline along with material improvement and rising literacy, paradoxically many such practices have become increasingly popular as peasant incomes have risen. There is now more money available to pay *fengshui* experts (geomancers) and fortune-tellers (Bruun 1996), to burn incense and spirit-money, and to hold local festivities that the state had tried to suppress as uncivilized and wasteful. The association with illegitimate and exploitative commerce is still used as a justification for the ideological condemnation and criminal prosecution of some of these activities, but at a local level officials often find themselves in a continual dialectic of conflict and accommodation with villagers whose ritual activity can be seen as resistance to the state's civilizing or disciplining mission.

However, this is not necessarily a 'revival' of traditional religion and ritual practice. State persecution of traditional religion, which has now lasted several generations, has disrupted the reproduction of local culture, and the 'social memory' of ritual practices has been attenuated, in some cases totally lost. Its resurgence in the post-Mao era shifts the process of social remembering from the 'natural' linkages between the generations to the abstracted knowledge of the folklorist and heritage specialist, as 'tradition' is reinvented (Feuchtwang 1993). As Siu (1990) puts it, cultural practices such as village rituals are not 'revived', but 'recycled' for new purposes in new circumstances.

Conclusion

The shape of cultural power in China has been changing throughout the twentieth century. Two generations of Communist revolution, following two or more previous generations of modernizing onslaughts on the beliefs and practices of the bulk of the population, drastically altered the conditions of cultural reproduction. The cultural power of old elites was dismantled, and the dominance of the Communist Party took its place. Divisions within the party made it impossible for a consistent policy, either of cultural egalitarianism or technocratic modernization, to be pursued, and it is also difficult to disentangle the effects of deliberate political cultural engineering from the effects of more diffuse factors such as new economic conditions and new communications technologies. The latter have accelerated in recent years, weakening the capacity, though not the desire, of the regime to control ideology. In any case, the memory of the Cultural Revolution has engendered disillusionment among much of the population in all forms of overt politicization, and this combines with the anti-Maoist policies of the government to leave space for a new, less politicized, cultural hegemony of commercialism and consumerism, with all its capacity for reinforcing and extending social division and social distinction. A new structure of cultural power is in the making, which sociologists will want to study carefully.

Further reading

Pepper (1996) provides the most comprehensive analysis of educational developments and policy. McDougall (1984) contains illuminating articles on cultural policy up to and including the Cultural Revolution. Kraus (1989, 1991) gives entertaining and unusual insights into the sociology and politics of culture through the examples of calligraphy and music. Zha (1995) presents the diversity of popular culture in the 1990s.

8

Changing Patterns of Social Inequality

Introduction

Twentieth-century China, a latecomer to the conflicts surrounding modern inequalities, experienced this transition in a particularly violent and radical way. Political and economic power, which in some industrial capitalist societies of the West remained relatively stable and lent a degree of continuity to patterns of social inequality, has in China been almost continually contested throughout the century. The Communist Party rose to power committed to a drastic restructuring of inequalities of life chances, the abolition of rural and urban poverty and destitution and the elimination of the gap in living standards between urban and rural populations. In practice, there have been considerable shifts in policy and strategy during the period of Communist rule. This chapter surveys the main trends in social inequalities from pre-revolutionary times to the present.

In order to provide a systematic framework for the analysis of this large and complex topic, the discussion draws on the neo-Weberian tradition in the study of social inequalities. Following Weber's classic distinction between class, status, and party, many sociologists have accepted that social inequality should be seen as multidimensional, thus recognizing the possibility that inequalities of one type might not correlate with inequalities of other types. The particular version of such a multidimensional approach to be used here draws on the work of Pierre Bourdieu (1986) and Reinhard Kreckel (1976,

1992). Kreckel distinguishes four dimensions of social inequality, or four unequally available strategic resources: (1) 'wealth', which approximates to a Weberian concept of class and to Bourdieu's 'economic capital', and includes all socially scarce material resources such as property and income; (2) 'knowledge', similar to Bourdieu's 'cultural capital', including all socially scarce symbolic resources such as literacy, educational qualifications, and professional expertise; (3) 'hierarchical organization', or positional power (related to Weber's concept of *Herrschaft*), which locates people in organized social relationships of command and obedience; when the organization concerned is a political party or a government department, this resource is sometimes called 'political capital'; and (4) 'selective association', similar to Bourdieu's 'social capital', and referring to relationships between people who think of each other as sharing membership of social groups or categories, from which 'non-members' may be excluded and thus deprived of life chances. Each of these resources can bring its own rewards to those who have access to them; they have a 'use value'. In addition, they may have an 'exchange value', in that each resource may be convertible into the others. The conditions of convertibility are themselves socially structured and regulated.

In western capitalist societies, inequalities of the first three kinds tend to be upheld by the legal order of the state: inequalities of wealth by laws of property and contract; inequalities of knowledge by state recognition of legitimately gained educational and professional qualifications; hierarchical organization by state guarantees of the rights of management and the legal standing of organizational structures. They are overt, public inequalities, and in that sense legitimate. The fourth, selective association, which in earlier European societies was often the basis of differences of legal estate (Weber's *Stand*), now operates by contrast in private, and may be illegitimate and even illegal, since it appears as the favouritism of nepotism and the iniquity of discrimination, such as that based on race or gender.

This chapter will thus investigate these four dimensions of inequality as they have appeared in twentieth-century China, both in themselves and in their interrelationships. It examines the implications for changing patterns of inequality of state policies towards wealth and income, towards knowledge, education and expertise, towards organizational hierarchies (in particular those of the Communist Party and the state itself), and towards the all-pervasive tendency to seek advantage by mobilizing relationships of selective association and to transfer disadvantage by discrimination.

Pre-revolutionary patterns of inequality

Wealth

As in all agrarian civilizations, the most important strategic material resource in imperial and Republican China was agricultural land. Land was mostly privately owned, had been a marketable commodity for many centuries, and was distributed highly unequally. Reliable information about the extent of this inequality is scarce and contested. However, evidence from a number of surveys carried out in the 1930s[1] suggests that landlords, making up around 4 per cent of rural households, owned 39 per cent of the land; rich peasants, those owning more land than they could farm with family members, accounted for 6 per cent of households and 17 per cent of the land; self-sufficient middle peasants 22 per cent of households owning 30 per cent of the land; while poor peasants, those with insufficient land to keep their families, made up 60 per cent of households. Of the poor peasants, around three-fifths owned some land (around 14 per cent of all land), while two-fifths were just tenants. The remaining 8 per cent of rural households were also landless, and members of them worked as agricultural labourers or maintained some other precarious existence. These figures are extremely crude and uncertain, and conceal wide variations between different parts of the country. In general, much higher proportions of land were rented out in southern provinces than in northern ones; in some less fertile northern areas, landlordism was almost unknown. Approximately 60 per cent of rented land was owned by absentee landlords, who tended to be the wealthier landowners (Esherick 1981).

Despite the relatively low rate of return for the landowner, from the peasant's point of view tenancy was very burdensome. Typical rents, though varying considerably from region to region, often amounted to half of the crop yield. The practice of dividing land on the death of the farmer, mentioned in chapter 5, not only hindered the growth of large estates, it also continually drove poorer peasants further into poverty, reproducing the pool of landless labourers and preventing the poorest from continuing their family line. In the 1930s a range of factors, including political instability, intensified exploitativeness of social relationships and the world depression, increased the pressures on the peasantry and deepened their poverty. There is no satisfactory evidence concerning the distribution of income in pre-revolutionary rural China; Perkins (1969: 122) assumes that it mirrored the proportion of land in the hands of landlords.

Apart from landowning and trade, the other main source of high income and wealth was through office-holding in the imperial bureaucracy. Official emoluments accruing to county magistrates were in themselves considerable, but in the nineteenth century they were far outweighed by unofficial, semi-legal and illegal exactions from the subject population in the form of fees, bribes, and other payments known as 'squeeze'. The opportunities open to a civil servant for accumulation of wealth that could be reinvested in land or business underlay the widely quoted saying that a family's prosperity would be guaranteed if it could produce one imperial official in every three generations.

Inequalities in urban wealth and income in late imperial and Republican China are very difficult to gauge. Many urban dwellers were in fact sojourners, whose economic circumstances were closely associated with that of their family back in their native place. Most wealthy urban residents gained their wealth from absentee landlordism, from official positions, and from trade and commerce; wealth from trade was regularly converted into official status and the lifestyle of the literati. The emergence of new economic opportunities in the first half of the twentieth century brought into existence a class of wealthy bourgeois with interests in manufacture, trade and finance, though no reliable statistics as to the size and wealth of this class exist. In the decades before 1949 much economic wealth remained in the hands of the state and of the Guomindang leadership. Among the new industrial labour force, skill at first brought with it returns in significantly higher income, but such differentials appear to have generally declined over the decades to the 1940s (Howe 1973). The cities also became the location of the poor and destitute, existing on casual work, begging, or the lowest forms of prostitution.

Knowledge

'Knowledge' as a strategic resource refers to any form of restriction of access to the symbolic culture of a society. Much of a society's cultural heritage, its language, customs, and basic productive techniques, can be the common property of all members of a society. But all elements of symbolic culture have to be learned, and to the extent that access to learning particular elements of symbolic culture is socially regulated and limited, the socially produced scarcity of symbolic goods generates inequalities in life chances.

For the vast majority of the population of Chinese agrarian society, access to the common heritage of customs and agricultural techniques was widely available, though young women were deprived of the chance to learn more complex aspects of agricultural technique on the grounds that their skills would be lost to their family of origin when they married out. Handicraft skills were the property of particular families and transmitted through the family. Other craft skills were the property of groups of urban workers, and guild regulations restricted the learning of such skills to members of the guild. Chinese traditional medicine was highly developed, and the knowledge and skills necessary for its practice were accessible only to the few, although knowledge of folk medicine of various kinds was more widespread. Religious skills were the property of ritual experts such as Daoist or Buddhist priests, geomancers, and others, and families were dependent on the services of such religious experts for the performance of life-cycle rituals.

Traditional elementary schooling was diffused throughout the countryside and was not confined to towns and cities.[2] However, such schooling reached only a very small proportion of the young population: approximately one per cent of the 7 to 14-year-old age group among boys in the middle of the nineteenth century, and a lower proportion of girls. Tutoring and schooling of various kinds produced literacy rates, defined on very minimal criteria, of 30 to 45 per cent of males and 2 to 10 per cent of females. The degree and form of this literacy varied widely, however, from a basic literacy sufficient for everyday life up to the sophistication of classical scholarship (Rawski 1979). To this must be added the fact that the language of the literati was completely different from the language of the everyday life of the people; early acquisition of this literary language was considered by officials' families to be essential for their children's future, and this cultural capital gave such children considerable advantage over those born into less literate families.

For a very small minority of males, schooling could proceed towards preparation for the imperial examinations. This endeavour required considerable time and thus freedom from the need to engage full-time in economic activity, and was available only to a very few. According to Ho, however, meritocratic Confucian ideology was sufficiently realized to allow able young men of humble social origin to be sponsored into higher education, and upward social mobility through success in the examinations was not uncommon (P. Ho 1962). Although the examination degrees were scarce commodities, they were not completely monopolized by families already high in the structure of inequality.

Professions requiring licensed certification, thereby excluding those without qualifications, did not exist in imperial China. Medicine, for example, could be practised by anyone who wished to do so and who could attract a clientele, and was unregulated either by the state or by an occupational organization (Unschuld 1979). Proposals for such organization, with a code of medical ethics to protect physicians and gain the trust of a clientele, were resisted by Confucian doctors on the grounds that specialization and specialized codes of ethics did not befit a gentleman. The practice of law as an independent profession was similarly unknown (MacCormack 1990). The criminal law was administered by county magistrates who had no more than a practical knowledge of the penal code, and who relied on private secretaries or clerks for legal advice. Such clerks could have legal training but they remained unpaid, dependent on customary fees and gifts, susceptible to local pressures and open to bribery, all features inimical to professionalization. In the civil law, the notarizing of documents, such as those of contract, was either the responsibility of the magistrate or was carried out according to local custom outside a formal legal framework.

Control over the practice of certain professions began to develop in the last decade of the empire or during the Republican period although, unlike in the Anglo-American framework, this control was exercised by the state rather than by the profession itself. The practice of law was recognized for the first time by regulations promulgated in 1912, though practice of the law by unlicensed persons was not a serious offence, and the range of qualifications accepted was wide and flexible (Conner 1994). Western-style scientific medicine also began to be professionalized, with the formation in 1915 of the National Medical Association of China and the support of the Nationalist government for the development of what were seen as modern public health services, but the bulk of medical practice remained in the hands of unlicensed and unsupervised practitioners of Chinese medicine (R. P. L. Lee 1982). Professional control over specialist knowledge developed late, and was only weakly and ineffectively institutionalized before 1949.

Hierarchical organization

In pre-revolutionary Chinese society, two institutions in particular were inherently hierarchical, universal in scope, and composed of positions which furnished their occupants with different degrees of positional power: the family and the imperial bureaucracy.[3] The hierarchical organization of the traditional family and lineage has already been described in chapter 5, and will not be repeated here. A third institutional area of hierarchical organization affected a smaller, yet significant and growing proportion of the population, namely non-familial work.

The imperial bureaucracy was erected on the fundamental dichotomy between the rulers and the ruled. Leaving aside the hereditary imperial and non-imperial nobilities, China was ruled through a complex, hierarchical, bureaucratic organization of officials. The hierarchy consisted of nine ranks of official positions, falling into three strata. Officials in each rank were furnished with specific rights, duties, powers, and obligations within the organizational structure. Occupation of a post in the hierarchy could only be achieved by the proper procedures of appointment (including appointment following purchase). The positional powers attaching to each office were laid down in law, and punishments for the abuse of such powers were also specified. To the lowest stratum of officials may also be added a whole array of unclassed clerks or sub-officials who could ascend to the lower-classed ranks through seniority or special tests. All officials, apart from the positional power appropriate to their rank, also had certain general privileges which marked them off from the rest of the commoner population, in particular exemption from labour services and from subjection to the ordinary penal code and corporal punishments.

Positions within the imperial bureaucracy were extremely scarce. During the Qing dynasty China was administered by no more than about 27,000 officials, including about 1300 district magistrates, the district being the lowest level of administration. Very few men, and no women, could avail themselves of the life chances that went with this scarce resource. The bureaucracy was not a socially closed group, and access to it was in principle regulated by competition. However, according to Ho's data, nearly 60 per cent of all higher degree holders over the whole Ming-Qing period came from families which had produced at least one official in the previous three generations (P. Ho 1962: 124), a statistic that indicates a rather high level of self-recruitment among the officialdom. The proportion of new holders of this degree who came from the commoner population decreased steadily over the period and was at its lowest in the last years of the empire.

The growth of central and municipal government and of modern industry and commerce in the Republican period added to the range of hierarchical organization and brought increasing numbers of people within its scope, although a relatively small proportion of the population had positions in formal organizations. The new forms of hierarchical organization that grew up, especially in the cities, included occupational hierarchies in the modern sectors of the economy, in modern industry, medicine, education, banking, and so on. Another form that began to be significant towards the end of the imperial era but became even more important as the Republican period wore on was the political party. Especially in those areas of China under the authority of the Nanjing government in the decade 1927–37, position within the Guomindang was an important resource for improving a person's life chances. Military reorganization and the growing militarization of society from the mid-nineteenth century onwards also increased the salience of hierarchical position in the army, which became an important route to power and wealth.

Selective association

Chinese social relationships were to a very considerable extent orientated by particularistic considerations.[4] Rather than relying on the performance of universalistic role-obligations by strangers, people would prefer whenever possible to draw on particularistic relationships with specific known others in any conceivable situation. The preference was to deal exclusively with family members, because the Chinese were taught that family members could be relied on, whereas non-family people were not to be trusted. The basic form of selective association was therefore rooted in family relationships, and family members could be expected to bond together for mutual support; for example, a young man might receive aid of various kinds from those kinsmen who had posts in the bureaucracy. Beyond the family, connections were assiduously cultivated, including affinal links made through marriage, since people knew that as soon as they moved outside the area where kinship and personal acquaintance held sway they would have to depend on such relationships in order to make their way or get anything done. Such connections were treated precisely as what Bourdieu means by 'social capital', and were clearly thought to affect the distribution of life chances. It appeared in all sorts of contexts: in networks of former classmates in the civil service, in dealings of commoners with the bureaucracy, in trading relationships, and so on. Relationships based on shared native-place were pervasive in employment practices and in mutual support networks among sojourners. After the collapse of the empire, local and provincial networks formed the basis for political factions and warlord cliques.

The mutual support maintained by selective association also implies discrimination against those thought to be outsiders or inferiors. The most pervasive and taken-for-granted form of discrimination in pre-revolutionary China was that based on gender (Stockman et al. 1995). Women were excluded from the vast majority of roles outside the immediate domestic context. The exceptions were activities of inferiority and immorality, such as prostitution and entertainment. With the emergence of the modern economy, women were mainly confined to routine manual work in such industries as textiles, and the few women who broke through into professions such as teaching, medicine or banking tended to be restricted to subordinate positions. Discrimination was also practised on the basis of ethnicity and native-place identity, as a corollary of the mutual support between those sharing such identity. Han superiority over non-Han minorities was assumed,[5] but even within the Han, according to Honig (1992), the stereotyping of and discrimination against Subei people in Shanghai, for example, amounted to ethnic discrimination and constituted an important aspect of social inequality.

Revolutionary transformations of social inequality

Wealth

Guided by the theories of Marxism–Leninism, adapted to Chinese circumstances by Mao Zedong, the Communist regime aimed to transform access to material resources through changing the balance of class forces. The result of the determined pursuit of this aim was the construction of a society characterized by an unusual degree of material equality. Inequalities of wealth and income were not entirely eradicated, but they existed within ranges that were narrow by comparison both with industrial capitalist and less developed societies (Parish 1984).

Land reform transformed the distribution of land ownership. Considerable dispute surrounds the amount of land redistributed from landlords to poor and middle peasants: Esherick (1981) suggests that the official figure of 700 million *mu* (47 million hectares) is only plausible on the assumption that land was also expropriated from some rich peasants or managerial farmers. None the less, it is agreed that landlordism was abolished, as was landlessness. A small class of rich peasants (2–3 per cent) remained in existence in the mid 1950s, cultivating approximately three times as much land on average as the average poor peasant and continuing to hire in some farm labour; around 30 per cent of peasant households were classified as 'poor', many of whom had insufficient land to provide family subsistence and had to hire out labour; but the bulk of the rural population (around 60 per cent) was classified as 'middle peasants', indicating that rural China had become a realm of smallholders. Inequalities in ownership of livestock and farm equipment also remained but, as a result of land distribution and taxation policies, the poorest 20 per cent of the peasantry doubled their share of rural income by the 1950s compared with the 1930s (Selden 1988: 9).

No sooner had this smallholder economy become established than it was transformed once again by co-operativization and collectivization. Private ownership of land and of all other forms of wealth except housing was abolished and material resources became the common property of the communes and brigades. The income of each accounting unit (usually production teams) was distributed according to the number of work-points accumulated by each member of each household and by the mid 1970s exhibited a very low degree of inequality at a local level. The most important form of material inequality in rural society was geographical; regions and localities varied enormously in their natural endowments and level of agricultural development, and the egalitarianism of the commune system was not designed to redistribute resources from richer to poorer regions. In fact the state policy of local self-reliance reinforced interregional inequalities. The material life chances of the Chinese peasantry depended almost entirely on where they happened to live.

The class structure of urban society was also transformed by the revolution. By the mid 1950s the property-owning classes had been expropriated (apart from those capitalists who had managed to transfer their interests to Taiwan, Hong Kong or overseas) and their wealth incorporated into state-owned organizations. Smaller businesses were collectivized. At the other extreme, destitution was eradicated by allocating the whole urban population to work-units through which welfare and social security was provided. The mass of the working population was paid according to a planned structure of income differentiation. In 1955 a wage structure for all state workers and staffs was introduced: government cadres were divided into twenty-six grades, technicians into seventeen grades, and workers into eight grades (Korzec and Whyte 1981). The span of income differentiation ranged from Y30 to Y560 among government cadres, and an official guideline set a ratio of 6:1 or 7:1 for top and bottom wages in an enterprise (Howe 1973: 36). Piece-rate systems were also used in the early years of planned industrialization. However, the extremes exaggerate the degree of income inequality. At the high point of egalitarianism before the economic reforms of the 1980s took effect, the overall distribution of urban income was highly concentrated in the middle of these scales. The Gini coefficient[6] for urban income distribution found in a World Bank study of 1981 was only 0.16, which is extraordinarily low by international standards (Riskin 1987: 249). Even though money incomes in China were an unreliable measure of access to material resources, the inclusion of decommodified collective goods provided to members of work-units would go only a small way to dent the impression of an urban society that had considerably reduced inequality of access to material benefits of many kinds. It had also become inappropriate for a person to strive for greater material comforts than others; the egalitarian ethos of the revolution encouraged asceticism and self-sacrifice, even if this value was often honoured in the breach as well as in the adherence (Oksenberg 1968).

Material inequalities between rural and urban areas continued to be great. *Hukou* regulations rigidified the division between town and country in the period after 1958.[7] The planning mechanism, the low proportion of national investment directed into agriculture, and the 'scissors gap' in the structure of relative prices of agricultural and industrial products, also reinforced material inequalities between rural and urban inhabitants, despite official pronouncements on the priority to be given to agriculture. The consequences of these planning policies are evident in the discrepancies between rural and urban incomes and levels of consumption, although there were also wide variations between and within regions.

Knowledge

The fluctuations of educational policy between meritocratic and radical egalitarian tendencies, discussed in the previous chapter, affected different cohorts of students differently, but it seems clear that by the late 1970s inequalities of educational opportunity had been significantly reduced, though inequalities of knowledge, in the sense of command over strategic symbolic resources, remained considerable.

The most basic of these resources was literacy. Drives to extend literacy were a recurrent feature of Communist modernization policies. Yet illiteracy remained widespread, excluding millions of mostly rural residents from all those activities requiring the ability to read and write. Statistics are made uncertain by many factors, including the operational definition of literacy itself. In 1956 the Minister of Education reported to the National People's Congress that illiterates made up 78 per cent of the total population. The 1982 Census produced a figure of 229 million illiterates over 15 years of age, approximately 35 per cent of the adult population. One can assume that this represents a real reduction in illiteracy, although the definition of literacy used was probably minimal, but it still reveals the very basic level at which inequalities of knowledge appeared in China, compared with the almost universal literacy of developed societies.

A similar situation existed by the early 1980s in relation to schooling. Whereas 94 per cent of children enrolled in primary schools, it seems (in the absence of precise statistics) that 60 to 70 per cent completed five or six years of primary schooling, and about 30 per cent graduated with satisfactory results. Access to junior middle school did however increase steadily up to the mid 1970s, when 90 per cent of graduates from primary school were going on to middle schools (Thøgersen 1990: 177). At the other extreme, higher education expanded five-fold from an enrolment of 137,000 in 1950 to 625,000 in 1977 (Pepper 1996: 487), but remained restricted to a small minority. The 1982 census showed that 0.6 per cent of Chinese adults had experienced higher education.

Absolute inequalities of knowledge, as measured by literacy and schooling rates, therefore remained high. These inequalities were socially structured. The gap of school provision between the towns and cities and the countryside remained very wide; primary schooling, and later junior middle schooling, became virtually universal in the cities but much more sparse in rural areas, especially remote ones. The policy pursued in the aftermath of the Cultural Revolution of establishing a senior middle school in every commune considerably increased the rates of senior secondary schooling in rural areas, but this policy did not last long. Gender gaps in literacy and schooling also remained considerable, especially in rural areas where schooling for daughters was often not considered worthwhile. But inequalities between social classes in their opportunity to gain regular schooling and formal educational qualifications were reduced in the first thirty years of the Communist regime. The policies of giving preference to children of workers and peasants and reducing the privileged access to education of the children of the wealthy and the highly educated had some effect. This equalization of opportunity increased over the decades, and reached its peak in the Cultural Revolution decade. The decline in the advantage of having a high-status father was greater for the sons of intellectuals than for the sons of cadres, suggesting that cadres were more successful in passing on privilege to their sons (Deng and Treiman 1997). None the less, Communist policies up to 1976 went some way to interrupting the inheritance of cultural capital and the transmission of advantage down the generations.

Schooling and educational qualifications lost much of their exchange value in the first three decades after 1949. Apart from specific scientific and technical occupations, formal education was not the way to get ahead and was not an important determinant of a person's level of income. More important was another, and uncredentialized, form of knowledge: the ability to read the political wind, to understand the terms of political debate, and to give the right impression in political meetings (Oksenberg 1968). In the highly charged atmosphere of the 'campaign phases' of the revolution, these abilities could have significant implications for life chances (sometimes literally), and not only for those with political ambitions.

Political considerations also produced other forms of inequality of knowledge. Information with any degree of political sensitivity was tightly restricted and controlled. A vast array of files and documentation, including regular reports and the results of specific investigations, was designated as classified information (*neibu*) and accessible only to cadres at appropriate levels of government and party. Inclusion in the ranks of those entitled to receive *neibu* publications was a mark of success; it could also be a reward in its own right.

Hierarchical organization

In the first decade after 1949 Chinese society was transformed according to principles of hierarchical organization (Schurmann 1968). Virtually the entire population was brought within the compass of two intertwined organizational systems, those of the state and the Communist Party. State administration and the state-planned economy, both urban and rural, came to be organized as a hierarchy of hierarchies in which everyone had a place in the transmission of command.

State administration was structured as a series of bureaucratic levels, from central government down to locality. At each level, administrative branches were established to control work organizations and co-ordinate economic activities. Every urban work-unit (*danwei*) belonged to one of these levels of administration: central government, ministry (*bu*), bureau (*ju*), division (*chu*), department (*ke*), or section (*gu*) (Bian 1994: 30). From the late 1950s, the commune system established a rural hierarchy of commune, brigade and production team. Each work-unit was in turn organized as a hierarchical arrangement of positions from director downwards. Thus all individuals at any given stage of their careers were located in this dual hierarchy: their place in the hierarchy of the work-organization itself, and the rank of their work-organization in the larger administrative hierarchy.

Each location within this dual hierarchy was formally vested with a degree of positional power. A person in a higher position within an organization had the formal right to command those lower in the structure, or to transmit commands from higher levels. Depending on the degree of centralization in force at a given time, many of these commands would themselves be transmitted from higher-ranking organizations. Higher-ranking organizations determined the allocation of resources for lower-ranking ones, had greater authority and larger budgets, and a greater capacity to acquire resources of all kinds. Lower-ranking organizations had to remit surpluses and taxes up the hierarchy to central government organizations which had the power to redistribute resources according to their own plans.

The direct use values of positional power, the ability to command others, to realize plans, to be relatively autonomous from superior authority, which exist in any system of hierarchical organization, were however not untrammelled. In every organization the Communist Party committee as a parallel hierarchy exercised political supervision over the management. In more turbulent times, political instability could result in the displacement or demotion of higher-ranking cadres who had failed to retain the confidence of the party. During the Cultural Revolution, the insecurity of rank reached a high point, as senior cadres, administrators and experts of all kinds were attacked and humiliated by Red Guards and forced to undergo re-education. In addition, the egalitarian ethic of the revolution normatively restrained the flaunting of authority and the excessive symbolic representation of rank. Once again, the Cultural Revolution accentuated this tendency to remove the trappings of hierarchy, though in practice the temporary disappearance of party control in many parts of the country allowed excesses of 'commandism' to reassert themselves.

Despite these political and ideological constraints on hierarchical organizational power, it was generally the case that higher rank brought its own rewards and was also convertible into other resources. Despite relatively low income differentiation, higher rank brought with it higher official salaries. Data from the later 1970s show that the rank of work-unit was a major determinant of inequalities of urban incomes (Walder 1990). More important than higher individual income was the fact that higher-ranking work-units were able to provide more substantial collective goods to their members. Higher-ranking units could offer better housing, facilities for health care, sports and recreation, child care, and many other aspects of welfare that were neither provided universally by the state nor available as commodities on the market. Higher-ranking units were also more likely to provide high-quality schooling for the children of members as well as training for the adult members themselves, allowing the conversion of inequalities of rank into inequalities of knowledge.

Selective association

In the social development of western European societies, equality before the law replaced the legal privilege and disprivilege of an order of feudal estates. The logic of formal legal equality is that social advantage and disadvantage based on selective association and discrimination is difficult to justify. Meritocracy demands that reward should depend on the public display of ability and effort, in which supposedly everyone has an opportunity to shine. If preference is given or denied to people on the basis of ascribed characteristics, this must happen in a private sphere of social inclusion and exclusion, concealed from public gaze. This meritocratic model has been a long time in the making; only relatively recently, in many societies, has the force of state legislation been brought to bear against discrimination based on race, gender, and sometimes religion. Other aspects of selective advantage based on private association appear to be much less amenable to legal remedy. The transmission of advantage through the inheritance of economic and cultural capital occupies a grey area, sometimes contested, partially restrained through inheritance taxation and educational policies, more often ignored.

China's revolutionary history in this respect is quite different. In its attempt to restructure the economic and social conditions of unequal life chances, the Communist regime identified privileged categories in the population whose privileges were to be removed. In the process the whole population was classified under a system of 'class labels' (*jieji chengfen*). Ostensibly based on the 'scientific' categories of Marxism–Leninism as adapted to Chinese circumstances, these were also imbued with the evaluative distinction between 'good class' (friends) and 'bad class' (enemies). During subsequent political campaigns a number of further evaluative labels, or 'hats' (*maozi*), were added to these class statuses, mostly derogatory (such as 'political pickpocket' or 'little reptile'), some commendatory (such as 'five-good commune member') (Kraus 1981: 58f). General labels such as 'bad element' or 'counterrevolutionary element' were also widely used. These labels, once attached to a person and recorded on their personal dossier, were difficult to escape. Many of them, especially the class statuses, were also hereditary, following the theory of 'family background'; the children of 'bad class' categories such as former landlord carried the stigma of their family's class status with them, even if they were born after the revolution. Persons thus stigmatized were repeatedly scapegoated during campaigns and discriminated against in the distribution of rewards and opportunities. It was important for anyone with career ambitions to avoid associating with persons of 'bad' categories. The categories became generally understood stereotypes, continually reinforced by their representation as characters in films, plays and novels as well as newspaper reports. This entire set of political labels can be interpreted as a state-sponsored system of quasi-legal unequal statuses (Billeter 1985). Rather than a meritocracy, China under Mao was a 'virtuocracy' (Shirk 1984), in which positive and negative discrimination was based on official judgements of revolutionary virtue.

The other main official form of selective association was membership of the Communist Party itself. Party membership, which before the establishment of the PRC had been associated with risk and personal sacrifice, afterwards came to mean privilege and opportunity. Membership was maintained at about 4 per cent of the adult population and was much sought after by ambitious young people. Party members were expected to take a leading role in their work-units and communities, and spent much time in each other's company. As well as constituting an organized hierarchy with different degrees of positional power, party members also formed complex networks of social relationships. Such networks affected the process by which new members were accepted; membership was more likely to be gained by those with personal relationships with branch secretaries, especially among members of higher-ranking work-units (Bian 1994). In turn, party membership was a resource that could be transformed into other advantages: party members were more likely to experience upward career mobility, to receive higher incomes, better housing and other material rewards, and to procure a better education for their children.

In principle, the egalitarian and universalistic ethos of the revolution discouraged other aspects of selective association and discrimination. In practice, policy or neglect allowed deep-rooted forms of discrimination to continue. Policy towards minority nationalities[8] rigidified ethnic distinctions, and the evolutionary framework of Marxist theory reinforced Han cultural superiority. The immobility of the population enforced by the *hukou* regulations did nothing to weaken local solidarities and regional stereotypes. Gender stereotypes were challenged by the (male-centred) slogan, 'female comrades can do what male comrades can do', but gender discrimination continued in many forms, and reinforced gender differentials in income, literacy and education, and access to organizational positions of power and influence.

Social inequalities in the era of economic reform

The egalitarianism of the Mao era had never been accepted by all the leaders of the Communist Party and was explicitly rejected after Mao died. Egalitarianism was blamed for a lack of incentives perceived to be at the root of slow economic development. The work-point system in the rural areas and the wage scales and job security in urban industry were thought to reward everyone irrespective of their commitment to work (Nolan 1988). The new leadership was determined to revive the economy by providing incentives for hard work and initiative. It was anticipated that this would increase the degree of inequality in Chinese society; Deng Xiaoping proclaimed that following the economic reforms, 'some would get rich first', implying a trickle-down theory according to which the rising incomes of the few would stimulate economic growth and ultimately benefit the many (Griffin and Zhao 1993). One would therefore expect that the period after 1978 would witness increasing gaps between the better and worse off, and that social inequality would increase. In part this has been the case but, as Whyte (1986) and others have argued, the overall situation is rather more complicated.

Wealth

Material inequalities at first remained relatively restricted in the countryside. Under the household responsibility system, agricultural land was not privatized and did not become a marketable commodity.

Instead it remained the property of the collective, and was contracted to households. This method of moving back to family farming tended to ensure that families contracted for no more land than they could farm. There was only restricted expansion of the scale of farming operations and hence little scope for the growth of a class of capitalist farmers. Nor has the household responsibility system favoured concentration of ownership of other assets such as equipment and livestock. Housing, which remained in private ownership throughout the revolution and after, has been a major form of investment for rural households and is somewhat more unequally distributed. The initial impact of the responsibility system on agricultural incomes was to reduce household inequalities that had been generated by differences in the gender composition of households, although inequalities began to rise again shortly after the dissolution of the communes (Griffin and Zhao 1993).

Rural industrialization, on the other hand, has had quite different consequences for material inequalities. A class of rural entrepreneurs has emerged (Unger 1994), some of whom directly own the businesses they run, while others gain material rewards from controlling nominally collective enterprises. Income inequalities have widened following the growth of rural industry (Khan 1993), partly from wage-earning and partly from self-employment, and the most recent evidence from a large-scale survey in 1995 shows that this trend is accelerating (Khan and Riskin 1998). Rural industrialization is very unevenly spread geographically, and has accentuated the material inequalities between regions and localities that were untouched or even reinforced by the decentralized commune system.

The rise in rural incomes that followed the new economic policies after 1978 was quite widely distributed and resulted in a reduction of absolute poverty in rural areas. None the less, considerable rural poverty remains. Estimates of rural poverty[9] suggest that around 12 per cent of rural households fall below the poverty line nation-wide (World Bank 1992; Riskin 1993). Poverty, like wealth, is unevenly spread geographically. The worst forms of rural poverty are rooted in the ecological conditions of mountain and desert areas and are concentrated in the provinces of the south-west and north-west, as well as the eastern provinces subject to periodic flooding, but more moderate poverty is experienced in all provinces, a fact not fully recognized by government poverty alleviation programmes which tend to be focused geographically.[10] Rural social security systems are less developed than urban ones, and old age and sickness provision have become more dependent on market conditions and private support since the dissolution of the communes. Social support in the countryside varies considerably with the wealth of the area, and many households depend primarily on kin, both agnatic and affinal, for support in case of need (Feuchtwang 1994).

The pattern of material inequality in urban areas is also complex. Precise information about wealth ownership is sparse. State-owned enterprises still dominate the urban economy, and the system of issuing shares is not conducive to the growth of private fortunes, though this may change as forms of ownership are diversified. A more feasible route to private wealth is through the expansion of private enterprises, and the newspapers have long been full of stories of millionaires who have built up their businesses through initiative and hard work. Such success stories are obviously exceptional and most private business remains on a very small scale (D. S. G. Goodman 1996). None the less, a class of wealthy entrepreneurs is coming into existence with control over material resources far in excess of the average urban resident, although no statistical measure of the size of this class or the amount of wealth concentrated in its hands is available.

Paradoxically, inequalities in urban incomes, which were already low in the 1970s, seem at first to have been further reduced in the early phases of the post-Mao era. Walder (1990) shows that money incomes in Tianjin were less unequal in 1986 than in 1976. Walder suggests that, as bonuses became more important as a proportion of total cash incomes for workers in the state and collective sectors, higher bonuses were paid to lower-income workers. However, later research in the same city reveals that income inequalities started to rise again at the end of the 1980s and, at a faster rate, in the 1990s (Bian and Logan 1996). The same tendency was found in a national sample of households studied in 1988, although at that time the degree of inequality was still modest by international standards (Knight and Song 1993).[11] A large-scale 1995 survey shows a marked increase in income inequality compared with 1988, partly due to wider wage differentials, but even more to the effects of policies on housing privatization and housing subsidies (Khan and Riskin 1998).

As urban work-units are forced further into a competitive economic environment, their managements' ability and willingness to continue to provide for 'non-productive' members is being reduced. Urban residents who are less attractive as employees are therefore driven closer to the margins of poverty. It became more difficult, for example, for state enterprises to meet pension obligations to their retired members, and although many pensioners have in fact benefited from pension reforms of the 1980s, many also have worries about financial security in the more commodified urban society of the 1990s (D. Davis 1994). The cost of medical care has risen and is not always covered by the sick person's work-unit, so that sickness can become a source of poverty (Grogan 1995). Unemployment, which officially did not exist under the Mao regime, has grown considerably as state enterprises have reduced manning levels, laying off personnel (especially women) and providing insufficient employment opportunities for school-leavers, and no adequate unemployment insurance system has yet been devised to prevent unemployment also being a cause of poverty for urban households (Schädler and Schucher 1994). All of these aspects of material inequality, typical of western capitalist societies, are likely to be accentuated in China in the coming years.

The gap between urban and rural incomes, which had been rigidly maintained during the Mao era, was at first narrowed by the change in policy after 1978 (Nolan and Paine 1987). Reforms were implemented more speedily in the rural economy and resulted in a rapid rise of rural incomes. However, this narrowing of the urban–rural gap was not continued beyond the first few years. The measurement of urban and rural incomes in a comparable manner is very difficult, since in both cases, but for different reasons, cash incomes are not a valid guide to real income levels. Money income measures tend to understate the advantage of urban residents. None the less, according to official statistics average rural incomes were 42 per cent of urban incomes in 1978, rose to 54 per cent by 1983, but then fell back again to 41 per cent of urban incomes by 1990 (Zhao 1993). These considerable income disparities underlie the very large migrations to the towns and cities discussed in chapter 3 and remain among the most fundamental aspects of inequality in contemporary China.

Knowledge

With government education policy after 1978 reverting to its old emphasis on selection and elitism, access to education continued to be structured according to the same social divisions as previously. The gap between urban and rural schooling remained as wide as ever. Knight and Li (1993), using data from a 1988 national household sample, estimate the average difference in years of schooling between rural and urban residents to be around four years, and this gap had not reduced in the youngest cohort. Fifty-five per cent of 14–19 year olds had dropped out of schooling in rural areas, compared with 25 per cent in urban areas. Among rural areas, educational provision varies according to the wealth of the province; urban school provision is more even, but varies somewhat with size of city or town. Cultural capital is still transmitted from generation to generation, with the length of schooling of children highly correlated with that of their parents. The children of intellectuals and cadres are still considerably more likely to go on to senior middle school and university than the offspring of other sections of the population. The gender gap remains wide, with girls less likely than boys to stay on longer at school, to be allocated to the academic rather than the vocational track, and to be admitted to university, even if they have similar grades at middle school level (Broaded and Liu 1996). Only among the top 10 per cent of examination scores, and among the children of cadres and intellectuals, does gender have a negligible affect on school attainment.

The exchange value of schooling has begun to change, though not as much as might have been hoped by the proponents of government policy, for whom the modernization strategy requires rewards to go to the more skilled and educated. For much of the 1980s, there continued to be relatively little correlation between level of education and income, partly because of the narrow differentials in income, partly because most of the more highly rewarded positions in industry and administration were held by people who had begun their careers with low educational qualifications and been promoted on the basis of seniority. As time went on, however, more highly educated people began to replace their seniors, and by the 1990s those with university education and special vocational training were receiving significantly more income than those with middle school education, at least in the urban economies (Bian and Logan 1996). The professionalization of expertise,[12] in complete reversal of Cultural Revolution policies, increases the value of credentialized knowledge for its holders.

As the return to education in terms of material rewards began to rise, so material investment in education came to be seen as worthwhile, with parents paying higher fees to have their child educated in schools perceived as better staffed and equipped. It is too soon for any research to have shown whether this development will contribute to the self-recruitment of the emerging entrepreneurial and professional classes, since existing social mobility studies cannot usefully look beyond cohorts born in the 1950s or 1960s (Y. Cheng and Dai 1995), but it seems likely that this will indeed take place. As in western capitalist societies, one would expect that the inheritance of economic and cultural capital will interact to maintain privilege despite the forms of meritocracy.

Hierarchical organization

The economic reforms were complemented by government attacks on 'commandism', in particular the positional power of local cadres to control the economic activity of producers, which was seen as encouraging authoritarianism and inhibiting initiative. The reduction of this power can be seen most clearly in the case of rural labour. Before the reforms, the individual peasant's labour was managed by the production team leader; in addition, labour (and other production team resources) could be commandeered by higher levels of the commune organization to carry out brigade or commune work. The reforms first increased the autonomy of production teams in dealing with brigade or commune authorities, and then increased the autonomy of each individual household to determine the nature of its economic activity (Zweig 1997). Thus 'hierarchical relations within the communes have been replaced by contractual relations' (Ghose 1987: 63). With the dissolution of the communes, cadres lost a considerable amount of their formal positional power. As mentioned in chapter 6, however, many local cadres have been able to maintain power as gatekeepers controlling access to valued agricultural materials and as directors of collectively owned rural industries (Oi 1986).

The situation in the cities is similarly ambiguous. The government has aimed to release economic initiative from the control of civil servants and cadres, but has also wanted to maintain party domination over the society. Thus organizational hierarchies have remained intact and in some cases, such as industrial management in state enterprises, even been strengthened (Zhao and Nichols 1996). Managements have been empowered to take certain decisions which hitherto would have been subject to the planning command structure, and have been able to gain some autonomy from party committees and trade union supervision, but the hierarchy of hierarchies remains in place in many respects, with lower-level organizations having to seek approval from higher ones before plans can be implemented. As in any complex urban industrial society, many activities in China continue to be co-ordinated by large-scale bureaucratic organizations with a hierarchy of offices, providing intrinsic rewards and career opportunities to those who wish to seek them.

Hierarchical rank clearly continues to have significant exchange value in China. Position within organizational hierarchies has a strong influence on a person's income and other material conditions. With the government bringing pressure on officials with long records of service but little formal expertise to retire and make way for younger and more educated cadres, seniority in itself appears to have a declining effect on incomes, but cadres may have seen an increase in their earnings relative to other workers, even taking into account their higher education. The bureaucratic rank of a person's work-unit has also increased in significance for income determination as income inequalities have widened in the 1990s (Bian and Logan 1996). Alongside the increasing commodification of housing, the power of higher-ranking work-units together with bureaucratic procedures of housing allocation continue to ensure that personnel with greater administrative authority, especially those working in government agencies and state enterprises, have access to more spacious and higher quality housing in the major cities (Bian et al. 1997). Party membership also continues to bring material rewards.

Selective association

The state-sponsored system of positive and negative discrimination, described earlier in this chapter, has been partially dismantled since the death of Mao. As part of its shift of emphasis from class struggle to technocratic modernization, the post-Mao regime moved swiftly after 1978 to rehabilitate the vast majority of cadres, intellectuals, and former landlords and capitalists who had been branded as enemies of the people in earlier political campaigns. Derogatory labels relating to class status or political unreliability in most cases ceased to have significance for a person's life chances. However, judgements of virtue have continued to play an important role in Chinese political discourse and to have distributive consequences. Positive discrimination favours those who show themselves to be abiding by state policies. Anagnost (1997) argues that representations of 'civility' have replaced those of class opposition in the moral vocabulary of the regime, so that those who demonstrate through their behaviour their willingness to contribute to the modernization process can expect to gain more favourable treatment than those who do not. Though less formalized and explicit than the previous system of labels and 'hats', a system of estate-like discriminations is still promoted that mixes elements of virtuocracy with the new emphasis on meritocracy.

As before, beyond this state-sponsored social capital lies an infinite range of bases for the mobilization of *guanxi* in the pursuit of advantage. *Guanxi* are particularly important in the process of finding a job. As the bureaucratic process of job allocation in the urban economy has been eroded and individuals are able to exercise their own initiative in seeking employment, social connections to those who can help have become crucial. At all levels of society, *guanxi* bind people together into networks of patron–client relationships. Access to officials who control any kind of resource can yield preferential treatment, and the people with the best such access are themselves likely to be cadres or former cadres. Mayfair Yang's (1994) argument[13] that *guanxixue* constitutes a kind of 'second society' or 'popular realm' (*minjian*), beneath and in resistance to the state, tells only part of the story. If there are '*guanxi* of the weak', there are also '*guanxi* of the powerful' which help those who occupy or have occupied positions of power to retain or extend their social advantages. Operating in private, these processes of selective association are difficult to document and to prove, apart from the cases of corruption that are brought to light by legal investigation or journalistic reportage.

Long-standing bases for discrimination remain intact. Despite a consolidation and extension of legislation to protect the rights of women,[14] gender discrimination in such fields as education and employment continues to be intense and may well be intensifying. Symptomatic of this is the absence of any controls over gender bias in recruitment, and jobs are explicitly advertised as suitable for one gender to the exclusion of the other. Higher grades are often required from girls to progress to a higher stage in education. The forms of meritocracy now common in many western societies,[15] such as equal opportunity monitoring, have not been adopted in China, nor are there many formal channels for women to assert their legal rights.

The theory of market transition and its critics

As the process of economic reform and modernization has unfolded, there has been considerable discussion of an interpretation of that process and its consequences for social inequality that goes by the name of 'market transition theory'.[16] Influenced by analysis of social and economic change in eastern Europe (Szelényi 1978), the development of this theory in the context of China is associated especially with the writings of Victor Nee (Nee 1989, 1992, 1996). Although Nee's argument has altered in detail over the years, the core of it remains the same: as a society with a planned economy shifts towards a market economy, power and the rewards that go with it shift away from state officials towards entrepreneurs, workers and farmers; away, that is, from those who redistribute the wealth of the society towards those who directly produce it. The direct producers are able to establish more secure property rights over the wealth they produce and are less vulnerable to the state's power to extract it by taxation and other means. As a consequence of the reduction in their power, cadres will experience a declining return to their political capital (or, to use Kreckel's terminology, a decline in the exchange value of their hierarchical rank); they will continue to enjoy some power and privilege, as state officials do in all societies, but relatively less than under the planned economy.

In general terms, it seems plausible that wealth inequalities become more salient as market transactions replace administrative planning (Stockman 1992a), and material inequalities in China have become greater as the economic reform programme has been extended. However, critics have questioned whether market transition theory really captures the dynamics of change in power and inequality, either in the former Soviet societies of eastern Europe or in China. Walder (1996) indeed suggests that market transition as such has no determinate consequences for patterns of social inequality.[17] In particular, Walder argues that market transition theory tends to ignore the extent to which cadres and former cadres are able to retain advantages in the emerging commercialized economy, even if they lose their formal power to allocate and redistribute economic resources. The social capital which they derive from their administrative experience can be of inestimable value in helping them to find new roles in the reformed economy, as entrepreneurs, brokers, advisers and intermediaries of all sorts. Highly developed capitalist societies have a wide range of financial institutions, business services and consultants that play important mediating roles in a complex economic system, and which are only beginning to emerge in China (Oberschall 1996). The functions these organizations perform therefore tend to be performed in China by party and state cadres and the wheeler-dealers who have the appropriate contacts. Market transition theory appears to operate with a model of a perfectly competitive market economy in which these mediating functions do not need to be performed, resulting, as Walder remarks, in tautological statements that, if cadres are still gaining returns to their political capital, this proves that market transition has not proceeded very far.

The stress in this chapter on the interplay between economic, cultural, political and social capital is consistent with the arguments of the critics of market transition theory. Social inequality is multidimensional and complex. The drive to eliminate class inequalities in the early phase of the Chinese revolution was partially successful in its own terms but also had unforeseen and unintended consequences. The change of course in the last twenty years is also having complex effects on patterns of social inequality that are not easily captured by any simple theory. Elements of meritocracy and re-emerging class divisions are compounded together with political and bureaucratic hierarchies, and all are permeated with unofficial networks of patronage and brokerage and with discriminatory practices. As in other societies, perhaps the best image with which to visualize this complex web of inequalities is that of a mosaic.

Further reading

Watson (1984) brings together articles on various aspects of class and stratification in post-1949 China, and also has some discussion on pre-revolutionary inequalities. Bian (1994) is a thorough study of urban inequalities, especially those derived from variations in work-units. Griffin and Zhao (1993) provides thorough research evidence on the changing distribution of income, while McKinley (1996) analyses material on the distribution of rural wealth. Thøgersen (1990) is a useful starting-point on educational inequalities. Krieg and Schädler (1994) is a collection of papers on various aspects of social security reforms and problems. *American Journal of Sociology*, vol. 101, no. 4 (1996) contains a symposium of papers on the theory of market transition.

9

The Differentiation of Chinese Society

Introduction

The second chapter of this book introduced some theoretical frameworks, especially Marxism and theories of modernization in their various forms, that are relevant for studying social continuity and social change in any society, and which have been used to interpret social developments in Chinese society in particular. Subsequent chapters have been devoted to continuities and changes in specific aspects of Chinese society, such as urban–rural differences, family relationships, power structures and patterns of inequality. In this final chapter, the focus widens once again. The purpose of this chapter is to examine the general development of Chinese social structure through the lens of theories of societal differentiation, theories that stress the increasing complexity and institutional differentiation that societies may take on in the course of historical development.[1] The approach is explicitly comparative, setting China in relation to the experience of modern western industrial societies which, despite considerable variation, share certain basic characteristics. Such a comparative approach is not merely of theoretical interest; it has also been, and continues to be, of considerable practical importance to those in China who have attempted to influence China's social development, since in doing so they explicitly or implicitly relate their vision of China's future to their interpretation of other societies, in a process that Robertson (1992) calls 'reflexive modernization'. The differentiation of Chinese society is not just an abstract sociological idea, it is also a battleground on which competing images of China's present and future social structure have confronted each other. This chapter aims, first, to sketch out some ways in which the historical development of Chinese society differed from that of the institutionally differentiated societies of Europe; second, to examine the structure of communist society and the types of differentiation sought by different elements of the party; third, to reflect on the legacy of a relatively undifferentiated social structure inherited by the Chinese in the present day.

The comparative framework is provided by a generalized model of western societies, according to which modern society emerged out of a process of social differentiation. Step by step, relatively autonomous and bounded realms of social life became demarcated from each other, in each of which different principles were relevant and different rules of the game held sway. In medieval Europe there began a gradual process of separation of the secular from the religious spheres of society, a process that culminated in the doctrine of the separation of church and state incorporated in some constitutions. Within the sphere of the state, which claims monopoly over the legitimate use of force, there developed further differentiation, the separation of powers between the realms of executive, legislature and judiciary, each with its own rules and competencies. Alongside church and state a third differentiated realm of social life was constructed, namely the economy, with the spread of free trade and markets, and eventually also industrialization. Each of these three major fields of social life came to operate primarily according to its own principles: the church on the basis of belief in revealed truth and God-given morality, the state on the basis of man-made law, eventually legitimated by principles of national sovereignty and democracy, the economy on the basis of the autonomous economic agent's search for monetary gain in terms of wages or profits. Other realms of social life also claimed autonomy from these three major institutional sectors, for example the realm of education and science, based on the search for and teaching of scientifically testable truth-claims independently of religious belief, political control or economic interest, and the realm of art, based on the freedom of cultural expression also independent of such forces and interests. Underpinning all of this differentiation of social spheres is a categorical distinction between the public and the private spheres of social life, with the boundedness of each dependent on demarcation from the other.

Central to these processes of institutional differentiation was the role of specific professions, estates or classes, whose material and ideal interests lay in pursuing the relative autonomy of their social realm. The differentiation of the sacred realm from the secular polity both produced and was produced by specialized priesthoods. The differentiation within the state was driven in part by the rivalry between monarchy, landed aristocracy and church, in part by the emergence of a powerful legal profession. The differentiation of a market economy was promoted by the desire of bourgeois merchants and industrialists for autonomy from political interference. The differentiation of institutions of scholarship and science, especially in universities, was bound up with the demand of scholars and researchers for freedom from religious and state control. The autonomy of cultural institutions related to the claims of artists and writers for independence from censorship or the direct control of religious, political or private patrons. In many if not all cases, these claims were pursued through the formation of associations of professionals who maintained that the distinctive values enshrined in their bounded realm of life required self-regulation and autonomy.

Sociological theories have often treated this process of differentiation as one of social evolution, a universal process affecting all societies. However, for latecomers to modernization such as China, the model of an institutionally differentiated society could provide a goal or a warning, a target to be achieved or an alien construct to be avoided. By viewing China through the filter of social differentiation, the sociologist can hope not only to cast light on aspects of China's social structure and social change, but also to gain a perspective on struggles and debates that have pervaded China's revolutionary experience and that still have great resonance today.

Differentiation in late imperial China

Imperial China was a developed civilization with a complex institutional structure. Its large territory and population were at least partially integrated by the political organization of the imperial state, by the state cult of Confucius and its local religious and educational manifestations, and by complex patterns of regional and interregional trade. None the less, its type of institutional structure did not result in relatively autonomous and bounded realms of social life such as are held to characterize western modernity. As in the case of other bureaucratic empires (Eisenstadt 1963), political, economic, religious and cultural roles and activities in China did become differentiated out from ascriptive kinship groups and partially also from each other, but only to a limited extent.

First, a strong differentiation between sacred and secular realms did not become established. At the apex of the social hierarchy, the emperor united both in his person. He was 'deemed unique in his capacity to link the realms of heaven, earth, and humanity' (Ebrey 1996: 79). He held his position as divine right through the Mandate of Heaven, and was responsible for propitiating the gods by calendrical rituals as well as for the government of the people. As Weber (1968 [1916]) put it, he was both Caesar and Pope. At the base of society, ancestor worship was carried out as part of normal family life without the mediation of priests, since a man had to worship his own ancestors directly. The empire did not tolerate the development of autonomous churches or priesthoods; the state controlled and licensed, or persecuted and banned them.[2] The licensed priests, such as the Buddhists, had no national organization up to the end of the empire. There was no tension between church and state as bounded institutional realms such as existed in European society.

Second, the state itself was not a highly differentiated set of institutions. At the centre there were only a small number of ministries concerned with only a narrow range of functions. There was no separation of powers, no separate legislative or judicial instances. Law was certainly deemed to be man-made rather than god-given; emperors could make new law and override existing law, although usually within a general framework that had the sanctity of tradition (MacCormack 1996: 21–2). Law was, however, not made by legislative assemblies, of which there were none, but by the emperor and his ministers. Nor was the law interpreted and applied by a separate, let alone an independent judiciary, but by civil servants with appeal up to the emperor in severe cases such as those carrying the death penalty. There were very few legal specialists in government, and no legal profession ever developed during the imperial epoch. The emphasis on harmony was a restraint on litigation, although a considerable amount of civil litigation was in fact heard and adjudicated by magistrates, and litigants were often supported by 'litigation brokers', despite official criticism of them for disturbing harmonious relationships (Macauley 1994). The imperial bureaucracy, from the district magistrates right up to the central ministries, was staffed not by specialists expert in particular branches of law or administration but by generalists with a classical Confucian education (C. K. Yang 1959a).

Third, there was relatively little institutional differentiation of the economy as a bounded sphere of social life, despite the relatively high degree of commercialization and the use of money for various trans-actions from at least the Song dynasty onwards. The most fundamen-tal aspect of this differentiation in European societies was the institutional separation of the enterprise, with its own legal and financial status, from the household. In predominantly peasant agri-culture, in China and elsewhere, this separation did not appear. But even in the Chinese urban economy the vast majority of enterprises took the form of family businesses with no clear difference between household and enterprise accounts, location or personnel.[3] Business associations and credit arrangements were not to any great extent detached from kinship ties, and commercial property was subject to the normal rules of inheritance, with each son having a legitimate claim on the father's business (Wong Sui-lun 1985). Even non-family members of the work-force were likely to live in dormitory accom-modation within the enterprise, often as sojourners from rural native places, as if they were domestic servants. In many situations, there could be no clear distinction between production and reproduction as demarcated phases of the social metabolism (Stockman 1994).

Private business, furthermore, had very little autonomy or protected status in law. The imperial legal codes took no interest in business transactions unless they involved punishable offences. Property rights were not guaranteed and the state could intervene in any economic activity if officials deemed it appropriate (Balazs 1964). Markets were associated in the official mind with the risk of disorder and subjected to rigorous control. The pursuit of private economic interests had no value within the Confucian ethical system and tended to be inter-preted as selfishness (*si*). The space that was carved out for private economic action in the emerging bourgeois societies of seventeenth- and eighteenth-century Europe, partially insulated on the one side from political interference and on the other from interpersonal ethical restraints (Habermas 1989b), scarcely existed in the late imperial Chinese social structure.

Fourth, cultural activities too had little institutionalized autonomy from the state.[4] The notion that intellectuals, scholars and artists could occupy a demarcated social sphere from within which they could express any ideas whatsoever, even those critical of emperor, government and official doctrine, had no resonance in Chinese tradi-tion. Scholars did 'claim a continuous right of independent judgment', but only 'within a strictly defined perimeter of values shared with authority' (Wakeman 1972); the price of overstepping this perimeter was political estrangement. Cultural production was to a considerable extent integrated with the functions of court and temple, or was the pursuit of the gentlemanly elite (Clunas 1997). Scientific enquiry was carried out as part of the attempts of artisans at technical improvement, or to satisfy the curiosity of men of leisure (Needham 1969). None of this is to dispute the extensiveness, subtlety, and coherence of Chinese intellectual endeavours, whether scientific, cultural or artistic; in contrast to the situation in early modern Europe, however, China did not experience the emergence of self-conscious knowledge professionals who sought and to some extent gained a relatively autonomous realm of freedom to investigate and publish what they claimed to be scientific or aesthetic truths.

By comparison with the evolution of European societies, then, imperial Chinese society did not experience the same degree of separation of the spheres of the state, the church, the economy, the sciences and the arts. Two more abstract sets of concepts can also be brought to bear on this comparison. One of these derives from the theoretical reflections of Jürgen Habermas (1989b), who has argued that, as the scale of social organization has increased, there has been a tendency for systemic modes of societal integration, especially those of the administrative state and the market economy, to become 'uncoupled' from the lifeworld, the world of interpersonal interaction governed by shared language and shared morality in which individual identities are formed. Action in the context of the state and the market becomes instrumental and detached from traditional norms. Symptomatic of this rationalization is a separation of law and morality; economic transactions and administrative processes are governed by systematic legal principles and procedures rather than by moral injunctions. Utilizing this approach, it is possible to suggest that in Chinese society systems became only partially uncoupled from the lifeworld.[5] The administrative behaviour of officials was indeed governed by law, but the law remained heavily imbued with Confucian moral principles. Economic action remained embedded in networks of personal relations, especially those of kinship, discouraging the growth of scale of operations and the development of systems of transactions based on impersonal contractual procedures. Scholarly reflection on statecraft and on livelihood reflected this; in China, unlike in early modern Europe, such reflections (apart from those in the Legalist tradition) remained essentially within frameworks of traditional morality rather than postulating realms of norm-free technical or strategic action with ambiguous moral implications, such as those discussed in the writings of Machiavelli or Adam Smith (Schwartz 1969; Negt 1988). This emphasis on social integration rather than system integration continues to resonate throughout the twentieth century.

The second more abstract conceptual framework that has increasingly been used in recent scholarship to reflect on the character of Chinese social structure relates to the distinction between public and private spheres. The concept of the 'public sphere' and the often related concept of 'civil society' have become highly topical because of their relevance to the question of democratic reforms in China in the post-Mao era.[6] Associated with it there has developed a debate over whether China ever had a public sphere (Huang 1993). Rankin (1993), for example, argues that in the late nineteenth century there emerged a sphere of non-state management of local affairs, including education, welfare and defence, by associations of local elites who debated issues to arrive at collective policies. She suggests that this development marks the partial differentiation out of a 'public' sphere (the Chinese term is *gong*), between the bureaucratic sphere of the imperial state (*guan*) and the realm of private interests (*si*). A similar argument has been advanced by Rowe (1990, 1993), although he is rather more circumspect about associating *gong* with 'public' in the western sense, and has been vigorously challenged by Wakeman (1993), who denies that local elites ever had much autonomy from the state bureaucracy.

Much of this debate refers to Habermas's (1989a) writings on the public sphere in modern Europe. As Habermas argues, the public sphere in Europe can only be identified in relation to a private sphere; the distinction between public and private marks another dimension of institutional differentiation of modern society. It might equally well be questioned, therefore, whether imperial China ever had a private sphere. This question has been discussed by Barrington Moore (Moore 1984; Stockman 1989), who suggests that, if the private sphere is conceived as an area in which individuals and their families can claim protected immunity from the intrusion of a larger societal authority, no such sphere was ever guaranteed in imperial China. The Legalist tradition of statecraft did indeed postulate an inherent conflict between the interest of the whole ('public') and that of the individual or family ('private'), but would subordinate the latter to the former absolutely. The Confucian tradition denied any contradiction between a public and a private sphere; some kind of distinction between them could be made, but the emphasis was on harmony and on patriarchal hierarchy as a microcosm of imperial and wider cosmic hierarchy. The Daoist tradition, with its stress on individual mystical self-cultivation and search for the Way, appeared thus to glorify a private sphere but did not differentiate it from a public realm, in which Daoism was not much interested. Thus, whatever

the truth of Rankin's thesis about the emergence of non-state associational activity among local elites towards the end of the empire, the
analogy of this to the public–private distinction in anything like its
western sense of a differentiation of societal spheres seems somewhat
weak.

Differentiation between the revolutions

In the short period between the collapse of the imperial regime and the
establishment of Communist power, developments took place which
might have resulted in greater differentiation of Chinese society and
the institutionalization of relatively autonomous social spheres. However, the forces promoting such differentiation turned out to be
weaker than powerful pressures acting against it. The result was a
continuing tendency to a relatively low level of societal differentiation.

The collapse of the empire itself might have been expected to result
in a clearer separation of the realms of the sacred and the secular. The
figure of the emperor uniting both in his person and his functions had
been removed from the scene, and imperial state religion simply
disappeared. However, there was little demand for autonomous religious organization that might have confronted the new Republican
secular powers. Those demands that existed came from religions that
could be identified as foreign and non-Chinese, and therefore associated either with imperialism (as in the case of the Christian
churches) or with resistance to Han domination (as in the case of
Islam). Republican governments tended to be hostile to organized
religion, and denied religious institutions rights of autonomy, especially in such areas as education. The promotion of the New Life
movement by the Guomindang government in the 1930s, with its
mixture of modern authoritarian ideology and traditional Confucianism, revealed the incomplete separation of the sacred and secular
realms in Republican China.

The political institutions of the Republic were more differentiated
than those of the empire. The establishment of elected representative
bodies of the Republic seemed to recognize a differentiation between
the government on the one hand and political movements and organizations among the people on the other. However, although these
institutions borrowed from the external forms of western constitutional regimes, the ideological underpinning of such forms had no
resonance in Chinese political thought. The leading reformist thinker,

Liang Qichao, for example, could not admit any inherent conflict between individual interests (that might be aggregated by political parties) and collective interests (that might be represented by the government) (Nathan 1986). The opposition of competing parties had little legitimacy, parties tended to become mere factional groupings of politicians, and the parliamentary system was always weak and fragile. The re-establishment of a centralized autocratic regime seemed to be the only alternative to warlord fragmentation.

Similarly, the Republican regime implemented Qing plans for a judiciary independent of the state administration, with a hierarchy of courts from county level up to a Supreme Court. However, the main purpose of this from the government's point of view was to bring to an end the immunity from Chinese justice of foreigners who claimed extraterritoriality. There was little real commitment to the principle of an independent judiciary, not least because of the weakness of the fledgeling legal profession. Gradually this constitutional innovation was restricted in its scope, the county courts were abolished and primary jurisdiction returned to county administrators (Young 1977: 194–5). The separation of powers, which appeared to be laid down in the constitution, in reality hardly existed.

The beginnings of industrialization in the last decades of the empire and its extension during the Republican period increased the complexity of the division of labour, with new occupations and technical differentiation in the more modern work-places. The institutions of finance and trade also became more complex. However, the differentiation of economic institutions as such was not well established. Much economic activity remained embedded in family and kinship networks. Agriculture continued to be dominated by peasant family farms, and family businesses made up the bulk of urban economies. Even when the scale of operations increased, there was a preference for employing kinsfolk or people from the same native place (Lang 1968). Employees in modern factories were often temporary migrants from the countryside, with dormitory accommodation provided by the enterprise (Hershatter 1986; Honig 1986). Furthermore, the economic and the political realms were only weakly insulated from each other. Throughout the Republican period there was a close interpenetration between the financial and business elites and the political and military leaders who were attempting to stabilize their control of state power. The Nationalist government was always short of money and dependent on its relationships with bankers and industrialists for funds needed for military purposes. The relationship was reciprocal:

in an unstable environment, owners of economic resources sought the protection of any regime that was likely to preserve their property rights, even at the expense of relinquishing some aspects of those rights. The warlord regimes were especially predatory in this respect, levying an enormous range of irregular taxes. There was no clearly demarcated sphere of economic decision-making in which considerations of productivity and profitability could hold sway, an indication that economic agents were not powerful or secure enough to shield themselves from non-economic pressures.

Finally, cultural and intellectual professionals of all kinds were subject to the hegemonic ambitions of the new political movements. Those who were educated in the West were aware of concepts of academic freedom, freedom of the press, art for art's sake, and other expressions of the relative autonomy of spheres of intellectual life. Educators such as Cai Yuanpei, president of Beijing University, for example, attempted to champion the notion of academic freedom (Schwarcz 1986). But such ideas had no roots in Chinese history, and were not attractive to the leaders of political movements intent on gaining power in a context of uncertainty and danger and on using that power to transform China and its relation to the outside world. Writers, artists, scientists and teachers, whether they liked it or not, found themselves under pressure to commit themselves to one of a variety of political programmes; many willingly and enthusiastically threw in their lot with a political movement. Involvement in politics from a standpoint of relative autonomy was not an easily available option for enlightened intellectuals.

Chinese cultural tradition provided little support for the bounded demarcation of economic interest or intellectual endeavour from moral restraint or state control, or for the institutionalization of political or legal rights independent of state interest. The first half of the twentieth century saw the emergence of modern classes and professions, such as entrepreneurs, lawyers, journalists, and academics, whose material and ideal interests might have led them to pursue some degree of insulation from the demands of interpersonal morality and of state policy, and this might have resulted in the acceptance of greater societal differentiation and pluralism. But the political conditions were not conducive to such developments; internal warfare and instability and external threat combined to deprive such groups of the resources they would have needed to establish and uphold specific ground rules for their own range of activities and maintain boundaries from others.

Differentiation and the Communist revolution

The fifty years since 1949 can be interpreted as a violent and fluctuating struggle over the differentiation of Chinese society. The threefold factional division within the Communist Party outlined in chapter 6 can also be seen as a divergence of approach to questions of societal differentiation. The advocates of a centrally planned economy rejected the model of a modern differentiated society on western lines, preferring the Soviet vision of a transformation of society under the exclusive control of the party and its state apparatuses. The party-state would penetrate all facets of society and break down any boundaries that might allow resistance to its rule. The radical Maoist component of the party also rejected western models of societal differentiation, but its concern was more moral and ideological. Its vision of a socialist society was of a moral collectivity on a grand scale, in which no specific group with its own ideal or material interests would be allowed to prevent the implementation of shared egalitarian values. The revolution was a continual struggle against such groups, including those that might develop within the party itself. The third element of the party, associated early on with pragmatic modernizers such as Liu Shaoqi and then, after the Cultural Revolution, with Deng Xiaoping and his successors, saw a much greater need for a differentiation of social spheres in the quest for economic development and modernization. This element is closest in its ideology to the evolutionary theory of social change advanced by many western sociologists, although considerable differences remain.

Central planning versus differentiation

The Soviet-orientated planners could agree with the pragmatic modernizers on the need for technical expertise and a specialized division of labour in the drive for industrialization. Societal differentiation, however, operates at a different level from the technical division of labour. For the planners it was essential that the party retain strict control over the whole society, and this precluded the emergence of relatively autonomous spheres of social life. The religious sphere was tightly controlled, or even abolished and replaced with the 'civil religion' of Marxism–Leninism–Mao Zedong Thought.[7] Any insulation between the political and the economic spheres was made impossible in the planned and administered economy (Bastid 1973). All decisions had to be made within the organizational structures of the party-state; no groups of professional experts could be allowed to follow principles insulated from party oversight. For example, the academic profession which had begun to gain some autonomy in the Republican period was subjected to party control and the universities brought within the planning process (Hayhoe 1996). The fledgeling legal profession, which, had it been more powerful, might have attempted to preserve not just its own autonomy but also a legal framework underpinning the relative autonomy of other social groups, was subjected to the public security organs of the state after the Anti-Rightist campaign of 1957 (V. Li 1972). The practical result of this centralizing approach was a set of highly undifferentiated structural forms.

The most ubiquitous of these forms, at least as far as urban society was concerned, was the urban work-unit (*gongzuo danwei*).[8] A *danwei* could be a factory or factory complex, an administrative agency, a school or university, a hospital, a publishing house, or any other of a host of apparently specialized organizations. Work-units combined, within one organizational setting, functions that in a more differentiated society would be considered to be economic, political, judicial, educational, ideological, welfare, recreational, and so on (Lu Feng 1989; Li Hanlin 1991). Work-units were often referred to as societies in miniature, and the people who worked in them were not so much employees as 'members' (Hebel and Schucher 1991). It was a basic principle of social life that, once an individual was allocated to a *danwei*, he or she remained a member for life. Unlike in the case of a capitalist enterprise, employment in which is eventually terminated by retirement if not sooner, membership in a *danwei* was not affected by the capacity of the member to continue to perform specialized work functions. Whether ill, disabled, or retired, a worker continued to be a member of the *danwei*.

Although the work-unit system was an expression of the undifferentiated administrative control by the Communist party-state over urban society, the consequences were not exactly in accord with the planners' aims. Urban social structure became increasingly segmented and cellular, with each work-unit demarcated both practically and symbolically from the wider society by high walls and supervised gates.[9] Each *danwei* developed an interest in its own continuing existence and improved conditions. *Danwei* leaders did all they could to retain within the unit funds that according to regulations should have been remitted up the hierarchical chain to the unit's superior agency, and to use them for their own purposes and for the provision of services to members. In this way the *danwei* can be seen as a 'minor public' (*xiao gong*) (Lü 1997), potentially at odds with the 'greater public' of the party-state. From the point of view of the central planners, this was a pathological development that should have been met by more stringent enforcement of administrative procedures and closer supervision of lower-level units by the higher levels.

Maoism versus differentiation

The Maoist interpretation of this contradiction was rather different. Mao's vision of socialism imagined an even more radical de-differentiation of society than that of the 'Stalinists'. Habermas's concepts of lifeworld and system are useful again here. Mao envisaged a society co-ordinated neither by the economic transactions of the market nor by the bureaucratic administration of the state. Socialist China would be a large-scale community held together by shared moral values and political purposes, co-ordinated through communicative principles of the lifeworld. The slogan of 'putting politics in command' can be seen as an attack on a society steered by blindly working mechanisms, whether of the market or of the administrative state. No aspect of social organization should be governed by principles withdrawn from the possibility of political discussion and criticism. Mao's emphasis on the need to build socialism on the ethical principles of selflessness, self-reliance, persistence, honesty, and faith (Starr 1979) is evidence of a social theory which, consonant with Confucian traditions, prefers to operate at the level of the lifeworld rather than that of systems.[10]

The Maoist tendency was dominant only during the brief periods of the Great Leap Forward and the Cultural Revolution, and was in a constant state of tension with bureaucratic planners and pragmatic reformers. However, the broad elements of Mao's radical de-differentiation can be sketched out. The fusion of economic and political spheres was interpreted in an anti-economistic and anti-bureaucratic manner. Markets were identified as encouraging the pursuit of self-interest and completely rejected or restricted to narrowly localized scope (Skinner 1985). Central planning was identified with the self-interest of party bureaucrats and was to be simplified and de-professionalized. The watchword of Maoist policy was 'self-reliance'. At every level, right down to the production brigade and the individual factory, the aim was to rely on the unit's own resources and capacity for collective problem-solving. Although self-reliance was not supposed to be equivalent to autarky and self-sufficiency, the consequence of Maoist de-differentiation was an even more thoroughgoing seg-mentalization and cellularity (Donnithorne 1972).

De-professionalization affected all aspects of specialization during the Cultural Revolution. Expertise of all kinds was identified with one-sided monopolization of knowledge and conducive to social divi-sions.[11] Many experts, such as medical doctors, were therefore forced to relinquish control of specialized activities to their juniors or their students, or were dispatched to the countryside to learn from the peasants. The idea that expertise required professional autonomy, since experts were the best judges of problems falling within their area of expertise, was rejected in favour of revolutionary democratic, or 'red', control and supervision of all specialized functions (Stock-man 1992b). The inherent tension between democracy and expertise, of which Max Weber (1978 [1922]: 999) was well aware, was resolved in favour of a version of 'democracy' that insisted on breaking down all the walls with which professionals protected their expertise.

One of the most striking aspect of this rejection of expertise was in the sphere of law. There had never been in imperial China an inde-pendent legal profession catering to private clients, but there had been a sophisticated and complex legal code applied and interpreted by magistrates and higher government officials. This 'experts' law' was extended during the Republican period and a legal profession began to develop. In the early years of the People's Republic, the Communists set out to reform the legal system to reflect new socialist values. Codification of law proceeded, culminating in the enactment of the Constitution of 1954. But there was a growing tension between legal specialists trained before 1949, many in the West, and new cadres appointed after 1949, who believed that law should be simple to understand, free of technicalities, and accessible to the people without the need for legal specialists (V. Li 1978). After the Anti-Rightist campaign of 1957, and especially during the Cultural Revolution, opposition to legal specialism won the day. Legal issues were seen entirely in terms of class domination, and lawyers' belief in universal legality transcending class characteristics was branded as bourgeois ideology. Legal specialists were removed from legal work, the process of codification of law was halted, and many legal functions were transferred from courts to other agencies. The control of crime and deviance was made the responsibility of a wide range of social institu-tions, such as neighbourhood committees, residents small groups, work-units, and the police who combined conventional police activ-ities with social work and education. Very few crimes reached the courts. Disputes were handled by informal or more organized media-tion. Law in the sense of norms of behaviour in a wide range of settings was taken out of the hands of specialists and made the subject of discussion and interpretation by myriads of small study groups in which the vast majority of the population were expected to take part (Whyte 1974). The legal system, rather than being a separate set of institutions staffed by specialists, was merged into the community under the supervision of the Communist Party.

Mao's model of an undifferentiated socialist community was rad-ically egalitarian. By rejecting the relative autonomy of different societal spheres he rejected also the privileges of the elites that might dominate each sphere. By denying the relative autonomy of the administrative state he challenged the privileges of the bureaucratic elite, in this case the Communist Party itself.[12] By denying the relative autonomy of the economy, he opposed the privileges of those who might control economic processes, for example a capitalist class or its socialist substitute, the party-state economic planners. By denying the relative autonomy of the legal sphere, he thwarted the privileges of a profession of lawyers and judges. By denying the relative autonomy of the sphere of education he denied the privileges of knowledge elites such as teachers, academics and scientists. In the Maoist undifferen-tiated moral community, all such supposedly privileged groups were to lose their capacity for autonomous action and become servants of the people, under the control of the people's representatives such as the revolutionary committees.

Market socialism and partial differentiation

The third tendency in the conflict over social differentiation, namely that of the market socialists, has come to dominate the period since the death of Mao. However, it seems that representatives of this tendency were advocating a greater degree of differentiation even in earlier years. During debates in the 1960s over the extent to which the PLA should become involved in non-military affairs, the 'Learn from the PLA' campaign of 1964 was opposed, for example, by Liu Shaoqi and Deng Xiaoping. Deng allegedly said: 'factories must produce, schools must run their classes, and commercial firms have their busi-ness to do – they are different from the PLA' (Gittings 1970: 395). It was not until Deng and his followers regained the commanding heights of the party in the years after 1976 that this alternative vision could be put into practice.

The extent to which the post-1978 reforms have resulted in a separation of the economic from the political sphere has already been examined in chapter 6. The picture that emerged was complex, and by no means one of straightforward differentiation. Despite some moves towards private enterprise, and some degree of autonomy of managerial decision-making in state enterprise, economic activities are still interwoven with state administration in a variety of ways. In some respects state involvement in economic life has increased, as with the growth of entrepreneurial ventures in the armed forces. The developing theory of the socialist market economic structure, as expounded for example in the Communist Party Fourteenth Central Committee decision adopted at its third plenum in November 1993 (Lieberthal 1995: 419–40), clearly does not envisage a high degree of insulation between economic and political processes, but rather a regularization of the interaction between them.

One might have expected that the economic reforms would have resulted in work-units shedding many of their functions and becoming more specialized organizations, and this has certainly been the intention of reformers (Lu Feng 1989). However, movement in this direction has been partial. According to Dittmer and Lu (1996), the control functions that units have performed on behalf of the state have indeed been eroded in recent years, especially since mobility of personnel between them has increased. In other respects, differentiation of *danwei* functions has not proceeded far. Work-unit leaders have found it difficult to relieve themselves of responsibilities for the welfare of their members. In fact, as the work-force of state-owned enterprises ages, units have had to become even more involved in welfare activities, providing new housing, retirement homes, clinics and even funeral homes for their members, as well as monetary pensions in the absence of a state pension system. The members of work-units expect these services to be provided by their organizations, which remain the focus of many people's identities and social networks (Li Hanlin and Wang Qi 1996). Work-units remain to a considerable extent 'small societies', between which relationships are fraught with difficulties and even dangers. Nor is this tendency to segmentalism and cellularity confined to older state-owned enterprises; Francis (1996) shows how even modern high-tech firms in the private sector are reproducing institutional features of the communist *danwei*, remaining the main providers to their personnel of housing, medical care, social security and insurance.

One of the reformers' main criticisms of the Maoist era was its tendency to arbitrariness and unpredictability. The reformers claim to

be introducing greater procedural regularity into political and economic affairs so that decision-making can be more rational (Christiansen and Rai 1996: 104ff). The quest for greater regularity involves
a degree of differentiation in the political system and in particular a
greater emphasis on a relatively autonomous legal order.

The 1982 Constitution, by omitting any direct mention of the
Communist Party,[13] and by providing that 'all political parties...
must abide by the Constitution and the Law', established a formal
separation of the party and the state administration (Dicks 1989).
Now it is formally possible to distinguish between the offices and
competencies of party and state organs and committees. Even in
well-established liberal democracies the boundary between governing
party and state is not always clear-cut and contentious activities of the
government are sometimes accused of stepping over the boundary. In
China, where the Communist Party is the dominant and leading party,
and where the party's principles (of socialism, democratic centralism,
and so on) are written into the constitution, the separation is even
more difficult to uphold. The party controls access to all state offices
and there is therefore a strong overlap of personnel between the two.
None the less, it is in principle now possible to distinguish between a
person's actions taken in the capacity of state official and those taken
in the capacity of party member, and this distinction enters into the
discourse of political debate and legal dispute.

Furthermore, political reality has begun to correspond somewhat
more to the constitutional separation of powers (executive, legislative
and judicial). The legislative process has become more differentiated,
and law-making can no longer be seen in terms of commands issued
from the top (Tanner 1995). The formal law-making body, the
National People's Congress, is no longer just a rubber stamp on laws
made by the government, but to some degree carries out its functions
of amending and even rejecting proposals brought to it from the State
Council. The whole process by which a law is made has become more
complex, with a variety of actors and agencies involved at different
stages, including specialists in legislative matters (Tanner 1994). This
gives a greater variety of organizations and interests access to the
legislative process, a development that both reflects and contributes
to greater social differentiation. The judiciary is in a rather different
situation. There is evidence of a somewhat more autonomous role
taken by the Supreme People's Court in laying down regulations for
the detailed interpretation of legislation (Tanner 1995), though the
significance of this is disputed (W. C. Jones 1994). Courts at lower
levels have little autonomy. They appear to be treated by non-judicial

officials as simply another branch of the administrative state (Clarke 1995), their judgements are often considered as no more definitive than the varied interpretations of legislation made by different bureaucratic agencies (Dicks 1995), and their day-to-day activities are still subject to regular intervention by Communist Party officials (Clarke and Feinerman 1995).

None the less, although 'legal work' is still seen primarily as a branch of state administration rather than as the practice of an auto-nomous profession (Alford 1995), it is beginning to detach itself from the state in some respects. The rapid expansion of the numbers of trained lawyers and legal para-professionals is in itself indicative of the differentiation out of the legal order from the administrative state. State law firms are ceasing to be administrative branches of the Ministry of Justice and are being converted to enterprise units which sell their legal services on the market, as do members of private or co-operative law firms. Lawyers have an association, the All-China Lawyers' Association, which operates a code of conduct, provides specialized training, publishes a magazine, and represents the interests of its members. However, it is partially financed by the state, member-ship is compulsory for licensed lawyers, and it is supervised by the Ministry of Justice, so the degree of its autonomy is debatable (White et al. 1996: 107). It seems that legal practice has still not attained the elite standing that it has in western societies and that Maoist egalitar-ianism was determined to prevent. Some individual lawyers and law firms may well be becoming rather wealthy, but the occupation as such is not a high status one; it is notable by its absence from studies of occupational prestige and professional status in Chinese cities (Bian 1996; Bian and Lu 1996).[14] Judges are also described as having low salaries and low status (Lubman 1995). Legal practice is only just beginning to take on characteristics of a profession in western terms.

The growth of legal occupations is a response to the increasing juridification of economic relationships, as enterprises of various kinds make contractual arrangements with each other outside the framework of state planning. It is also a response to the increasing willingness of many elements in the population to seek legal redress in a wide range of dispute situations. These include 'private' affairs such as disputes over family property and inheritance, divorce cases with their implications for property division and child custody, as well as contested outcomes of individual economic transactions (Palmer 1995). But a growing type of litigation involves complaints about the misconduct of state officials. The state has provided the legal framework for citizens to bring such suits, the 1990 Administrative

Litigation Law (P. B. Potter 1994), and reports are emerging of its use. For example, in rural areas villagers are using the law as a last resort to pursue complaints against government departments that sell fake fertilizers and other agricultural inputs, and against township cadres who extort excessive fees or use illegal coercive means in their dealings with villagers (O'Brien and Li 1995). However, the resort to legal procedures to further disputes or complaints does not necessarily point to a belief in the autonomy and independence of the legal order, or in the role of such an order in upholding the rights of citizens. Li and O'Brien (1996) suggest that, as far as the villagers they have interviewed are concerned, complainants and litigants see themselves as something between citizens and subjects, using legal and other procedures to appeal over the heads of local officials to higher authorities whose existence and arbitrariness is accepted fatalistically.

As can be seen from the discussion in chapter 7, the differentiation out of relatively autonomous cultural spheres, such as education, science and religion, has also made only partial headway. The state still attempts to maintain firm control over activities in all these spheres, partly to lock them into the state's modernization strategy, partly to preclude any challenge to the power of the Communist Party. But this is a far cry from the radical Maoist de-differentiation campaign to subject all cultural affairs to the goals of the revolution and to interpret all aspects of culture in class terms. Spaces have opened up for a degree of autonomy in cultural matters, although this is fragile and state intervention is an ever-present possibility. The banning of the Falun Gong movement, which combines Buddhist teachings with *qigong* exercises, and which mounted a demonstration in 1999 at the government compound at Zhongnanhai, was just one prominent example of the vulnerability of religious and other cultural associations.

Social differentiation and 'civil society'

The perspective of social differentiation can also cast light on an issue that has been much discussed in recent years: whether, in the wake of the economic reforms and the accompanying legal and political changes, China has been developing a 'civil society' (Strand 1990; Huang 1993; White et al. 1996; Brook and Frolic 1997). The question of civil society in China is inextricably linked to discussions of the possibility of democratization (He 1996), and is consequently another major battleground in the complex process of reflexive modernization. Comparisons have been made between developments in eastern Europe and China, between the role of autonomous organizations such as Solidarity in Poland in the collapse of the Communist regimes at the end of the 1980s, and the movements of popular protest in China at the same time that culminated in their forcible suppression in June 1989. The assumption is often made, especially in western writings on China, that the emergence of associations and organizations that have some degree of autonomy from the state is a sign of incipient or potential democratization. Underlying this assumption is an interpretation of the growth of liberal democracy in the West, according to which the rise of the capitalist economic system created the conditions for a realm of free association that could limit the power of the state and make it responsive to a range of social interests. The debate over civil society is thus very wide-ranging, since it raises complex issues of democratic political theory as well as historical questions of the connection between capitalism and liberal democracy (Keane 1988; J. Cohen and Arato 1992). It is impossible to enter into all these discussions here. It is, however, possible to make a few concluding remarks about civil society and its relationship to the differentiation of society in the Chinese context.

Many different definitions of civil society can be found in the literature that has burgeoned in the last ten years, but most of them encompass some conception of the differentiation of societal spheres. Typical of these is the one advanced by White et al. (1996: 3). Without denying the political implications of any notion of civil society, they define a specifically sociological conception as 'an intermediate associational realm situated between the state on the one side and the basic building blocks of society on the other (individuals, families and firms), populated by social organizations which are separate, and enjoy some autonomy, from the state and are formed voluntarily by members of society to protect or extend their interests or values'. They use this conception to explore the hypothesis that the Chinese market reforms of the 1980s and 1990s have opened up a social space where such an associational realm can flourish. What they find is far more complicated, much of it not in accord with the hypothesis. There has indeed been an enormous growth in the number of apparently non-state associations, which represents a considerable change from the earlier phase of the Communist regime when no organizations outside the scope of party and state were permitted to exist. Much of this associational growth is in the fields of economic, technical, professional and cultural life. It includes professional (or quasi-professional) associations similar to the lawyers' association mentioned before, associations of various branches of production, technology, business and trade, associations in many realms of the arts, sports, and hobbies, and associations pursuing particular issues, such as consumer and environmental organizations.

However, the extent to which these associations are actually autonomous from the state is variable and mostly very limited. White et al. (1996: 30–7) endeavour to capture this variation by identifying four sectors of 'civil society': first, the caged sector of mass organizations; second, the incorporated sector of new social organizations; third, the interstitial 'limbo' world, more or less tolerated by the state, a kind of counter-culture in waiting; and fourth, the suppressed sector of illegal associations and activities, making up underground civil society. What this classification is designed to capture is not autonomy, but the attempt of the state to control Chinese society in new ways. The first sector is made up of the old transmission belt mass organizations, such as the trade unions and the women's federation. The second sector, that of new social organizations (*shehui tuanti*), comprises a vast array of organizations that are officially registered with the government at national, provincial and county levels, and therefore are sponsored (as the law on social organizations requires) by an official body that supervises their day-to-day activities. Such associations, by agreeing to this supervision, have thrown in their lot with the state; this is more like 'corporatism' than 'civil society' or, to use Frolic's (1997) paradoxical-sounding phrase, 'state-led civil society'. The third sector is made up of groups that are not registered and incorporated in this way, and are therefore open to harassment or discretionary toleration and manipulation by officials. It includes networks of women outside the official women's organizations, of artists and musicians, of homosexuals, of martial arts specialists, as well as networks based on lineages and religious temples and shrines that are revivals of pre-revolutionary forms of association. The fourth sector is subject to more active surveillance or repression by state authorities, and includes oppositional political groups, underground 'spontaneous' churches, secret societies and criminal gangs. As White et al. (1996: 208) point out, none of the organizations they studied 'operates in a political context which guarantees them the right to do so'.

On this evidence, which is also supported by other studies (Brook and Frolic 1997), civil society in the western sense, a bounded sphere of a differentiated social structure, has not developed in China. The contrast between European and Chinese history, summarized earlier in this chapter, is relevant here.[15] The institutionalization of civil society in western societies was the result not of gradual evolution nor of an intrinsically democratic culture but of intense struggles and social divisions. Only powerful sectors of society could attain relative autonomy from a powerful state. In the West, such powerful sectors have included the churches, guilds, merchants and entrepreneurs, and the knowledge professions in fields such as law, medicine, education, science and technology, publishing and journalism. All of these elite groups competed and conflicted both with each other and with the rulers of states for autonomy to pursue their material and ideal interests, and out of these fields of tension emerged the institutions of civil society and the public sphere as an aspect of the differentiation of society. Among these elites there was diversified control of the various resources that could help to maintain relative autonomy for participants in civil society; and the differentiation of political and economic powers helped to establish what Etzioni-Halevy (1993) refers to as the 'meta-principle of the relative autonomy of elites', the recognition that the ability of each elite to retain autonomy in its own sphere depended on a collective agreement that there should be separate spheres.

This division of power centres, or what Aron (1972: 58) termed a 'plurality of ruling minorities', is inherently fragile; even in the most established liberal democracies, powerful political and economic interests may attempt to subordinate other sectors of society, such as the independent professions and the media of public debate, and thus weaken the institutions of civil society. This is all the more true in China, where no such development of a plurality of elites, either in material or symbolic terms, ever became established in pre-revolutionary China, and where the revolutionary regimes actively sought to prevent it. Control over resources, although no longer entirely in the hands of the all-embracing party-state, is still concentrated in overlapping and interpenetrating party, state and corporate institutions, and there is still little legitimacy for relatively autonomous bases for social organization in any area that might infringe on the state. In these circumstances there is little scope or incentive for independent action or initiative to carve out a public space between state and economy. This is not to say that no such attempts have been or will be made. The formation of autonomous students' and workers' associations in 1989 clearly demonstrates that, at least at times of great social tension, there are those who will dare to claim rights to independent association and communication in a prototype of civil society. But such attempts are not typical, and their violent suppression in June 1989 and recurrent harassment since then demonstrate the risks involved. Many sectors of society will find the more attractive alternative is judicious manoeuvring within the parameters set by the state.[16] This is particularly true of the media of critical public discussion, which occupy a vital place in the theory of civil society; studies of potentially independent journals have stressed the compromises that their promoters had to make with the state authorities, and the mandarin-like role they were prepared to play (Li Cheng and White 1991; Gu 1998). The prospects for civil society in China are, to say the least, uncertain.

If Etzioni-Halevy (1993) is right to argue that western democracy rests on two principles, the overt electoral principle and the implicit meta-principle of the relative autonomy of elites, then there also seems to be little concern for democracy of this kind in China.[17] There may be concern that the government should act according to law, that government officials should obey the state's law, and that there should be some mechanisms for checking the monopoly power of the Communist Party. This may also include the operation of the electoral principle in some contexts. But the idea that democracy embodies a tension and balance between competing values pursued by autonomous elements in a differentiated social structure does not find much favour. A division of power centres would conflict with the long-standing assumption, reinforced by modern Chinese communism, that the unity and harmony of China depends on a single centre of power that enforces an optimal social order (Eisenstadt 1978). The theory of 'neo-authoritarianism', which postulated the need for a strong central power capable of forcing through economic modernization and which was popular among some party leaders and intellectuals in the late 1980s and beyond, is a reflection of that principle (Sautman 1992). And not just leaders and intellectuals: those with limited economic bargaining power in the new commodified economy may look to a strong state to maintain whatever can be maintained of pre-reform welfare egalitarianism, which would be swept aside in a rapid shift to democratization and privatization on the Russian model (White 1994). The decline of state power discussed in chapter 6 is, from this point of view, a problem rather than a solution.

Conclusion

The discussion in this chapter of societal differentiation and civil society highlights three issues that have recurred at various points throughout the book, and that can be restated in its final paragraphs.

First, there is always a complex interplay between social continuity and social change. The most overtly revolutionary periods do not necessarily produce the greatest social changes, though they may pave the way for them. In some respects revolutionary de-differentiation reinforced pre-revolutionary tendencies to a homogeneous social structure, while post-revolutionary developments have begun to result in increased social complexity. A similar dynamic was seen, for example, in chapter 3, where it was argued that the period of economic reform has loosened urban–rural divisions that had been rigidified by Maoist policies despite an explicit commitment to their abolition. As Marx and Engels said in the Communist Manifesto, the dynamics of capitalism created a powerful social solvent, dissolving old social structures; this appears to be true also of the 'socialism with capitalist characteristics' now prevalent in China.

Second, the study of any society requires consideration of its global context. This is not just a matter of a national society's incorporation into, or isolation from, global economic and political systems, although in the case of China the 'Open Door' policy has shifted China from isolation to incorporation and intensified both external influence on China and China's influence on the world. It is also a matter of cultural interaction between China and the rest of the world. In this chapter, one focus for attention has been the various Chinese responses to images of other societies with complex, pluralistic social structures and liberal democratic political institutions. The selective appropriation and selective rejection of foreign models, and the way this enters into discourses of 'Chinese' identity, would repay further study. Similar issues have been raised in previous chapters too: images of 'western individualism' confronted with 'Asian values' and 'Chinese' commitment to family solidarity, for example.

Third, the future is open. Sociological theories, such as theories of societal differentiation, can focus attention on particular significant aspects of social structure and social processes, but they do not (as yet) extend to the statement of determinate sequences that might warrant predictions. Many of the social changes discussed in this book have been the result, even if not the immediate result, of large-scale and violent conflicts associated with revolution and civil war. They have also been the outcome of the decisions of large numbers of people trying to shape their own lives, for example young men and women seeking to escape the patriarchal control of their families, or rural people migrating to the cities. The varying conditions in which Chinese people have lived their lives would have been difficult to predict. This will continue to be the case. Following a twentieth century full of instability and uncertainty, it would be rash to forecast what the twenty-first century might hold. Only time will tell.

Further reading

Parsons (1977) provides a brief statement of his interpretation of the level of societal differentiation in imperial China, in the context of his theory of social evolution. Sun et al. (1995) give a contemporary Chinese sociological view of the importance of this issue. Lü and Perry (1997) is a useful collection of up-to-date papers on the phenomenon of work-units (*danwei*). *The China Quarterly*, no. 141 (1995) contains accessible papers on the law and recent legal reforms. White et al. (1996) provide the most thorough study yet on the civil society issue.

Notes

Chapter 1   The Study of Chinese Society

1   According to the 'population clock' on the China Population Information and Research Centre website: http://www.cpirc.org.cn/eindex.htm.

2   See Dirlik (1993) for a critical discussion.

3   I am indebted to Reinhard Kreckel for this succinct formulation of methodological debates within sociology.

4   See chapter 3 for further discussion of urbanization.

5   See King (1978), Wong Siu-lun (1979), and Gransow (1992) for useful accounts of this history.

6   See Schwartz (1969) and H. Chang (1971) for discussions of this Chinese appropriation of western social thought.

7   Arkush (1981) provides a survey of Fei's life and work. Some of his writings are available in English: see Fei (1986, 1992).

8   Especially those in Hunan Province; see Mao (1967: I, 23–59).

9   See Gransow (1993).

10 Martin Albrow, then editor of the journal *International Sociology*, argued at the time of the Madrid World Congress of Sociology in 1990 that sociology was developing through five stages: the *'universalism'* of its founders Comte and Spencer, aiming to create a universal natural science of society; the *'national sociologies'* of the late nineteenth and early twentieth centuries, institutionalized in professional academic associations with their role in national systems of higher education and research; the *'internationalization'* of the post-World War Two period, attempting to overcome the disaster of national rivalries by means of international associations bringing together national representatives, such as the various United Nations organizations

and, in sociology, the International Sociological Association, founded in 1949; the '*indigenization*' of the 1970s and 1980s, especially in the newly independent countries of the Third World, where sociologists aimed to draw on their indigenous culture without importing inappropriate models of social science from the imperialist first world; and finally, the stage-in-the-making of '*globalization*', which would be neither national nor international, but would be created by networks of sociologists operating on a global scale (Albrow 1990). The 'sinification of sociology', which also had strong proponents in Taiwan and Hong Kong, appears to be a version of the stage of 'indigenization', though political factors considerably affected the nature of claims to represent China's indigenous culture.

11 Hong Kong is since 1997 a Special Administrative Region of the PRC, but its history gives it an enduring special relationship to Britain and other English-speaking countries.

12 Chapter 7 will return to this theme.

13 See chapter 5 for discussion of this policy.

Chapter 2   Which China? Whose China?

1 See Lam (1995) for a thorough discussion of ideological debates in the party up to 1994. The section of *The China Quarterly* entitled 'Quarterly Chronicle and Documentation' is a useful source of contemporary developments and debates.

2 *Heshang* will be discussed further in chapter 7.

3 See, for example, Sydie (1987) on feminist critiques.

4 For alternative approaches to this issue see, for example, Bhabha (1994) and, on China specifically, R. Chow (1991, 1993).

5 We shall return to the relation of the Orient to the Occident in chapter 4.

6 Discussion of this theory forms the basis of the final chapter of this book.

7 Macau returned to PRC sovereignty as a special Administrative Region on 20 December 1999.

8 A more comprehensive study of Chinese society than is possible in this book would have to give greater consideration to both Hong Kong and Taiwan, on each of which there is an extensive sociological literature. It would also take up the question of 'Greater China', on which see the symposium of papers in *The China Quarterly*, no. 136, 1993.

9 See Gladney (1991). It must be stressed that people of Hui nationality have in practice developed a wide variety of stances towards both Islam and their non-Islamic social environment; these Sino-Muslim identities are discussed by Lipman (1996).

10 The same is true of the relatively smaller group of Shanghainese, who are widely distrusted and disliked by inhabitants of other parts of China. At a more local level, Shanghainese themselves have a derogatory stereotype of 'Subei' people (roughly, those from Jiangsu Province north of the Yangzi River), a situation Honig (1992) analyses as a form of emergent ethnicity creating a cleavage within the shared 'Han' nationality.

11 Fairbank (1987), Gray (1990), Phillips (1996), Smith (1991) and J. D. Spence (1990) may all be profitably consulted.

Chapter 3 Rural and Urban in China

1 A relatively low estimate by Elvin (1973: 176) found around 6 to 7.5 per cent of the population dwelling in large cities of over 100,000 in the Song dynasty.
2 e.g. Whyte and Parish (1984: 10).
3 For further information, see various chapters in Skinner (1977).
4 Skinner's influential model, based on central place theory in economic geography, has been much discussed and criticized by later scholars, but many aspects of it remain of sociological significance.
5 For example, P. C. C. Huang (1985) has argued that in the north China plain villages varied in their degree of commercialization and in their internal social structure, so that self-sufficient 'middle peasant' families would have least need to be involved in either trading networks or labour markets, while both richer and poorer peasants would have wider linkages within and beyond their local area.
6 On which, see chapter 6.
7 The rigid division of Chinese society into urban and rural sectors is also widely discussed in Chinese sociology and anthropology under the rubric 'dualistic urban–rural social structure' and is seen as one of the major legacies of the post-revolutionary period (Li Yingsheng 1994; Zhou Daming 1995–6: 10ff).
8 There were many detailed variations in the way this system worked, at different times and in different places: see, for example, Chan, Madsen and Unger (1992); Parish and Whyte (1978); Potter and Potter (1990).
9 The urban–rural dimension of social inequality will be further taken up in chapter 8.
10 This paragraph is drawn from material in Sausmikat (1999).
11 The question of property ownership will be taken up further in chapters 6 and 8.
12 This is another example of *li tu bu li xiang*; see above, p. 59.
13 But see Chang and Feuchtwang (1996) and Feuchtwang (1998) for discussion of the most systematic comparative study of villages available in English. Chapter 8 will return to this aspect of the structure of social inequality.
14 The material in this section is derived from various chapters of Ginsburg et al. (1991).
15 See below, chapter 5.

Chapter 4 Individual and Society in China

1 Reference was often made to the *ti-yong* formula introduced in the 1880s by the reformer Zhang Zhidong, according to whom Chinese culture should be

the goal or the essence, while western culture was the means. The assumption was that China could import western technology and organizational techniques without affecting the essence of its social morality. See Levenson (1958–65, I).

2 I use this term in the sense given it by Roland Robertson (1992: 12).

3 See, for example, Nathan (1993) and Dirlik (1997).

4 There is now an immense literature on this subject, which may be approached through Berger and Hsiao (1988) and Tu (1996).

5 Traditional Chinese family relationships, and the distinct role of male and female within them, will be further discussed in the next chapter.

6 Yan'an was one of the communist base areas where the survivors of the Long March had settled in 1935. See Selden (1971).

7 See chapter 6 for further discussion of this diversity of policy lines within the Communist Party.

8 Discussed in chapter 3 above.

9 The concept of 'civil society' has become a focus for discussion in China in recent years, and is discussed further in chapter 9.

10 *Renqing* (literally meaning 'human feelings') is another term from the 'Confucian' moral vocabulary, and is used to refer to the intrinsically social character of human existence, in which social relations are laden with emotionally tinged attitudes of propriety and reciprocity, obligation and indebtedness.

11 The specific features of the Chinese administrative hierarchy are outlined in chapter 8.

12 Some leading Confucian theorists outside China, notably Tu Wei-ming, support this interpretation, while others dispute it. De Bary, especially, has long argued that Confucianism contained a liberal strand which upheld popular participation in government and moral criticism of wrong policies. See de Bary (1998) and de Bary and Tu (1998).

13 The one-child family policy is discussed in more detail in the next chapter.

14 On Nationalist ideology in Taiwan, see Chun (1995).

Chapter 5 Chinese Family: Continuity and Change

1 There is a large literature on critical approaches to the family. A useful overview drawing on Marxist and feminist perspectives is Eisenstein (1979), which contains an article by Stacey foreshadowing her book (Stacey 1983) which is discussed later in this chapter.

2 Although they are also disputed; see for example Wong Siu-lun (1988b).

3 As contrasted with 'neolocal' marriage, where the newly married couple sets up a new household, the norm in most modern western societies. 'Virilocal' stresses the husband; 'patrilocal' stresses the husband's father or grandfather.

4 The encounter between western anthropologists who built up models of lineage organization from the 1940s on the evidence of detailed fieldwork among relatively poor rural communities, especially in south-east China, and

social historians who have studied the operations of the literate elites in the Song, Ming and Qing dynasties from written evidence, has resulted in complex and technical debates which are beyond the scope of this book. See Ebrey and Watson (1986) and its bibliography.

5   This term has gained considerable currency; see for example Judd (1994: 187ff).

6   See chapter 7 for further discussion of schools.

7   Land reform is discussed further in chapter 6.

8   Perhaps precisely because marriage was considered to be an ideological issue, superstructural rather than part of the basic economic structure.

9   For discussion of class labels, see chapter 8.

10 Evans (1997) provides a detailed analysis of discourses of sexuality in China in the 1950s and 1980s, stressing the 'naturalized' and 'scientific' approach of official discourse and the subordination of women's sexuality to male drives.

11 These 'societies in miniature' are discussed further in chapter 9.

12 See further discussion in chapter 8.

13 Croll also mentions that aggregate families might further combine into revived lineage organizations, which have been reported in southern China (G. E. Johnson 1993), though she thinks it unlikely.

14 Discussed further in chapter 8.

15 There is a relation here with the debate over Asian values discussed in chapter 4.

Chapter 6   Power and Revolution: Economic and Political

1   An overview of debates concerning this concept may be found in Lukes (1986).

2   As reviewed in Poggi (1990: 3–18). Mann (1986) prefers a fourfold classification by separating *military* from *political* power. There are cogent reasons for both approaches, and for others that cannot be discussed here.

3   Skocpol (1979) provides a stimulating comparative discussion of the conditions for revolutionary change in China, France and Russia, emphasizing the interplay of both internal and external factors.

4   The distribution of land ownership is further discussed in chapter 8.

5   Wittfogel's (1957) theory, mentioned in chapter 2, linked despotic empire to the need for irrigation agriculture and large-scale hydraulic works, especially canal building, flood defences and river-valley irrigation systems. The theory has been thoroughly discredited, especially in China where most irrigation systems were on a very small scale requiring no more than local co-operative organization.

6   This confrontation has lasted for the whole period since the early 1920s, apart from short episodes of uneasy co-operation in United Fronts: first, between 1923 and 1927, in order to defeat the warlord regimes and unify the country; second, between 1937 and 1945, in order to resist the Japanese occupation.

7   See, among others, Bianco (1971), *CHOC* vol. 13, Gray (1990), and Spence (1990).

8   The distributional consequences of land reform will be discussed in chapter 8.

9   The class labels are further discussed in chapter 8.

10 Many such businesses, especially those located in Shanghai, were transferred to Hong Kong where they formed the basis for the latter's economic development.

11 The factionalism model was the subject of a symposium published in *The China Journal*, 34, July 1995.

12 This will be discussed in more detail in chapter 7.

13 As mentioned in chapter 4, Walder (1986) refers to this state of affairs as 'communist neo-traditionalism', and explores in detail its manifestations in the patterns of authority and social control in Chinese factories in the 1970s.

14 The 'Four Modernizations' slogan is explained in chapter 2 above. The 'Open Door' slogan refers to policies of reopening relationships with the outside world in trade, investment, education and training, and other matters.

15 These will be discussed in chapter 8.

16 The theory of market transition, and its attempt to explain changes in social inequality, is further discussed in chapter 8.

17 There are also various other forms of ownership in rural industry including hybrid forms (Nee 1992).

18 This clientelism is often interpreted as corruption, which is discussed further below.

19 Industrial relations in joint ventures and foreign-owned companies appear to vary according to the country of the foreign management, with workers preferring to work under American and European managements to Asian ones (A. Chan 1995).

20 This point refers back to issues discussed in chapter 4.

Chapter 7   Power and Revolution: Cultural

1   The latter are what is often referred to as 'culture' in the narrow sense (as contrasted with the wider, anthropological sense).

2   The writings of Pierre Bourdieu and Antonio Gramsci are voluminous and complex and have generated much discussion and criticism. This paragraph is intended merely to point to the main aspects relevant to the themes of this chapter. Interested readers are encouraged to consult the writings of both authors, and commentaries on them, for further information.

3   Cultural capital is a key term of Bourdieu's theory (Bourdieu 1986), and refers to those particular cultural elements in a society that can be used a resource to claim cultural and social superiority. The selection of cultural elements is ultimately arbitrary from a sociological point of view, and the value of cultural capital is upheld by state power and potentially subject to social struggle for that power.

4   A fuller discussion would reveal that the 'Confucian orthodoxy' was in fact hybridized with other religions and world-views, and developed in complex ways throughout the imperial era.

5   Yan Fu, mentioned in chapter 1, originally went to Britain to study naval technology but made his main contribution as a translator and interpreter of the major writings of western social theory.

6   The fragile development of an intelligentsia claiming intellectual autonomy and academic freedom is further discussed in chapter 9.

7   The reasons behind the launching of the Cultural Revolution in 1966 have been much discussed. See, for example, MacFarquhar (1974, 1980, 1997).

8   Such inequalities are further discussed in the next chapter.

9   However, in 1999 the sect called Falun Gong, which combines Buddhist teaching with *qigong* practices, was banned when it appeared to pose a threat to the regime.

10 See the discussion of Islam in chapter 2.

Chapter 8   Changing Patterns of Social Inequality

1   Discussed by Esherick (1981).

2   See previous chapter for a general description of pre-revolutionary schooling.

3   As Mann (1993: 559) remarks, hierarchical organization of any scale was rare in agrarian societies. Imperial China presents only a partial contrast to this generalization.

4   See the discussion in chapter 4.

5   See chapter 2 for further discussion of ethnicity.

6   The Gini coefficient is a standard measure of the distribution of a value, such as income, in a population. It varies between zero and one; the closer to zero, the more equally distributed is the value.

7   See chapter 3.

8   See chapter 2.

9   As everywhere, the measurement of poverty is fraught with conceptual and practical problems.

10 There are signs that government poverty policy is changing to a more realistic view of the extent and spread of poverty. See John Gittings, 'China faces a hard truth: some of its people are desperate', *The Guardian*, 2 September 1999, p. 15.

11 The data from household surveys of money income must be treated with caution: apart from the range of rewards in kind available to many people, income surveys tend to underestimate income from private business and self-employment as well as other unofficial or even illegal sources of income (Oberschall 1996).

12 Discussed further in chapter 9.

13 See chapter 4.

14 See chapter 5.

15　It is of course disputable that these procedures have much practical effect on gender or racial inequalities.

16　See also chapter 6, where this theory was introduced.

17　The market societies of western (and eastern) capitalism, after all, vary considerably in their patterns of inequality.

Chapter 9　The Differentiation of Chinese Society

1　Although often criticized, the theory of societal differentiation continues to be discussed and developed by sociologists from various perspectives. Sztompka (1993) provides a useful overview of the debates.

2　See chapter 7.

3　There were exceptions to this, such as the large-scale porcelain factories of Jingdezhen.

4　See chapter 7.

5　Hayhoe (1987) pursues this line of thought in specific relation to educational institutions.

6　See below for further discussion of the public sphere and civil society in contemporary China.

7　Thrower (1992) explores the analogy between American ideas of 'civil religion' and Soviet Marxist–Leninist scientific atheism.

8　For various analyses of the origins and nature of work-units, see the articles in Lü and Perry (1997).

9　Dutton (1998) contains useful illustrations of the cellularity of work-units.

10　It is therefore not surprising that Parsons associated Maoist de-differentiation (and its following in the western student movements of 1968) with historical regression (Parsons 1978).

11　See also the discussions of professional expertise in chapters 7 and 8, from the points of view of cultural power and social inequality.

12　In practice, this egalitarian theory was negated by the privileges that Mao and his associates arrogated to themselves.

13　The preamble to the constitution does, however, mention the leading role of the Communist Party.

14　The high earnings of some lawyers have made the law a prime goal for ambitious young people, but it is not clear whether this ambition includes a belief in the professional autonomy of the law.

15　The difference in historical and cultural experience, it has been suggested, underlies the difficulty Chinese intellectuals have had in finding an adequate translation for the term 'civil society' itself (Ma 1994).

16　Another possibility, increasingly prevalent especially among urban employees and laid-off workers, is street protest and 'collective bargaining by riot', but this is not usually included within the concept of 'civil society'.

17　There is a strong tendency, especially in the western literature, to take western liberal democracy as a model against which China should be measured and found wanting (Huang 1991; Gu 1993–4).

Glossary of Chinese Terms

A list of Chinese terms used in the text (with chapter in which the term is mainly used in parentheses)

baihua   vernacular language (7)

bao   reciprocity (4)

biaoxian   literally 'display, manifest': in Communist usage, refers to display of appropriate attitude or commitment (4)

bu   ministry (administrative rank) (8)

chao gupiao   'stir-fry shares', actively deal in shares (7)

chu   division (administrative rank) (8)

cun   village (6)

dang'an   personnel dossiers (9)

danwei   unit, work-unit (see *gongzuo danwei*) (5, 8, 9)

duozi duofu   many sons (to bring) much happiness (5)

fa   law (formal, public, written) (4)

fengshui   geomancy (3)

fenjia   division of the family or family estate (5)

getihu   individual household enterprise (employing fewer than 8 employees) (5)

gong   'public', associational (9)

gongzuo danwei   work-unit (5, 9)

gu   section (administrative rank) (8)

guan   official, bureaucratic (9)

guanxi   social relationships, connections (4, 8)

guanxiwang   networks of connections (4)

guanxixue   the art of social relationships, *guanxi* practices, 'connectology', networking (4, 8)

Guomindang   Nationalist Party (or National People's Party) (passim)

han minzu   Han nationality (2)
Heshang   'River Elegy', 'Deathsong of the River', (television series) (2, 7)
huaqiao   overseas Chinese (2)
huiguan   native place association (3)
hukou   household registration (3, 8)
jieji chengfen   class labels (8)
ju   bureau (administrative rank) (8)
ke   department (administrative rank) (8)
Kewang   'Yearnings' (television series) (7)
la guanxi   'pull' connections, to network (4)
li   ritual, propriety, etiquette (4)
li tu bu li xiang   to leave the land but not to leave the rural areas (3)
lian   face, moral reputation (4)
lieshen   bad gentry (6)
liwu   gift, ritual object (4)
lun   order based on differential categorization (4)
maozi   'hats' or labels (8)
mianzi   face, prestige (4)
minban   run by the people (7)
minban gongzhu   run by the people with public assistance (7)
mingong   peasant-workers (3)
minjian   popular sphere (4, 8)
minzu   nationality, people (2)
mu   land measure, one-fifteenth of a hectare, one-sixth of an acre (8)
neibu   internal classified document (1, 8)
niangjia   married woman's parental home (5)
nongmin   peasant (3)
putonghua   common language (2)
qigong   exercises that mobilize the body's vital energies (7, 9)
ren   humanity, basic Confucian virtue (4)
Renmin Ribao (*People's Daily*)   (main government newspaper) (7)
renqing   literally 'human feelings' (4)
Sanminzhuyi   Three Principles of the People (7)
shangshan-xiaxiang   up to the mountains and down to the countryside, rustication (3)
shaoshu minzu   minority nationality (2)
shehui tuanti   social associations, social organizations (9)
shexue   community schools (7)
shu   reciprocity (4)
shuyuan   local academies (7)
si   private, selfish (9)
sishu   private schools (7)
siying qiye   private enterprises (employing more than 8 employees) (6)
tongzhi   comrade, literally 'same ambition' (4)
wen   civil, civility, civilian; culture (6, 7)

wenyan   scholarly classical language (7)

wu   military (6)

wu fan   'Five Anti' campaign, 1952 (6)

wu lun   five cardinal relationships (4)

wushu   traditional martial arts (7)

xiang   township, officially designated; residents have rural *hukou* (3, 6)

xiao   filial piety (4)

xiao gong   'minor public' (9)

xiaozu   small groups (used for political study and mutual criticism) (4)

xuanchuan   propaganda (5, 7)

xue   study (4)

xuegong   Confucian temple-schools (in imperial times) (7)

yamen   magistrate's hall, residence, office (3)

yin   (hereditary) privilege of upper rank officials (8)

zhen   town, officially designated; residents have urban *hukou* (3)

Bibliography

Albrow, M. 1990: Introduction. In M. Albrow and E. King (eds), *Globalization, Knowledge and Society*, London: Sage in association with the ISA, 3–13.

Alford, W. P. 1995: Tasselled loafers for barefoot lawyers: transformation and tension in the world of Chinese legal workers. *The China Quarterly*, 141, 22–38.

Alitto, G. S. 1986: *The Last Confucian: Liang Shu-ming and the Chinese dilemma of modernity*. 2nd edn. Berkeley: University of California Press.

Anagnost, A. S. 1985: The beginning and end of an emperor: a counterrepresentation of the state. *Modern China*, 11 (2), 147–76.

Anagnost, A. S. 1987: Politics and magic in contemporary China. *Modern China*, 13 (1), 40–61.

Anagnost, A. [S.] 1997: *National Past-times: narrative, representation, and power in modern China*. Durham, NC and London: Duke University Press.

Anderson, B. 1983: *Imagined Communities: reflections on the origin and spread of nationalism*. London: Verso.

Anderson, P. 1974: *Lineages of the Absolutist State*. London: New Left Books.

Andrews, J. F. and Gao Minglu 1995: The avant-garde's challenge to official art. In Davis et al. (eds), 221–78.

Arkush, D. 1990: The moral world of Hebei village opera. In P. A. Cohen and M. Goldman (eds), *Ideas Across Cultures: essays on Chinese thought in honor of Benjamin I. Schwartz*, Cambridge, MA: Council on East Asian Studies, Harvard University Press, 87–107.

Arkush, R. D. 1981: *Fei Xiaotong and Sociology in Revolutionary China*. Harvard East Asian Monographs 98. Cambridge, MA: Council on East Asian Studies, Harvard University.

Aron, R. 1972: *Progress and Disillusion: the dialectics of modern society*. Harmondsworth: Penguin.

Bailey, P. 1988: The Chinese work-study movement in France. *The China Quarterly*, 115, 441–61.

Bailey, P. 1990: *Reform the People: changing attitudes towards popular education in early 20th-century China*. Edinburgh: Edinburgh University Press.

Baker, H. D. R. 1968: *A Chinese Lineage Village: Sheung Shui*. Stanford: Stanford University Press.

Baker, H. D. R. 1979: *Chinese Family and Kinship*. London: Macmillan.

Balazs, E. 1964: *Chinese Civilization and Bureaucracy: variations on a theme*. New Haven: Yale University Press.

Banister, J. 1987: *China's Changing Population*. Stanford: Stanford University Press.

Bastid, M. 1973: Levels of economic decision-making. In S. R. Schram (ed.), *Authority, Participation and Cultural Change in China*, Cambridge: Cambridge University Press, 159–97.

Bastid, M. 1984: Chinese educational policies in the 1980s and economic development. *The China Quarterly*, 98, 189–219.

Bastid, M. 1987: Servitude or liberation? The introduction of foreign educational practices and systems to China from 1840 to the present. In R. Hayhoe and M. Bastid (eds), *China's Education and the Industrialized World: studies in cultural transfer*, Armonk, NY: M. E. Sharpe, 3–20.

Benton, G. and Pieke, F. N. (eds) 1997: *The Chinese in Europe*. Basingstoke: Macmillan.

Berger, P. L. and Hsiao, Hsin-Huang M. (eds) 1988: *In Search of an East Asian Development Model*. New Brunswick, NJ: Transaction Publishers.

Bergère, M.-C. 1983: The Chinese bourgeoisie, 1911–37. In *CHOC* 12, 722–825.

Bernstein, T. 1977: *Up to the Mountains and Down to the Villages*. New Haven and London: Yale University Press.

Berry, C. 1991: Market forces: China's 'Fifth Generation' faces the bottom line. In C. Berry (ed.), *Perspectives on Chinese Cinema*, London: British Film Institute, 114–40.

Bhabha, H. K. 1994: *The Location of Culture*. London: Routledge.

Bian Yanjie 1989: A preliminary analysis of the basic features of the life styles of China's single-child families. *Social Sciences in China*, 8 (3), 189–209.

Bian, Yanjie 1994: *Work and Inequality in Urban China*. Albany, NY: State University of New York Press.

Bian, Yanjie 1996: Chinese occupational prestige: a comparative analysis. *International Sociology*, 11 (2), 161–86.

Bian, Yanjie and Logan, J. R. 1996: Market transition and the persistence of power: the changing stratification system in urban China. *American Sociological Review*, 61 (5), 739–58.

Bian, Yanjie and Lu, Hanlong 1996: Reform and socioeconomic inequality: status perception in Shanghai. In Jixuan Hu, Zhaohui Hong and E. Stavrou (eds), *In Search of a Chinese Road towards Modernization: economic and educational issues in China's reform process*, New York: Mellen University Press, 109–42.

Bian, Yanjie, Logan, J. R., Lu, Hanlong, Pan, Yunkang and Guan, Ying 1997: Work units and housing reform in two Chinese cities. In Lü and Perry (eds), 223–50.

Bianco, L. 1971: *Origins of the Chinese Revolution 1915–1949*. Stanford: Stanford University Press.

Bianco, L. and Hua Chang-ming 1988: Implementation and resistance: the single-child family policy. In S. Feuchtwang, A. Hussain and T. Pairault (eds), *Transforming China's Economy in the Eighties*. Vol. 1: *The Rural Sector, Welfare and Employment*, London: Zed Books, 147–68.

Bickford, T. 1994: The Chinese military and its business operations: the PLA as entrepreneur. *Asian Survey*, 34 (5), 460–74.

Billeter, J.-F. 1985: The system of 'class status'. In S. R. Schram (ed.), *The Scope of State Power in China*, London: School of Oriental and African Studies, University of London, 127–69.

Blecher, M. 1997: *China Against the Tides: restructuring through revolution, radicalism and reform*. London and Washington: Pinter.

Bourdieu, P. 1985: *Distinction: a social critique of the judgement of taste*. London: Routledge & Kegan Paul.

Bourdieu, P. 1986: Three forms of capital. In J. G. Richardson (ed.), *Handbook of Theory and Research for the Sociology of Education*, New York: Greenwood Press, 241–58.

Broaded, C. M. and Liu, Chongshun 1996: Family background, gender and educational attainment in urban China. *The China Quarterly*, 145, 53–86.

Brook, T. (ed.) 1989: *The Asiatic Mode of Production in China*. Armonk, NY: M. E. Sharpe.

Brook, T. and Frolic, B. M. (eds) 1997: *Civil Society in China*. Armonk, NY: M. E. Sharpe.

Browne, N., Pickowicz, P. G., Sobchack, V. and Yau, E. (eds) 1994: *New Chinese Cinemas: forms, identities, politics*. Cambridge: Cambridge University Press.

Brugger, B. 1990: Do we need to reassess the Chinese regime after the events of mid 1989? *Asian Studies Review*, 14 (1), 36–40.

Bruun, O. 1993: *Business and Bureaucracy in a Chinese City: an ethnography of private business households in contemporary China*. China Research Monograph 43. Berkeley: University of California Institute of East Asian Studies.

Bruun, O. 1995: Political hierarchy and private entrepreneurship in a Chinese neighborhood. In A. G. Walder (ed.), *The Waning of the Communist State: economic origins of political decline in China and Hungary*, Berkeley: University of California Press, 184–212.

Bruun, O. 1996: The *fengshui* resurgence in China: conflicting cosmologies between state and peasantry. *The China Journal*, 36, 47–65.

Burns, J. P. (ed.) 1994: *Renshi Dang'an*: China's cadre dossier system. *Chinese Law and Government*, 27 (2).

Cabestan, J.-P. 1996: Taiwan's mainland policy: normalization, yes; reunification, later. *The China Quarterly*, 148, 1260–83.

Calhoun, C. 1994: *Neither Gods nor Emperors: students and the struggle for democracy in China*. Berkeley: University of California Press.

Calhoun, C. 1997: *Nationalism*. Buckingham: Open University Press.

Cambridge History of China (CHOC). Cambridge: Cambridge University Press. Vol. 10, *Late Ch'ing, 1800–1911, Part 1*, ed. J. K. Fairbank, 1978; vol. 11, *Late Ch'ing, 1800–1911, Part 2*, ed. D. Twitchett and J. K. Fairbank, 1980; vol. 12, *Republican China 1912–1949, Part 1*, ed. J. K. Fairbank, 1983; vol. 13, *Republican China 1912–1949, Part 2*, ed. J. K. Fairbank and A. Feuerwerker, 1986; vol. 14, *The People's Republic, Part 1: The emergence of revolutionary China, 1949–1965*, ed. R. MacFarquhar and J. K. Fairbank, 1987; vol. 15, *The People's Republic, Part 2: Revolutions within the Chinese Revolution, 1966–1982*, ed. R. MacFarquhar and J. K. Fairbank, 1991.

Chamberlain, H. B. 1998: Civil society with Chinese characteristics? *The China Journal*, 39, 69–81.

Chan, A. 1985: *Children of Mao: personality development and political activism in the Red Guard generation*. Seattle: University of Washington Press.

Chan, A. 1993: Revolution or corporatism? Workers and trade unions in post-Mao China. *Australian Journal of Chinese Affairs*, 29, 31–61.

Chan, A. 1995: The emerging patterns of industrial relations in China and the rise of two new labor movements. *China Information*, 9 (4), 36–59.

Chan, A., Madsen, R. and Unger, J. 1984: *Chen Village: the recent history of a peasant community in Mao's China*. Berkeley: University of California Press.

Chan, A., Madsen, R. and Unger, J. 1992: *Chen Village under Mao and Deng*. Berkeley: University of California Press.

Chan, A., Rosen, S. and Unger, J. 1980: Students and class warfare: the social roots of the Red Guard conflict in Guangzhou (Canton). *The China Quarterly*, 83, 397–446.

Chan Hoiman 1993: Some metasociological notes on the sinicisation of sociology. *International Sociologist*, 8 (1), 113–9.

Chan, Kam Wing 1994: *Cities with Invisible Walls: reinterpreting urbanization in post-1949 China*. Hong Kong: Oxford University Press.

Chan, Kam Wing 1999: Internal migration in China: a dualistic approach. In Pieke and Mallee (eds), 49–72.

Chan Kim-Kwong and Hunter, A. 1994: Religion and society in mainland China in the 1990s. *Issues and Studies*, 30 (8), 52–68.

Chang, Chung-li 1974: *The Chinese Gentry: studies on their role in nineteenth-century Chinese society*. Seattle: University of Washington Press.

Chang, Hao 1971: *Liang Ch'i-ch'ao and Intellectual Transition in China 1890–1907*. Cambridge, MA: Harvard University Press.

Chang, Xiangqun and Feuchtwang, S. 1996: *Social Support in Rural China (1979–1991): a statistical report on ten villages*. London: China Research Unit, City University.

Chen, N. N. 1995: Urban spaces and experiences of *qigong*. In Davis et al. (eds), 347–61.

Cheng, L. and So, A. 1983: The reestablishment of sociology in the PRC: toward the sinification of Marxian sociology. *Annual Review of Sociology*, 9, 471–98.

Cheng, Yuan and Dai, Jianzhong 1995: Intergenerational mobility in modern China. *European Sociological Review*, 11 (1), 17–35.

Chesneaux, J. 1968: *The Chinese Labor Movement 1919–1927*. Stanford: Stanford University Press.

Chesneaux, J. 1973: *Peasant Revolts in China 1840–1949*. London and New York: Thames and Hudson and W. W. Norton.

CHOC: see *Cambridge History of China*.

Chow, R. 1991: *Woman and Chinese Modernity: the politics of reading between West and East*. Minnesota: University of Minnesota Press.

Chow, R. 1993: *Writing Diaspora*. Bloomington and Indianapolis: Indiana University Press.

Chow Tse-tsung 1960: *The May Fourth Movement: intellectual revolution in modern China*. Cambridge, MA: Harvard University Press.

Christiansen, F. 1989: The justification and legalization of private enterprises in China, 1983–1988. *China Information*, 4 (2), 78–91.

Christiansen, F. 1991: Social division and peasant mobility in mainland China: the implications of the hu-k'ou system. *Issues and Studies*, 26, 23–42.

Christiansen, F. and Rai, S. 1996: *Chinese Politics and Society: an introduction*. London: Prentice Hall Harvester Wheatsheaf.

Chu, Yiu-kong 1996: Triad societies and the business community in Hong Kong. *International Journal of Risk, Security and Crime Protection*, 1 (1), 33–40.

Chun, A. 1995: An oriental orientalism: the paradox of tradition and modernity in Nationalist Taiwan. *History and Anthropology*, 9 (1), 27–56.

Clarke, D. C. 1995: The execution of civil judgments in China. *The China Quarterly*, 141, 65–81.

Clarke, D. C. and Feinerman, J. V. 1995: Antagonistic contradictions: criminal law and human rights in China. *The China Quarterly*, 141, 135–54.

Cleverley, J. F. 1991: *The Schooling of China: tradition and modernity in Chinese education*. 2nd edn. Boston: George Allen & Unwin.

Clunas, Craig 1997: *Art in China*. Oxford: Oxford University Press.

Cohen, J. and Arato, A. 1992: *Civil Society and Political Theory*. Cambridge, MA: MIT Press.

Cohen, M. L. 1991: Being Chinese: the peripheralization of traditional identity. *Daedalus*, 120 (2), 113–34.

Cohen, M. L. 1992: Family management and family division in contemporary rural China. *China Quarterly*, 130, 357–77.

Cohen, M. L. 1993: Cultural and political inventions in modern China: the case of the Chinese 'peasant'. *Daedalus*, 122 (2), 151–70.

Cohen, P. A. 1978: Christian missions and their impact to 1900. In *CHOC* 10: 543–90.

Cohen, P. A. 1984: *Discovering History in China: American historical writing on the recent Chinese past*. New York: Columbia University Press.

Cohen, P. A. 1988: The post-Mao reforms in historical perspective. *Journal of Asian Studies*, 47 (3), 518–40.

Conner, A. W. 1994: Lawyers and the legal profession during the republican period. In K. Bernhardt and P. C. C. Huang, (eds), *Civil Law in Qing and Republican China*, Stanford: Stanford University Press, 215–48.

Cotterell, A. 1989: *The First Emperor of China*. Harmondsworth: Penguin.

Croll, E. 1978: *Feminism and Socialism in China*. London: Routledge & Kegan Paul.

Croll, E. 1981: *The Politics of Marriage in Contemporary China*. Cambridge: Cambridge University Press.

Croll, E. 1983: Production versus reproduction: a threat to China's development strategy. *World Development*, 11 (6), 467–81.

Croll, E. 1987: Some implications of the rural economic reforms for the Chinese peasant household. In Saith (ed.), 105–36.

Croll, E. 1994: *From Heaven to Earth: images and experiences of development in China*. London: Routledge.

Croll, E., Davin, D. and Kane, P. (eds) 1985: *China's One-Child Family Policy*. London: Macmillan.

Dai Kejing 1993: The vicissitudes of sociology in China. *International Sociology*, 8 (1), 91–9.

Davin, D. 1976: *Woman-Work: women and the party in revolutionary China*. Oxford: Clarendon Press.

Davin, D. 1988: The implications of contract agriculture for the employment and status of Chinese peasant women. In S. Feuchtwang, A. Hussain and T. Pairault (eds), *Transforming China's Economy in the Eighties*. Vol. 1: *The Rural Sector, Welfare and Employment*, London: Zed Books, 137–46.

Davin, D. 1990: The early childhood education of the only child generation in urban areas of mainland China. *Issues and Studies*, 26 (4), 83–104.

Davin, D. 1996: Gender and urban-rural migration in China. *Gender and Development*, 4 (1), 24–30.

Davin, D. 1998: *Internal Migration in Contemporary China*. Basingstoke: Macmillan.

Davis, D. 1993: Urban households: supplicants to a socialist state. In Davis and Harrell (eds), 50–76.

Davis, D. 1994: Financial security of urban retirees. In Krieg and Schädler (eds), 186–205.

Davis, D. and Harrell, S. (eds) 1993: *Chinese Families in the post-Mao Era*. Berkeley: University of California Press.

Davis, D. S., Kraus, R., Naughton, B. and Perry, E. J. (eds) 1995: *Urban Spaces in Contemporary China*. Cambridge: Cambridge University Press.

Davis, Fei-ling 1977: *Primitive Revolutionaries of China: a study of secret societies of the late nineteenth century*. Honolulu: The University Press of Hawaii.

Davis, K. 1948: *Human Society*. London: Macmillan.

Davis-Friedmann, D. 1983: *Long Lives: Chinese elderly and the Chinese revolution*. Cambridge, MA: Harvard University Press.

Dawson, R. 1981: *Confucius*. Oxford: Oxford University Press.

De Bary, Wm. T. 1998: *Asian Values and Human Rights: a Confucian communitarian perspective*. Cambridge, MA: Harvard University Press.

De Bary, Wm. T. and Tu Weiming (eds) 1998: *Confucianism and Human Rights*. New York: Columbia University Press.

Deng, Zhong and Treiman, D. J. 1997: The impact of the Cultural Revolution on trends in educational attainment in the People's Republic of China. *American Journal of Sociology*, 103 (2), 391–428.

Dennerline, J. 1986: Marriage, adoption, and charity in the development of lineages in Wu-hsi from Sung to Ch'ing. In Ebrey and Watson (eds), 170–209.

Diamond, N. 1975: Collectivization, kinship, and the status of women in rural China. *Bulletin of Concerned Asian Scholars*, 7 (1), 25–32.

Dicks, A. 1989: The Chinese legal system: reforms in the balance. *The China Quarterly*, 119, 540–76.

Dicks, A. 1995: Compartmentalized law and judicial restraint: an inductive view of some jurisdictional barriers to reform. *The China Quarterly*, 141, 82–109.

Dikötter, F. (ed.) 1997: *The Construction of Racial Identities in China and Japan*. London: Hurst.

Ding, A. S. 1996: China's defence finance: content, process and administration. *The China Quarterly*, 146, 428–42.

Ding Jinhong and Stockman, N. 1999: On floating population and the integration of the city community: a survey on the attitudes of the Shanghai residents to recent migrants. In Pieke and Mallee (eds), 119–33.

Dirlik, A. (ed.) 1993: *What is in a Rim? Critical perspectives on the Pacific region idea*. Boulder, CO and Oxford: Westview Press.

Dirlik, A. 1995: Confucius in the borderlands: global capitalism and the reinvention of Confucianism. *boundary 2*, 22 (3), 229–73.

Dirlik, A. 1997: *The Postcolonial Aura: third world criticism in the age of Global Capitalism*. Boulder, CO: Westview Press.

Dirlik, A. and Prazniak, R. 1990: Socialism is dead, so why must we talk about it? Reflections on the 1989 insurrection in China, its bloody suppression, the end of socialism and the end of history. *Asian Studies Review*, 14 (1), 3–25.

Dittmer, L. and Kim, S. (eds) 1993: *China's Quest for National Identity*. Ithaca: Cornell University Press.

Dittmer, L. and Lu Xiaobo 1996: Personal politics in the Chinese *danwei* under reform. *Asian Survey*, 36 (3), 246–67.

Donnithorne, A. 1972: China's cellular economy: some economic trends since the Cultural Revolution. *The China Quarterly*, 52, 605–19.

Duara, P. 1988: *Culture, Power, and the State: rural North China, 1900–1942*. Stanford: Stanford University Press.

Duara, P. 1995: *Rescuing History from the Nation: questioning narratives of modern China*. Chicago: University of Chicago Press.

Dutton, M. 1992: *Policing and Punishment in China: from patriarchy to 'the People'*. Cambridge: Cambridge University Press.

Dutton, M. 1997: 'The basic character of crime in contemporary China'. *The China Quarterly*, 149, 160–77.

Dutton, M. 1998: *Streetlife China*. Cambridge: Cambridge University Press.

Eberhard, W. 1966: *Conquerors and Rulers*. Leiden: Brill.

Eberhard, W. 1975: The upper-class family in traditional China. In C. E. Rosenberg (ed.), *The Family in History*, University of Pennsylvania Press, 59–94.

Ebrey, P. [B.] 1991a: The Chinese family and the spread of Confucian values. In G. Rozman (ed.), *The East Asian Region: Confucian heritage and its modern adaptation*, Princeton, NJ: Princeton University Press, 45–83.

Ebrey, P. B. 1991b: Introduction. In R. S. Watson and P. B. Ebrey (eds), *Marriage and Inequality in Chinese Society*, Berkeley: University of California Press, 1–24.

Ebrey, P. B. 1996: *The Cambridge Illustrated History of China*. Cambridge: Cambridge University Press.

Ebrey, P. B. and Watson, J. L. (eds) 1986: *Kinship Organization in Late Imperial China 1000–1940*. Berkeley: University of California Press.

Eisenstadt, S. N. 1963: *The Political Systems of Empires*. New York: The Free Press of Glencoe.

Eisenstadt, S. N. 1978: *Revolution and the Transformation of Societies: a comparative study of civilizations*. New York and London: The Free Press and Macmillan.

Eisenstein, Z. R. (ed.) 1979: *Capitalist Patriarchy and the Case for Socialist Feminism*. New York: Monthly Review Press.

Elegant, R. 1990: *Pacific Destiny: inside Asia today*. London: Hamish Hamilton.

Elias, N. and Scotson J. L. 1965: *The Established and the Outsiders*. London: Frank Cass.

Elliot, F. R. 1986: *The Family: change or continuity?* London: Macmillan.

Elman, B. A. 1991: Political, social, and cultural reproduction via civil service examinations in late imperial China. *Journal of Asian Studies*, 50 (1), 7–28.

Elvin, M. 1973: *The Pattern of the Chinese Past*. London: Eyre Methuen.

Elvin, M. 1974a: Introduction. In Elvin and Skinner (eds), 1–15.

Elvin, M. 1974b: The administration of Shanghai, 1905–1914. In Elvin and Skinner (eds), 239–62.

Elvin, M. 1985: Between the earth and heaven: conceptions of the self in China. In M. Carrithers, S. Collins and S. Lukes (eds), *The Category of the Person: anthropology, philosophy, history*, Cambridge: Cambridge University Press, 156–89.

Elvin, M. and Skinner, G. W. (eds) 1974: *The Chinese City between Two Worlds*. Stanford: Stanford University Press.

Entwisle, B., Henderson, G. E., Short, S. E., Bouma, J. and Zhai Fengying 1995: Gender and family businesses in rural China. *American Sociological Review*, 60 (1), 36–57.

Esherick, J. 1981: Numbers games: a note on land distribution in prerevolutionary China. *Modern China*, 7 (4), 387–411.

Etzioni-Halevy, E. 1993: *The Elite Connection: problems and potential of western democracy*. Cambridge: Polity Press.

Evans, H. 1997: *Women and Sexuality in China*. Cambridge: Polity Press.

Fairbank, J. K. 1987: *The Great Chinese Revolution 1800–1985*. London: Chatto & Windus.

Fairbank, J. K., Reischauer, E. O. and Craig, A. M. 1965: *East Asia: the modern transformation*. Boston: Houghton Mifflin.

Faure, D. 1986: *The Structure of Chinese Rural Society: lineage and village in the Eastern New Territories, Hong Kong*. Hong Kong: Oxford University Press.

Fei Hsiao Tung [Fei Xiaotong] et al. 1986: *Small Towns in China: functions, problems and prospects*. Beijing: New World Press.

Fei Xiaotong 1992 [1947]: *From the Soil: the foundations of Chinese society*. Berkeley: University of California Press.

Feng Tongqing 1996: Workers and trade unions under the market economy: perspectives from grassroots union cadres. Edited and translated by Zhao Minghua. *Chinese Sociology and Anthropology*, 28 (3), 3–96.

Feuchtwang, S. 1992: *The Imperial Metaphor: popular religion in China*. London and New York: Routledge.

Feuchtwang, S. 1993: The persistence of village religion in China: questions of social memory. Paper given to the University of Aberdeen Chinese Studies Group. Unpublished.

Feuchtwang, S. 1994: Social support arrangements among households in rich and poor villages: some preliminary results of an enquiry. In Krieg and Schädler (eds), 141–58.

Feuchtwang, S. 1998: What is a village? In E. B. Vermeer, F. N. Pieke and Woei Lien Chong (eds), *Cooperative and Collective in China's Rural Development: between state and private interests*, Armonk, NY: M. E. Sharpe, 46–74.

Feuchtwang, S. and Wang Ming-ming 1991: The politics of culture or a contest of histories: representations of Chinese popular religion. *Dialectical Anthropology*, 16, 251–72.

Feuerwerker, A. 1983: Economic trends, 1912–49. In *CHOC* 12: 28–127.

Fitzgerald, C. P. 1972: *The Southern Expansion of the Chinese People*. London: Barrie and Jenkins.

Francis, C.-B. 1996: Reproduction of *danwei* institutional features in the context of China's market economy: the case of Haidian District's high-tech sector. *The China Quarterly* 147, 839–59.

Franke, W. 1960: *The Reform and Abolition of the Traditional Chinese Examination System*. Cambridge, MA: East Asian Research Center, Harvard University.

Friedman, E. 1982: Maoism, Titoism, Stalinism. In M. Selden and V. Lippit (eds), *The Transition to Socialism in China*, Armonk, NY: M. E. Sharpe, 159–214.

Friedman, E. 1994. Reconstructing China's national identity: a southern alternative to Mao-era anti-imperialist nationalism. *Journal of Asian Studies*, 53 (1), 67–91.

Friedman, E., Pickowicz, P. G., Selden, M., with Johnson, K. A. 1991: *Chinese Village, Socialist State*. New Haven and London: Yale University Press.

Frolic, B. M. 1980: *Mao's People: sixteen portraits of life in revolutionary China*. Cambridge, MA: Harvard University Press.

Frolic, B. M. 1997: State-led civil society. In T. Brook and B. M. Frolic (eds), *Civil Society in China*, Armonk, NY: M. E. Sharpe, 46–67.

Fukuyama, F. 1992 : *The End of History and the Last Man*. London: Hamish Hamilton.

Furth, C. 1983: Intellectual change: from the Reform movement to the May Fourth movement, 1885–1920. In *CHOC* 12: 322–405.

Gamble, J. E. 1997: Stir-fried stocks: share dealers, trading places and new options in contemporary Shanghai. *Modern China*, 23 (2), 181–215.

Gamble, S. D. and Burgess, J. S. 1921: *Peking: a social survey*. New York: Doran.

Gao, Mobo C. F. 1994: Maoist discourse and a critique of the present assessments of the Cultural Revolution. *Bulletin of Concerned Asian Scholars*, 26 (3), 13–31.

Gardner, J. 1969: The *Wu-fan* campaign in Shanghai: a study in the consolidation of urban control. In A. D. Barnett (ed.), *Chinese Communist Politics in Action*, Seattle: University of Washington Press, 477–539.

Gates, H. 1993: Cultural support for birth limitation among urban capital-owning women. In Davis and Harrell (eds), 251–74.

Gellner, E. 1996: *Conditions of Liberty: civil society and its rivals*. Harmondsworth: Penguin.

Ghose, A. K. 1987: The People's Commune, responsibility systems and rural development in China, 1965–1984. In Saith (ed.), 35–80.

Ginsburg, N., Koppel, B. and McGee, T. G. (eds) 1991: *The Extended Metropolis: settlement transition in Asia*, Honolulu: University of Hawaii Press.

Gittings, J. 1970: Army–Party relations in the light of the Cultural Revolution. In J. W. Lewis (ed.), *Party Leadership and Revolutionary Power in China*, Cambridge: Cambridge University Press, 373–403.

Gladney, D. C. 1991: *Muslim Chinese: ethnic nationalism in the People's Republic*. Cambridge, MA: Council on East Asian Studies, Harvard University.

Gladney, D. C. 1994: Representing nationality in China: refiguring majority/minority identities. *Journal of Asian Studies*, 53 (1), 92–123.

Goffman, E. 1967: *Interaction Ritual*. New York: Doubleday.

Gold, T. [B.] 1980: Back to the city: the return of Shanghai's educated youth. *The China Quarterly*, 84, 755–70.

Gold, T. B. 1985: After comradeship: personal relations in China since the Cultural Revolution. *The China Quarterly*, 104, 657–75.

Gold, T. B. 1986: *State and Society in the Taiwan Miracle*. Armonk, NY: M. E. Sharpe.

Gold, T. B. 1996: Taiwan society at the *fin de siècle*. *The China Quarterly*, 148, 1091–114.

Goldman, M. 1981: *China's Intellectuals: advise and dissent*. Cambridge, MA: Harvard University Press.

Goldstein, S. 1990: Urbanization in China, 1982–87: effects of migration and reclassification. *Population and Development Review*, 16 (4), 673–701.

Goode, W. J. 1982: *The Family*. 2nd edn. Englewood Cliffs, NJ: Prentice-Hall.

Goodman, B. 1995: *Native Place, City, and Nation: regional networks and identities in Shanghai, 1853–1937*. Berkeley: University of California Press.

Goodman, D. S. G. 1996: The People's Republic of China: the party-state, capitalist revolution and new entrepreneurs. In R. Robison and D. S. G. Goodman (eds), *The New Rich in Asia: mobile phones, McDonald's and middle-class revolution*, London and New York: Routledge, 225–42.

Goodman, D. S. G. and Segal, G. (eds) 1994: *China Deconstructs: politics, trade and regionalism*. London and New York: Routledge.

Goody, J. 1973: Bridewealth and dowry in Africa and Eurasia. In J. Goody and S. J. Tambiah (eds), *Bridewealth and Dowry*, Cambridge: Cambridge University Press, 1–58.

Goody, J. 1976: *Production and Reproduction: a comparative study of the domestic domain*. Cambridge: Cambridge University Press.

Goody, J. 1990: *The Oriental, the Ancient and the Primitive: systems of marriage and the family in the pre-industrial societies of Eurasia*. Cambridge: Cambridge University Press.

Goody, J. 1996: *The East in the West*. Cambridge: Cambridge University Press.

Gramsci, A. 1971: *Selections from the Prison Notebooks*. Edited and translated by Q. Hoare and G. Nowell Smith. London: Lawrence & Wishart.

Gransow, B. 1992: *Geschichte der chinesischen Soziologie*. Frankfurt: Campus Verlag.

Gransow, B. 1993: Chinese sociology: sinicisation and globalisation. *International Sociology*, 8 (1), 101–12.

Gray, J. 1990: *Rebellions and Revolutions: China from the 1800s to the 1980s*. Oxford: Oxford University Press.

Greenhalgh, S. 1990: Land reform and family entrepreneurship in east Asia. In G. McNicoll and M. Cain (eds), *Rural Development and Population: institutions and policy*, New York and Oxford: Oxford University Press, 77–118.

Greenhalgh, S. 1993: The peasantization of the one-child policy in Shaanxi. In Davis and Harrell (eds), 219–50.

Greenhalgh, S. 1994a: Controlling births and bodies in village China. *American Ethnologist*, 21 (1), 3–30.

Greenhalgh, S. 1994b: De-orientalizing the Chinese family firm. *American Ethnologist*, 21 (4), 746–75.

Greenhalgh, S. and Li, Jiali 1993: *Engendering Reproductive Practice in Peasant China: the political roots of the rising sex ratios at birth*. Population Council Research Division: Working Paper No. 57. New York: The Population Council.

Grieder, J. B. 1981: *Intellectuals and the State in Modern China: a narrative history*. New York and London: The Free Press and Collier Macmillan.

Griffin, K. and Zhao Renwei (eds) 1993: *The Distribution of Income in China*. Basingstoke: Macmillan.

Grogan, C. M. 1995: Urban economic reform and access to health care coverage in the People's Republic of China. *Social Science and Medicine*, 41 (8), 1073–84.

Gu Xin 1993–94: A civil society and public sphere in post-Mao China? an overview of western publications. *China Information*, 8 (3), 38–52.

Gu, E. X. 1998: 'Non-establishment' intellectuals, public space, and the creation of non-governmental organizations in China: the Chen Ziming-Wang Juntao saga. *The China Journal*, 39, 39–58.

Guthrie, D. 1998: The declining significance of *guanxi* in China's economic transition. *The China Quarterly*, 154, 254–82.

Habermas, J. 1989a: *The Structural Transformation of the Public Sphere: an inquiry into a category of bourgeois society*. Cambridge, MA: MIT Press.

Habermas, J. 1989b: *The Theory of Communicative Action*. Vol. 2: *The Critique of Functionalist Reason*. Cambridge: Polity Press.

Hankiss, E. 1990: *East European Alternatives*. Oxford: Oxford University Press.

Harrell, S. 1995: Introduction: civilizing projects and the reaction to them. In S. Harrell (ed.), *Cultural Encounters on China's Ethnic Frontiers*, Seattle and London: University of Washington Press, 3–36.

Harris, C. C. 1983: *The Family and Industrial Society*. London: George Allen & Unwin.

Harrison, D. 1988: *The Sociology of Modernization and Development*. London: Unwin Hyman.

Hayhoe, R. 1987: Past and present in China's educational relations with the industrialized world. In R. Hayhoe and M. Bastid (eds), *China's Education and the Industrialized World: studies in cultural transfer*, Armonk, NY: M. E. Sharpe, 271–90.

Hayhoe, R. 1996: *China's Universities 1895–1995: a century of cultural conflict*. New York: Garland Publishing.

Hayhoe, R. and Zhong, Ningsha 1997: University autonomy and civil society. In Brook and Frolic (eds), 99–123.

He, Baogang 1996: *The Democratization of China*. London and New York: Routledge.

Hebel, J. and Schucher, G. 1991: From unit to enterprise? – the Chinese *tan-wei* in the process of reform. *Issues and Studies*, 27 (4), 24–43.

Hershatter, G. 1986: *The Workers of Tianjin, 1900–1949*. Stanford: Stanford University Press.

Hershatter, G., Honig, E., Lipman, J. N. and Stross R. (eds) 1996: *Remapping China: fissures in historical terrain*. Stanford: Stanford University Press.

Hinton, W. 1966: *Fanshen: a documentary of revolution in a Chinese village*. New York: Vintage Books.

Ho, D. Yau-fai 1976: On the concept of face. *American Journal of Sociology*, 81 (4), 867–84.

Ho, Ping-ti 1962: *The Ladder of Success in Imperial China: aspects of social mobility, 1368–1911*. New York: Columbia University Press.

Ho Yin-ping 1995: Foreign trade and China's growing international presence. In Lo Chi Kin, S. Pepper and Tsui Kai Yuen (eds), *China Review 1995*, Hong Kong: The Chinese University Press, 23.1–23.41.

Hong, Fan 1997: *Footbinding, Feminism and Freedom: the liberation of women's bodies in modern China*. London: Frank Cass.

Honig, E. 1986: *Sisters and Strangers: women in the Shanghai cotton mills, 1919–1949*. Stanford: Stanford University Press.

Honig, E. 1992: *Creating Chinese Ethnicity: Subei people in Shanghai 1850–1980*. New Haven: Yale University Press.

Hooper, B. 1992: Rethinking contemporary China. *Asian Studies Review*, 16 (1), 89–105.

Hooper, B. 1994: Women, consumerism and the state in post-Mao China. *Asian Studies Review*, 17 (3), 73–83.

Howe, C. 1973: *Wage Patterns and Wage Policy in Modern China 1919–1972*. Cambridge: Cambridge University Press.

Howell, J. 1993: *China Opens its Doors: the politics of economic transition*. Hemel Hempstead: Harvester Wheatsheaf.

Hsiao, Kung-chuan 1975: *A Modern China and a New World: K'ang Yu-wei, reformer and utopian, 1852–1927*. Seattle: University of Washington Press.

Hsu, F. L. K. 1969: *The Study of Literate Civilizations*. New York: Holt, Rinehart and Winston.

Hsu, F. L. K. 1971: *Under the Ancestors' Shadow: kinship, personality and social mobility in China*. Stanford: Stanford University Press.

Hsu, F. L. K. 1985: The self in cross-cultural perspective. In A. J. Marsella, G. DeVos and F. L. K. Hsu (eds), *Culture and Self: Asian and Western Perspectives*, New York and London: Tavistock, 24–55.

Hu Hsien Chin 1944: The Chinese concepts of 'face'. *American Anthropologist*, N.S., 46, 45–64.

Huang, P. C. C. 1985: *The Peasant Economy and Social Change in North China*. Stanford: Stanford University Press.

Huang, P. C. C. 1991: The paradigmatic crisis in Chinese studies: paradoxes in social and economic history. *Modern China*, 17 (3), 299–341.

Huang, P. C. C. (ed.) 1993: Symposium: 'Public sphere'/'civil society' in China? *Modern China*, 19 (2).

Huang, P. C. C. 1995: Rural class struggle in the Chinese revolution: representational and objective realities from the land reform to the Cultural Revolution. *Modern China*, 21 (1), 105–43.

Huang Shu-min 1989: *The Spiral Road: change in a Chinese village through the eyes of a Communist Party leader*. Boulder, CO: Westview Press.

Hughes, J. A., Martin, P. J. and Sharrock, W. W. 1995: *Understanding Classical Sociology: Marx, Weber, Durkheim*. London: Sage.

Hymes, R. P. 1986: Marriage, descent groups, and the localist strategy in Sung and Tuan Fu-chou. In Ebrey and Watson (eds), 95–136.

Ikels, C. 1993: Settling accounts: the intergenerational contract in an age of reform. In Davis and Harrell (eds), 307–33.

Ikels, C. 1996: *The Return of the God of Wealth: the transition to a market economy in urban China*. Stanford: Stanford University Press.

Investigation Group of the Department of Sociology of Nankai University 1989: Report on nationwide demand for sociology graduates during the period of the Seventh Five-Year Plan. *International Sociology*, 4 (4), 393–418.

Jacka, T. 1997: *Women's Work in Rural China: continuity and change in an era of reform*. Cambridge: Cambridge University Press.

Jacobs, J. B. 1979: A preliminary model of particularistic ties in Chinese political alliances: *kan-ch'ing* and *kuan-hsi* in a rural Taiwanese township. *The China Quarterly*, 78, 237–73.

Jenkins, Richard 1997: *Rethinking Ethnicity: arguments and explorations*. London: Sage.

Jenner, W. J. F. 1994: *The Tyranny of History: the roots of China's crisis*. London: Penguin.

Johnson, A. 1997: Business ethics in China. *China Review*, 7, 15–18.

Johnson, D., Nathan, A. J. and Rawski, E. S. (eds) 1985: *Popular Culture in Late Imperial China*. Berkeley: University of California Press.

Johnson, G. E. 1993: Family strategies and economic transformation in rural China: some evidence from the Pearl River delta. In Davis and Harrell (eds), 103–36.

Johnson, K. A. 1983: *Women, the Family and Peasant Revolution in China*. Chicago: University of Chicago Press.

Johnson, K. [A.] 1996: The politics of the revival of infant abandonment in China, with special reference to Hunan. *Population and Development Review*, 22 (1), 77–98.

Jones, A. F. 1992: *Like a Knife: ideology and genre in contemporary Chinese popular music*. Ithaca: Cornell University East Asia Program.

Jones, W. C. 1994: The significance of the Opinion of the Supreme People's Court for civil law in China. In P. B. Potter (ed.), *Domestic Law Reforms in Post-Mao China*, Armonk, NY: M. E. Sharpe, 97–108.

Jowitt, K. 1983: Soviet neotraditionalism: the political corruption of a Leninist regime. *Soviet Studies*, 35 (3), 275–97.

Judd, E. R. 1989: *Niangjia*: Chinese women and their natal families. *Journal of Asian Studies*, 48 (3), 525–44.

Judd, E. R. 1992: Land divided, land united. *The China Quarterly*, 130, 338–56.

Judd, E. R. 1994: *Gender and Power in Rural North China*. Stanford: Stanford University Press.

Kao, Ying-mao 1974: Urban and rural strategies in the Chinese communist revolution. In J. W. Lewis (ed.), *Peasant Rebellion and Communist Revolution in Asia*, Stanford: Stanford University Press, 253–70.

Karmel, S. M. 1994: Emerging securities markets in China: capitalism with Chinese characteristics. *The China Quarterly*, 140, 1105–20.

Keane, J. (ed.) 1988: *Civil Society and the State*. London: Verso.

Keith, R. C. 1997: Legislating women's and children's 'rights and interests' in the PRC. *The China Quarterly*, 149, 29–55.

Kelliher, D. 1992: *Peasant Power in China: the era of rural reform, 1979–1989*. New Haven: Yale University Press.

Kerr, C., Dunlop, J. T., Harbison, F. and Myers, C. A. 1973: *Industrialism and Industrial Man*. 2nd edn. Harmondsworth: Penguin.

Khan, A. R. 1993: The determinants of household income in rural China. In Griffin and Zhao (eds), 95–115.

Khan, A. R. and Riskin, C. 1998: Income and inequality in China: composition, distribution and growth of household income, 1988 to 1995. *The China Quarterly*, 154, 221–53.

King, A. Y. C. 1985: The individual and group in Confucianism: a relational perspective. In D. J. Munro (ed.), *Individualism and Holism: studies in Confucian and Taoist values*, Ann Arbor: Centre for Chinese Studies, The University of Michigan, 57–70.

King, A. Yeo-chi 1991: Kuan-hsi and network-building: a sociological interpretation. *Daedalus*, 120 (2), 63–84.

King, A. Yeo-chi (with Wang Tse-sang) 1978: The development and death of Chinese academic sociology: a chapter in the history of sociology. *Modern Asian Studies*, 12 (1), 37–58.

Kipnis, A. B. 1997: *Producing Guanxi: sentiment, self, and subculture in a North China village*. Durham and London: Duke University Press.

Kirby, W. C. 1984: *Germany and Republican China*. Stanford: Stanford University Press.

Kirkby, R. J. R. 1985: *Urbanisation in China: town and country in a developing economy 1949–2000 AD*. London and Sydney: Croom Helm.

Kirkby, R. [J. R.] and Bradbury, I. 1996: Small towns, big issues. *China Review*, 3, 14–19.

Knight, J. and Li Shi 1993: The determinants of educational attainment in China. In Griffin and Zhao (eds), 285–330.

Knight, J. and Song Lina 1993: Why urban wages differ in China. In Griffin and Zhao (eds), 216–84.

Knight, N. 1983: The form of Mao Zedong's 'sinification of Marxism'. *Australian Journal of Chinese Affairs*, 9, 17–33.

Knight, N. 1985a: Mao Zedong and the 'sinification of Marxism'. In C. Mackerras and N. Knight (eds), *Marxism in Asia*, London and Sydney: Croom Helm, 62–93.

Knight, N. 1985b: Mao Zedong and the Chinese road to socialism. In C. Mackerras and N. Knight (eds), *Marxism in Asia*, London and Sydney: Croom Helm, 94–123.

Korzec, M. and Whyte, M. K. 1981: Reading notes: the Chinese wage system. *The China Quarterly*, 86, 248–73.

Kraus, R. C. 1981: *Class Conflict in Chinese Socialism*. New York: Columbia University Press.

Kraus, R. C. 1989: *Pianos and Politics in China: middle-class ambitions and the struggle over Western music*. New York and Oxford: Oxford University Press.

Kraus, R. C. 1991: *Brushes with Power: modern politics and the Chinese art of calligraphy*. Berkeley: University of California Press.

Kreckel, R. 1976: Dimensions of social inequality: conceptual analysis and theory of society. *Sociologische Gids*, 6, 338–62.

Kreckel, R. 1992: *Politische Soziologie der sozialen Ungleichheit*. Frankfurt: Campus Verlag.

Krejcí, J. 1994: *Great Revolutions Compared: the outline of a theory*. 2nd edn. New York and London: Harvester Wheatsheaf.

Krieg, R. and Schädler, M. (eds) 1994: *Social Security in the People's Republic of China*. Hamburg: Institut für Asienkunde.

Kuhn, P. A. 1975: Local self-government under the republic: problems of control, autonomy, and mobilization. In F. Wakeman, jun. and C. Grant (eds), *Conflict and Control in Late Imperial China*, Berkeley and Los Angeles: University of California Press, 257–98.

Lam, W. Wo-Lap 1995: *China after Deng Xiaoping*. Singapore: J. Wiley.

Lang, O. 1968 [1946]: *Chinese Family and Society*. Archon Books [Yale University Press].

Lardy, N. 1983: *Agriculture in China's Modern Economic Development*. Cambridge: Cambridge University Press.

Lau, D. C. (trans.) 1970: *Mencius*. Harmondsworth: Penguin.

Lau Siu-kai 1984: *Society and Politics in Hong Kong*. Hong Kong: The Chinese University Press.

Lau, Tuen-yu and Wang, Jiangang 1992–3: The First National Survey of Mass Media Use in China's Underdeveloped Areas. *Chinese Law and Government*, 25 (4), 3–97.

Lavely, W. and Wong, R. Bin 1992: Family division and mobility in north China. *Comparative Studies in Society and History*, 34, 439–63.

Lee, L. Ou-Fan 1990: In search of modernity: some reflections on a new mode of consciousness in twentieth-century Chinese history and literature. In P. A. Cohen and M. Goldman (eds), *Ideas Across Cultures: essays on Chinese thought in honor of Benjamin I. Schwartz*, Cambridge, MA: Council on East Asian Studies, Harvard University Press, 109–35.

Lee, L. Ou-Fan and Nathan, A. J. 1985: The beginnings of mass culture: journalism and fiction in the late Ch'ing and beyond. In Johnson et al. (eds), 360–95.

Lee, R. P. L. 1982: Comparative studies of health care systems. *Social Science and Medicine*, 16, 629–42.

Lee, R. P. L. 1986: Bureaucratic corruption in Asia: the problem of incongruence between legal norms and folk norms. In L. V. Caiño (ed.), *Bureaucratic*

Corruption in Asia: causes, consequences and controls, Quezon City: JMC Press, 69–106.

Lee, Yok-shiu F. 1992: Rural transformation and decentralized urban growth in China. In G. E. Guldin (ed.), *Urbanizing China*, New York: Greenwood Press, 89–118.

Levenson, J. R. 1958–65: *Confucian China and its Modern Fate*. 3 vols. London: Routledge & Kegan Paul.

Levy, H. S. 1966: *Chinese Footbinding: the history of a curious erotic custom*. New York: Walton Rawls.

Levy, M. J., jun. 1963 [1949]: *The Family Revolution in Modern China*. New York: Octagon Books [Cambridge, MA: Harvard University Press].

Levy, M. J., jun. 1966: *Modernization and the Structure of Societies*. Princeton: Princeton University Press.

Li Cheng and White, L. T., III 1991: China's technocratic movement and the *World Economic Herald*. *Modern China*, 17 (3), 342–88.

Li Hanlin 1991: *Die Grundstruktur der chinesischen Gesellschaft: vom traditionellen Klansystem zur modernen Danwei-Organisation*. Opladen: Westdeutscher Verlag.

Li Hanlin and Wang Qi 1996: *Research on the Chinese Work Unit Society*. Frankfurt am Main: P. Lang Europäischer Verlag der Wissenschaften.

Li, Lianjiang and O'Brien, K. J. 1996: Villagers and popular resistance in contemporary China. *Modern China*, 22 (1), 28–61.

Li Lulu 1989: Theoretical theses on 'social modernisation'. *International Sociology*, 4 (4), 365–77.

Li, V. H. 1972: The evolution and development of the Chinese legal system. In J. M. H. Lindbeck (ed.), *China: management of a revolutionary society*, London: George Allen & Unwin, 221–55.

Li, V. H. 1978: *Law without Lawyers: a comparative view of law in China and the United States*. Boulder, CO: Westview Press.

Li Yingsheng 1994: An investigation of the dualistic nature of urban–rural society in China. *Social Sciences in China*, 15 (3), 161–70.

Lieberthal, K. G. 1980: *Revolution and Tradition in Tientsin, 1949–1952*. Stanford: Stanford University Press.

Lieberthal, K. [G.] 1995: *Governing China: from revolution through reform*. New York: W. W. Norton.

Lin, Nan 1995: Local market socialism: local corporatism in action in rural China. *Theory and Society*, 24, 301–54.

Linder, S. B. 1986: *The Pacific Century: economic and political consequences of Asian–Pacific dynamism*. Stanford: Stanford University Press.

Link, P. 1992: *Evening Chats in Beijing: probing China's predicament*. New York: W. W. Norton.

Lipman, J. N. 1996: Hyphenated Chinese: Sino-Muslim identity in modern China. In Hershatter et al. (eds), 97–112.

Lippit, V. D. 1974: *Land Reform and Economic Development in China*. White Plains, NY: International Arts and Sciences Press.

Lippit, V. D. 1978: The development of underdevelopment in China. *Modern China*, 4 (1), 251–328.

Litwak, E. 1965: Extended kin relations in an industrial democratic society. In E. Shanas and G. Streib (eds), *Social Structure and the Family*, Englewood Cliffs, NJ: Prentice-Hall, 290–323.

Liu, A. P. L. 1991: Communications and development in post-Mao mainland China. *Issues and Studies*, 27 (2), 73–99.

Liu, A. P. L. 1996: *Mass Politics in the People's Republic: state and society in contemporary China*. Boulder, CO and Oxford: Westview Press.

Liu Hui-chen Wang 1959: An analysis of Chinese clan rules: Confucian theories in action. In D. S. Nivison and A. F. Wright (eds), *Confucianism in Action*, Stanford: Stanford University Press, 63–96.

Loewe, M. 1966: *Imperial China: the historical background to the modern age.* London: Allen & Unwin.

Lu Feng 1989: *Dan Wei* – a special form of social organization. *Social Sciences in China*, 10 (3), 100–22.

Lu Feng 1993. The origins and formation of the unit (danwei) system. *Chinese Sociology and Anthropology*, 25 (3), 7–92.

Lu Hanlong 1997: To be privately comfortable in an egalitarian society: a study of Chinese urban consumer culture. Translated by K. K. Liu. Shanghai Academy of Social Sciences: unpublished.

Lü, Xiaobo 1997: Minor public economy: the revolutionary origins of the *danwei*. In Lü and Perry (eds), 21–41.

Lü, Xiaobo and Perry, E. J. (eds) 1997: *Danwei: the changing Chinese workplace in historical and comparative perspective.* Armonk, NY: M. E. Sharpe.

Lubman, S. 1995: Introduction: the future of Chinese law. *The China Quarterly*, 141, 1–21.

Lukes, S. (ed.) 1986: *Power.* Oxford: Basil Blackwell.

Lutz, J. G. 1971: *China and the Christian Colleges, 1850–1950.* Ithaca: Cornell University Press.

Ma, Shu-yun 1994: The Chinese discourse on civil society. *The China Quarterly*, 137, 180–93.

Ma, Shu-yun 1996: The role of power struggle and economic changes in the 'Heshang phenomenon' in China. *Modern Asian Studies*, 30 (1), 29–50.

Macauley, M. A. 1994: Civil and uncivil disputes in southeast coastal China. In K. Bernhardt and P. C. C. Huang, (eds), *Civil Law in Qing and Republican China*, Stanford: Stanford University Press, 85–121.

MacCormack, G. 1990: *Traditional Chinese Penal Law.* Edinburgh: Edinburgh University Press.

MacCormack, G. 1996: *The Spirit of Traditional Chinese Law.* Athens, GA and London: University of Georgia Press.

MacFarlane, A. 1978: *The Origins of English Individualism.* Oxford: Basil Blackwell.

MacFarquhar, R. 1974, 1980, 1997: *The Origins of the Cultural Revolution.* 3 vols. New York: Columbia University Press.

Madsen, R. [P.] 1984: *Morality and Power in a Chinese Village.* Berkeley: University of California Press.

Madsen, R. [P.] 1991: The countryside under communism. In CHOC 15: 619–81.

Madsen, R. P. 1995: Forward. In Chihua Wen, *The Red Mirror: children of China's Cultural Revolution*, Boulder, CO: Westview Press, xi–xix.

Mallee, H. 1995: China's household registration system under reform. *Development and Change*, 26, 1–29.

Mallee, H. 1995/96: In defence of migration: recent Chinese studies of rural population mobility. *China Information*, 10 (3/4), 108–40.

Mann, M. 1986: *The Sources of Social Power.* Vol. 1: *A history of power from the beginning to A.D. 1760.* Cambridge: Cambridge University Press.

Mann, M. 1993: *The Sources of Social Power.* Vol. 2: *The rise of classes and nation-states, 1760–1914.* Cambridge: Cambridge University Press.

Mann, S. 1987: *Local Merchants and the Chinese Bureaucracy, 1750–1950.* Stanford: Stanford University Press.

Mao Zedong 1966: *Quotations from Chairman Mao Tse-tung.* Peking: Foreign Languages Press.

Mao Zedong 1967: *Selected Works of Mao Tse-tung*. 4 vols. Peking: Foreign Languages Press.

Mao Zedong 1990: *Report from Xunwu*. Stanford: Stanford University Press.

Marx, K. 1970 [1859]: *A Contribution to the Critique of Political Economy*. Moscow: Progress Publishers.

McDougall, B. S. 1984: Writers and performers, their works, and their audiences in the first three decades. In B. S. McDougall (ed.), *Popular Chinese Literature and Performing Arts in the People's Republic of China, 1949–1979*, Berkeley: University of California Press, 269–304.

McDougall, B. S. and Louie, K. 1997: *The Literature of China in the Twentieth Century*. London: Hurst.

McKinley, T. 1996: *The Distribution of Wealth in Rural China*. Armonk, NY: M. E. Sharpe.

Mead, G. H. 1934: *Mind, Self and Society*. Chicago: University of Chicago Press.

Meijer, M. J. 1971: *Marriage Law and Policy in the Chinese People's Republic*. Hong Kong: Hong Kong University Press.

Meisner, M. 1967: *Li Ta-chao and the Origins of Chinese Marxism*. Cambridge, MA: Harvard University Press.

Meisner, M. 1977: *Mao's China: a history of the People's Republic*. New York: The Free Press.

Metzger, T. A. 1973: *The Internal Organization of Ch'ing Bureaucracy: legal, normative, and communication aspects*. Cambridge, MA: Harvard University Press.

Metzger, T. A. 1977: *Escape from Predicament: Neo-Confucianism and China's evolving political culture*. New York: Columbia University Press.

Milwertz, C. 1997: *Accepting Population Control*. Richmond, Surrey: Curzon Press.

Mok, Ka-ho 1997: Private challenges to public dominance: the resurgence of private education in the Pearl River delta. *Comparative Education*, 33 (1), 43–60.

Moore, B., jun. 1984: *Privacy: studies in social and cultural history*. Armonk, NY: M. E. Sharpe.

Morgan, D. H. J. 1985: *The Family, Politics and Social Theory*. London: Routledge & Kegan Paul.

Mote, F. W. 1970: The city in traditional Chinese civilization. In J. T. C. Liu and Wei-ming Tu (eds), *Traditional China*, Englewood Cliffs, NJ: Prentice-Hall, 42–9.

Mote, F. W. 1977: The transformation of Nanking, 1350–1400. In Skinner (ed.), 101–53.

Mumford, L. 1961: *The City in History*. New York: Harcourt, Brace.

Murphey, R. 1974: The treaty ports and China's modernization. In Elvin and Skinner (eds), 17–71.

Murphy, R. 2000: Return migrant entrepreneurship and local state corporatism in rural China: the experience of two counties in south Jiangxi. *Journal of Contemporary China*, 9.

Naquin, S. 1985: The transmission of White Lotus sectarianism in late imperial China. In Johnson et al. (eds), 255–91.

Nathan, A. J. 1973: A factionalism model for CCP politics. *The China Quarterly*, 54, 34–66.

Nathan, A. J. 1986: *Chinese Democracy*. Berkeley: University of California Press.

Nathan, A. J. 1993: Is Chinese culture distinctive? – a review article. *Journal of Asian Studies*, 52 (4), 923–36.

Nee, V. 1989: A theory of market transition: from redistribution to markets in state socialism. *American Sociological Review*, 54, 663–81.

Nee, V. 1992: Organizational dynamics of market transition: hybrid forms, property rights, and mixed economy in China. *Administrative Science Quarterly*, 37, 1–27.

Nee, V. 1996: The emergence of a market society: changing mechanisms of stratification in China. *American Journal of Sociology*, 101 (4), 908–49.

Needham, J. 1969: *The Grand Titration*. London: George Allen & Unwin.

Negt, O. 1988: *Modernisierung im Zeichen des Drachen: China und der europäische Mythos der Moderne*. Frankfurt am Main: Fischer Wissenschaft.

Nevitt, C. E. 1996: Private business associations in China: evidence of civil society or local state power? *The China Journal*, 36, 25–43.

Nolan, P. 1988: *The Political Economy of Collective Farms*. Cambridge: Polity Press.

Nolan, P. 1995: *China's Rise, Russia's Fall: politics, economics and planning in the transition from Stalinism*. Basingstoke: Macmillan.

Nolan, P. and Paine, S. 1987: Towards an appraisal of the impact of rural reform in China, 1978–1985. In Saith (ed.), 81–104.

O'Brien, K. J. and Li, Lianjiang 1995: The politics of lodging complaints in rural China. *The China Quarterly*, 143, 756–83.

Oberschall, A. 1996: The great transition: China, Hungary and sociology exit socialism into market. *American Journal of Sociology*, 101 (4), 1028–41.

Oi, J. C 1986: Commercializing China's rural cadres. *Problems of Communism*, 35 (5), 1–15.

Oi, J. C. 1989: *State and Peasant in Contemporary China: the political economy of village government*. Berkeley: University of California Press.

Oi, J. C. 1992: Fiscal reform and the economic foundations of local state corporatism in China. *World Politics*, 45, 99–126.

Oksenberg, M. 1968: The institutionalisation of the Chinese communist revolution: the ladder of success on the eve of the Cultural Revolution. *The China Quarterly*, 36, 61–92.

Palmer, M. 1995: The re-emergence of family law in post-Mao China: marriage, divorce and reproduction. *The China Quarterly*, 141, 110–34.

Pan, L. 1991: *Sons of the Yellow Emperor: the story of the overseas Chinese*. London: Mandarin.

Parish, W. L. 1984: Destratification in China. In Watson (ed.), 84–120.

Parish, W. L. and Whyte, M. K. 1978: *Village and family in contemporary China*. Chicago: University of Chicago Press.

Parsons, T. 1977: *The Evolution of Societies*. Edited by J. Toby. Englewood Cliffs, NJ: Prentice-Hall.

Parsons, T. 1978: The university 'bundle': a study in the balance between differentiation and integration. In T. Parsons, *Action Theory and the Human Condition*, New York: The Free Press, 133–53.

Peng Xizhe 1989: Major determinants of China's fertility transition. *The China Quarterly*, 117, 1–37.

Pepper, S. 1995: Regaining the initiative for education reform and development. In Lo Chi Kin, S. Pepper and Tsui Kai Yuen (eds), *China Review 1995*, Hong Kong: The Chinese University Press, 18.1–18.49.

Pepper, S. 1996: *Radicalism and Education Reform in 20th-Century China: the search for an ideal development model*. Cambridge: Cambridge University Press.

Perkins, D. H. 1969: *Agricultural Development in China 1368–1968*. Edinburgh: Edinburgh University Press.

Perry, E. J. 1993: *Shanghai on Strike: the politics of Chinese labor*. Stanford: Stanford University Press.

Perry, E. J. 1994: Shanghai's strike wave of 1957. *The China Quarterly*, 137, 1–27.

Perry, E. J. 1995: Labor's battle for political space: the role of worker associations in contemporary China. In Davis et al. (eds), 302–25.

Perry, E. J. 1997: From native place to workplace: labor origins and outcomes of China's *danwei* system. In Lü and Perry (eds), 42–59.

Perry, E. J. and Li Xun 1997: *Proletarian Power: Shanghai in the Cultural Revolution*. Boulder, CO and Oxford: Westview Press.

Phillips, R. T. 1996: *China since 1911*. Basingstoke: Macmillan.

Pieke, F. N. 1995: Bureaucracy, friends, and money: the growth of capital socialism in China. *Comparative Studies in Society and History*, 37 (3), 494–518.

Pieke, F. N. and Mallee, H. (eds) 1999: *Internal and International Migration: Chinese perspectives*. Richmond, Surrey: Curzon Press.

Poggi, G. 1990: *The State: its nature, development and prospects*. Cambridge: Polity Press.

Potter, J. M. 1968: *Capitalism and the Chinese Peasant*. Berkeley: University of California Press.

Potter, P. B. 1994: The Administrative Litigation Law of the PRC: judicial review and bureaucratic reform. In P. B. Potter (ed.), *Domestic Law Reforms in Post-Mao China*, Armonk, NY: M. E. Sharpe, 270–304.

Potter, S. H. 1983: The position of peasants in modern China's social order. *Modern China*, 9 (4), 465–99.

Potter, S. H. and Potter, J. M. 1990: *China's Peasants: the anthropology of a revolution*. Cambridge: Cambridge University Press.

Preston, P. W. 1998: *Pacific Asia in the Global System*. Oxford: Blackwell.

Pye, L. W. 1968: *The Spirit of Chinese Politics: a psychocultural study of the authority crisis in political development*. Cambridge, MA: MIT Press.

Pye, L. W. with M. W. Pye 1985: *Asian Power and Politics: the cultural dimensions of authority*. Cambridge, MA: Harvard University Press.

Rai, S. 1991: *Resistance and Reaction: university politics in post-Mao China*. Hemel Hempstead: Harvester Wheatsheaf.

Rankin, M. B. 1993: Some observations on a Chinese public sphere. *Modern China*, 19 (3), 158–82.

Rapp, J. 1989: Editor's introduction, China's debate on the Asiatic mode of production. *Chinese Law and Government*, 22 (2), 3–26.

Rawski, E. S. 1979: *Education and Popular Literacy in Ch'ing China*. Ann Arbor: University of Michigan Press.

Riley, N. E. 1997: Gender equality in China: two steps forward, one step back. In W. A. Joseph (ed.), *China Briefing 1995–96: the contradictions of change*, Armonk, NY: M. E. Sharpe, 79–108.

Riskin, C. 1987: *China's Political Economy: the quest for development since 1949*. Oxford: Oxford University Press.

Riskin, C. 1993: Income distribution and poverty in rural China. In Griffin and Zhao (eds), 135–70.

Robertson, R. 1992: *Globalization: social theory and global culture*. London: Sage.

Rose, A. M. (ed.) 1962: *Human Behavior and Social Processes: an interactionist approach*. London: Routledge & Kegan Paul.

Rosen, S. (ed.) 1993: Youth Studies (II). *Chinese Education and Society*, 26 (2).

Rosen, S. and Chu, D. 1987: *Survey Research in the People's Republic of China*. Washington, DC: United States Information Agency.

Rowe, W. T. 1984: *Hankow: commerce and society in a Chinese city, 1796–1889*. Stanford: Stanford University Press.

Rowe, W. T. 1989: *Hankow: conflict and community in a Chinese city, 1796–1895*. Stanford: Stanford University Press.

Rowe, W. T. 1990: The public sphere in modern China. *Modern China*, 16 (3), 309–29.

Rowe, W. T. 1993: The problem of 'civil society' in late imperial China. *Modern China*, 19 (3), 139–57.

Rozman, G. (ed.) 1981: *The Modernization of China*. New York: The Free Press.

Ruan, Danching 1993: Interpersonal networks and workplace controls in urban China. *Australian Journal of Chinese Affairs*, 29, 89–105.

Said, E. W. 1978: *Orientalism*. London: Routledge & Kegan Paul.

Saith, A. (ed.) 1987: *The Re-emergence of the Chinese Peasantry*. London: Croom Helm.

Sausmikat, N. 1999: Female autobiographies from the Cultural Revolution: returned *xiaxiang* educated women in the 1990s. In Pieke and Mallee (eds), 297–314.

Sautman, B. 1992: Sirens of the strongman: neo-authoritarianism in recent Chinese political theory. *The China Quarterly*, 129, 72–102.

Schädler, M. and Schucher, G. 1994: Unemployment and provisions for unemployment in a phase of transition: the Chinese case. In Krieg and Schädler (eds), 217–53.

Schluchter, W. 1981: *The Rise of Western Rationalism: Max Weber's developmental history*. Berkeley: University of California Press.

Schurmann, F. 1968: *Ideology and Organization in Communist China*. 2nd edn. Berkeley: University of California Press.

Schwarcz, V. 1986: *The Chinese Enlightenment: intellectuals and the legacy of the May Fourth Movement of 1919*. Berkeley: University of California Press.

Schwartz, B. 1969: *In Search of Wealth and Power: Yen Fu and the West*. New York: Harper & Row.

Selden, M. 1971: *The Yenan Way in Revolutionary China*. Cambridge, MA: Harvard University Press.

Selden, M. (ed.) 1979: *The People's Republic of China: a documentary history of revolutionary change*. New York: Monthly Review Press.

Selden, M. 1988: *The Political Economy of Chinese Socialism*. Armonk, NY: M. E. Sharpe.

Selden, M. 1993: Family strategies and structures in rural north China. In Davis and Harrell (eds), 139–64.

Shambaugh, D. 1996: China's military in transition: politics, professionalism, procurement and power projection. *The China Quarterly*, 146, 265–98.

Sheridan, J. E. 1983: The warlord era: politics and militarism under the Peking government, 1916–28. In *CHOC* 12: 284–321.

Shirk, S. L. 1982: *Competitive Comrades: career incentives and student strategies in China*. Berkeley: University of California Press.

Shirk, S. L. 1984: The decline of virtuocracy in China. In Watson (ed.), 56–83.

Shue, V. 1988: *The Reach of the State: sketches of the Chinese body politic*. Stanford: Stanford University Press.

Sidel, R. 1972: *Women and Child Care in China*. London: Sheldon Press.

Siu, H. F. 1990: Recycling tradition: culture, history and political economy in the chrysanthemum festivals of south China. *Comparative Studies in Society and History*, 32 (4), 765–94.

Siu, H. F. 1993: Reconstituting dowry and brideprice in south China. In Davis and Harrell (eds), 165–88.

Skinner, G. W. 1964: Marketing and social structure in rural China (part I). *Journal of Asian Studies*, 24 (1), 3–43.

Skinner, G. W. 1971: Chinese peasants and the closed community: an open and shut case. *Comparative Studies in Society and History*, 13 (3), 270–81.

Skinner, G. W. (ed.) 1977: *The City in Late Imperial China*. Stanford: Stanford University Press.

Skinner, G. W. 1985: Rural marketing in China: repression and revival. *The China Quarterly*, 101, 391–413.

Sklair, L. 1994: The culture-ideology of consumerism in urban China: some findings from a survey in Shanghai. *Research in Consumer Behavior*, 7, 259–92.

Sklair, L. 1995: *Sociology of the Global System*. 2nd edn. Hemel Hempstead: Prentice Hall/Harvester Wheatsheaf.

Skocpol, T. 1979: *States and Social Revolutions: a comparative analysis of France, Russia and China*. Cambridge: Cambridge University Press.

Smith, C. J. 1991: *China: people and places in the land of one billion*. Boulder, CO: Westview Press.

Solinger, D. J. 1984a: *Chinese Business under Socialism*. Berkeley: University of California Press.

Solinger, D. J. (ed.) 1984b: *Three Visions of Chinese Socialism*. Boulder, CO: Westview Press.

Solinger, D. J. 1992: Urban entrepreneurs and the state: the merger of state and society. In A. G. Rosenbaum (ed.), *State and Society in China: the consequences of reform*, Boulder, CO: Westview Press, 121–42.

Solinger, D. J. 1993: China's transients and the state: a case of civil society. *Politics and Society*, 21, 91–122.

Solinger, D. J. 1995: The floating population in the cities: chances for assimilation? In Davis et al. (eds), 113–39.

Solomon, R. H. 1971: *Mao's Revolution and the Chinese Political Culture*. Berkeley: University of California Press.

Spence, J. D. 1990: *The Search for Modern China*. London: Hutchinson.

Spence, J. D. 1997: *God's Chinese Son: the Taiping Heavenly Kingdom of Hong Xiuquan*. London: Flamingo.

Stacey, J. 1983: *Patriarchy and Socialist Revolution in China*. Berkeley: University of California Press.

Stafford, C. 1995: *The Roads of Chinese Childhood: learning and identification in Angang*. Cambridge: Cambridge University Press.

Starr, J. B. 1979: *Continuing the Revolution: the political thought of Mao*. Princeton: Princeton University Press.

Stockman, N. 1989: Intruding on Barrington Moore's *Privacy*: a review essay. *Theory, Culture and Society*, 6, 125–44.

Stockman, N. 1992a: Market, plan and structured social inequality in China. In R. Dilley (ed.), *Contesting Markets: analyses of ideology, discourse and practice*, Edinburgh: Edinburgh University Press, 260–76.

Stockman, N. 1992b: Red, blue or expert: cultural revolution in China and Britain. Paper read at colloquium 'From 1956 to 1968: Some Origins of Today's World', University of Aberdeen. Unpublished.

Stockman, N. 1994: Gender inequality and social structure in urban China. *Sociology*, 28 (3), 759–77.

Stockman, N., Bonney, N. and Sheng Xuewen 1995: *Women's Work in East and West: the dual burden of employment and family life*. London: UCL Press.

Strand, D. 1990: Protest in Beijing: civil society and public sphere in China. *Problems of Communism*, 39 (3), 1–19.

Stross, R. 1990: The return of advertising in China: a survey of the ideological reversal. *The China Quarterly*, 123, 485–502.

Su Xiaokang and Wang Luxiang 1991: *Deathsong of the River: a reader's guide to the Chinese TV series Heshang*. Introduced, translated and annotated by R. W. Bodman and Pin P. Wang. Ithaca: Cornell University East Asia Program.

Sun Liping, Wang Hansheng, Wang Sibin, Lin Bin and Yang Shanhua 1995: Changes in China's social structure following the reforms. *Social Sciences in China*, 16 (2), 70–80.

Sydie, R. A. 1987: *Natural Women, Cultured Men: a feminist perspective on sociological theory*. Milton Keynes: Open University Press.

Szelényi, I. 1978: Social inequalities in state socialist redistributive economies. *International Journal of Comparative Sociology*, 19, 63–87.

Sztompka, P. 1993: *The Sociology of Social Change*. Oxford: Blackwell.

Tanner, M. S. 1994: Organizations and politics in China's post-Mao lawmaking system. In P. B. Potter (ed.), *Domestic Law Reforms in Post-Mao China*, Armonk, NY: M. E. Sharpe, 56–96.

Tanner, M. S. 1995: How a bill becomes a law in China: stages and processes in lawmaking. *The China Quarterly*, 141, 39–64.

Taylor, J. R. 1988: Rural employment trends and the legacy of surplus labour, 1978–86. *The China Quarterly*, 116, 736–65.

Thøgersen, S. 1989: Through the sheep's intestines – selection and elitism in Chinese schools. *Australian Journal of Chinese Affairs*, 21, 29–56.

Thøgersen, S. 1990: *Secondary Education in China after Mao: reform and social conflict*. Aarhus: Aarhus University Press.

Thøgersen, S. 1998: Reconstructing society: Liang Shuming and the Rural Reconstruction Movement in Shandong. In K.-E. Brødsgaard and D. Strand (eds), *Reconstructing Twentieth-Century China: state, society and nation*, Oxford: Oxford University Press, 139–62.

Thrower, J. 1992: *Marxism–Leninism as the Civil Religion of Soviet Society*. Lewiston, Queenston and Lampeter: The Edwin Mellen Press.

Tien, Hung-mao and Chu, Yun-han 1996: Building democracy in Taiwan. *The China Quarterly*, 148, 1141–70.

Tilly, C. 1985: War making and state making as organized crime. In P. Evans, D. Rueschemeyer and T. Skocpol (eds), *Bringing the State Back In*, Cambridge: Cambridge University Press, 169–91.

Tu Wei-ming 1985: Selfhood and otherness in Confucian thought. In A. J. Marsella, G. DeVos and F. L. K. Hsu (eds), *Culture and Self: Asian and Western Perspectives*, New York and London: Tavistock, 231–51.

Tu Wei-ming (ed.) 1991: The Living Tree: the changing meaning of being Chinese today. *Daedalus*, 120 (2).

Tu Wei-ming (ed.) 1996: *Confucian Traditions in East Asian Modernity*. Cambridge, MA: Harvard University Press.

Unger, J. 1989: Review article: state and peasant in post-revolution China. *Journal of Peasant Studies*, 17 (1), 114–136.

Unger, J. 1993: Urban families in the eighties: an analysis of Chinese surveys. In Davis and Harrell (eds), 25–49.

Unger, J. 1994: 'Rich man, poor man': the making of new classes in the countryside. In D. S. G. Goodman and B. Hooper (eds), *China's Quiet Revolution: new interactions between state and society*, New York: St Martin's Press, 43–63.

Unger, J. and Chan, A. 1995: China, corporatism, and the East Asia model. *Australian Journal of Chinese Affairs*, 33, 29–53.

Unschuld, P. U. 1979: *Medical Ethics in Imperial China: a study in historical anthropology*. Berkeley: University of California Press.

Van der Pijl, K. 1989: The international level. In T. Bottomore and R. J. Brym (eds), *The Capitalist Class: an international study*, Hemel Hempstead: Harvester Wheatsheaf, 237–66.

Vogel, E. F. 1965: From friendship to comradeship: the change in personal relations in Communist China. *The China Quarterly*, 21, 46–60.

Vogel, E. F. 1980 [1969]: *Canton under Communism: programs and politics in a provincial capital, 1949–1968*. Third printing with a new Preface. Cambridge, MA: Harvard University Press.

Vogel, E. F. 1989: *One Step Ahead in China: Guangdong under reform*. Cambridge, MA: Harvard University Press.

Vogel, E. F. 1991: *The Four Little Dragons: the spread of industrialization in East Asia*. Cambridge, MA: Harvard University Press.

Wakeman, F., jun. 1972: The price of autonomy: intellectuals in Ming and Ch'ing politics. *Daedalus*, 101 (2), 35–70.

Wakeman, F., jun. 1993: The civil society and public sphere debate: western reflections on Chinese political culture. *Modern China*, 19 (3), 108–38.

Wakeman, F., jun. 1995: Licensing leisure: the Nationalists' attempt to regulate Shanghai, 1927–49. *Journal of Asian Studies*, 54 (1), 19–42.

Wakeman, F., jun. 1997: A revisionist view of the Nanjing decade: Confucian fascism. *The China Quarterly*, 150, 395–422.

Wakeman, F., jun. and Yeh, Wen-hsin (eds) 1992: *Shanghai Sojourners*. China Research Monograph 40. Berkeley: University of California Institute of East Asian Studies.

Walder, A. G. 1986: *Communist Neo-traditionalism: work and authority in Chinese industry*. Berkeley: University of California Press.

Walder, A. [G.] 1989: Factory and manager in an era of reform. *China Quarterly*, 118, 242–64.

Walder, A. G. 1990: Economic reform and income distribution in Tianjin, 1976–1986. In D. Davis and E. F. Vogel (eds), *Chinese Society on the Eve of Tiananmen*, Cambridge, MA: Harvard University Press, Council on East Asian Studies, 135–56.

Walder, A. G. 1994: The decline of communist power: elements of a theory of institutional change. *Theory and Society*, 23 (2), 297–323.

Walder, A. G. 1995: Local governments as industrial firms: an organizational analysis of China's transitional economy. *American Journal of Sociology*, 101 (2), 263–301.

Walder, A. G. 1996: Markets and inequality in transitional economies: towards testable theories. *American Journal of Sociology*, 101 (4), 1060–73.

Walder, A. G. and Gong Xiaoxia 1993: Workers in the Tiananmen protests: the politics of the Beijing Workers' Autonomous Federation. *Australian Journal of Chinese Affairs*, 29, 3–29.

Wang Gungwu 1991: *China and the Chinese Overseas*. Singapore: Times Academic Press.

Wang, Jing 1996: *High Culture Fever: politics, aesthetics, and ideology in Deng's China*. Berkeley: University of California Press.

Wang Jinling 1994: New characteristics of marriages between Zhejiang farmers and women from outside the province. *Social Sciences in China*, 15 (2), 59–64.

Wang Shaoguang 1995a: *Failure of Charisma: the Cultural Revolution in Wuhan*. Hong Kong: Oxford University Press.

Wang Shaoguang 1995b: The rise of the regions: fiscal reform and the decline of central state capacity. In A. G. Walder (ed.), *The Waning of the Communist State: economic origins of political decline in China and Hungary*, Berkeley: University of California Press, 87–113.

Wang, Yi Chu 1966: *Chinese Intellectuals and the West, 1872–1949*. Chapel Hill: University of North Carolina Press.

Wang Zhonghui 1990: Private enterprise in China: an overview. *Journal of Communist Studies*, 6 (3), 83–98.

Wank, D. L. 1995: Bureaucratic patronage and private business: changing networks of power in urban China. In A. G. Walder (ed.), *The Waning of the Communist State: economic origins of political decline in China and Hungary*, Berkeley: University of California Press, 153–83.

Wasserstrom, J. 1984: Resistance to the one-child family. *Modern China*, 10 (3), 345–74.

Wasserstrom, J. N. and Perry, E. J. (eds) 1994: *Popular Protest and Political Culture in Modern China*. 2nd edn. Boulder, CO and Oxford: Westview Press.

Watson, J. L. (ed.) 1984: *Class and Social Stratification in Post-revolution China*. Cambridge: Cambridge University Press.

Watson, J. L. 1991: The renegotiation of Chinese cultural identity in the post-Mao era: an anthropological perspective. In K. Lieberthal et al. (eds), *Perspectives on Modern China: four anniversaries*, Armonk, NY: M. E. Sharpe, 364–86.

Watson, J. L. 1993: Rites or beliefs? The construction of a unified culture in late imperial China. In Dittmer and Kim (eds), 80–103.

Watson, R. S. 1985: *Inequality among Brothers: class and kinship in south China*. Cambridge: Cambridge University Press.

Weber, M. 1930: *The Protestant Ethic and the Spirit of Capitalism*. London: George Allen & Unwin.

Weber, M. 1968 [1916]: *The Religion of China: Confucianism and Taoism*. New York and London: The Free Press and Macmillan.

Weber, M. 1978: *Economy and Society: an outline of interpretive sociology*. Edited by G. Roth and C. Wittich. Berkeley: University of California Press.

Weller, R. P. 1987: *Unities and Diversities in Chinese Religion*. London: Macmillan.

White, G. 1993: *Riding the Tiger: the politics of economic reform in post-Mao China*. London: Macmillan.

White, G. 1994: Democratization and economic reform in China. *The Australian Journal of Chinese Affairs*, 31, 73–92.

White, G. 1995: *Chinese Trade Unions in the Transition from Socialism: the emergence of civil society or the road to corporatism?* Institute of Development Studies Working Paper 18. Brighton: IDS at the University of Sussex.

White, G. 1996: Corruption and the transition from socialism in China. *Journal of Law and Society*, 23, 149–69.

White, G., Howell, J. and Shang Xiaoyuan 1996: *In Search of Civil Society: market reform and social change in contemporary China*. Oxford: Clarendon Press.

White, T. 1994: The origins of China's birth planning policy. In C. K. Gilmartin, G. Hershatter, L. Rofel and T. White (eds), *Engendering China: women, culture and the state*, Cambridge, MA: Harvard University Press, 250–78.

Whyte, M. K. 1972: 'Red vs. expert': Peking's changing policy. *Problems of Communism*, 21 (6), 18–27.

Whyte, M. K. 1974: *Small Groups and Political Rituals in China*. Berkeley: University of California Press.

Whyte, M. K. 1979: Revolutionary social change and patrilocal residence in China. *Ethnology*, 18 (3), 211–27.

Whyte, M. K. 1984: Sexual inequality under socialism: the Chinese case in perspective. In Watson (ed.), 198–238.

Whyte, M. K. 1986: Social trends in China: the triumph of inequality? In A. D. Barnett and R. N. Clough (eds), *Modernizing China: post-Mao reform and development*, Boulder, CO and London: Westview Press, 103–23.

Whyte, M. K. 1992: *From Arranged Marriages to Love Matches in Urban China*. Hong Kong: Institute of Asia-Pacific Studies.

Whyte, M. K. 1995: The social roots of China's economic development. *The China Quarterly*, 144, 999–1019.

Whyte, M. K. 1996: The Chinese family and economic development: obstacle or engine? *Economic Development and Cultural Change*, 45 (1), 1–30.

Whyte, M. K. 1997: The fate of filial obligations in urban China. *The China Journal*, 38, 1–31.

Whyte, M. K. and Parish, W. L. 1984: *Urban Life in Contemporary China*. Chicago: University of Chicago Press.

Wittfogel, K. A. 1957: *Oriental Despotism*. New Haven: Yale University Press.

Wolf, A. P. and Huang Chieh-shan 1980: *Marriage and Adoption in China, 1845–1945*. Stanford: Stanford University Press.

Wolf, M. 1970: Child training and the Chinese family. In M. Freedman (ed.), *Family and Kinship in Chinese Society*, Stanford: Stanford University Press, 37–62.

Wolf, M. 1972: *Women and the Family in Rural Taiwan*. Stanford: Stanford University Press.

Wolf, M. 1987 [1985]. *Revolution Postponed: women in contemporary China*. London: Methuen.

Wong, A. K. 1979: The modern Chinese family – ideology, revolution and residues. In Man Singh Das and Panos D. Bardis (eds), *The Family in Asia*, London: George Allen & Unwin, 245–76.

Wong, C. 1988: Interpreting rural industrial growth in the post-Mao period. *Modern China*, 14 (1), 3–30.

Wong, J. 1973: *Land Reform in the People's Republic of China*. New York: Praeger.

Wong Siu-lun 1979: *Sociology and Socialism in Contemporary China*. London: Routledge & Kegan Paul.

Wong Siu-lun 1985: The Chinese family firm: a model. *British Journal of Sociology*, 36 (1), 58–72.

Wong Siu-lun 1988a: *Emigrant Entrepreneurs*. Hong Kong: Oxford University Press.

Wong Siu-lun 1988b: The applicability of Asian family values to other sociocultural settings. In Berger and Hsiao (eds), 134–52.

World Bank 1992: *China: strategies for reducing poverty in the 1990s*. Washington, DC: IBRD/The World Bank.

Wu, D. Y. H. 1990: Minority or Chinese? Ethnicity and cultural change among the Bai of Yunnan, China. *Human Organization*, 49, 1–13.

Wu Jun 1992: Analysis of the current conditions of Chinese children. *Social Sciences in China*, 13 (4), 128–37.

Xiang Biao 1999: Zhejiang village in Beijing: creating a visible non-state space through migration and marketized networks. In Pieke and Mallee (eds), 215–50.

Yahuda, M. 1996: The international standing of the Republic of China on Taiwan. *The China Quarterly*, 148, 1319–39.

Yan Yunxiang 1996: *The Flow of Gifts: reciprocity and social networks in a Chinese village*. Stanford: Stanford University Press.

Yang, C. K. [Yang Qingkun] 1959a: Some characteristics of Chinese bureaucratic behavior. In D. S. Nivison and A. F. Wright (eds), *Confucianism in Action*, Stanford: Stanford University Press, 134–64.

Yang, C. K. 1959b: *The Chinese Family in the Communist Revolution*. Cambridge, MA: MIT Press.

Yang, C. K. 1961: *Religion in Chinese Society*. Berkeley: University of California Press.

Yang Lien-sheng 1957: The concept of pao as a basis for social relations in China. In J. K. Fairbank (ed.), *Chinese Thought and Institutions*, Chicago: University of Chicago Press, 291–309.

Yang, M. Mei-hui 1994. *Gifts, Favors and Banquets: the art of social relationships in China*. Ithaca: Cornell University Press.

Yeh, Wen-hsin 1990: *The Alienated Academy: culture and politics in Republican China, 1919–1937*. Cambridge, MA: Council on East Asian Studies Publications, Harvard University Press.

Yin Qiping and White, G. 1993: *The 'Marketization' of Chinese Higher Education: a critical assessment*. Institute of Development Studies Discussion Paper 335. Brighton: IDS at University of Sussex.

You Ji 1998: *China's Enterprise Reform: changing state/society relations after Mao*. London: Routledge.

Young, E. P. 1977: *The Presidency of Yuan Shih-k'ai: liberalism and dictatorship in early Republican China*. Ann Arbor: University of Michigan Press.

Young, L. C. 1974: Mass sociology: the Chinese style. *American Sociologist*, 9 (4), 117–25.

Yuan, V. and Wong, Xin 1999: Migrant construction teams in Beijing. In Pieke and Mallee (eds), 103–18.

Zha, Jianying 1995: *China Pop: how soap operas, tabloids, and bestsellers are transforming a culture*. New York: The New Press.

Zhang Qingwu 1988: Basic facts on the household registration system. Edited and introduced by M. Dutton. *Chinese Economic Studies*, 22 (1).

Zhang, Yunqiu 1997: From state corporatism to social representation: local trade unions in the reform years. In Brook and Frolic (eds), 124–48.

Zhao, Minghua and Nichols, T. 1996: Management control of labour in state-owned enterprises: cases from the textile industry. *The China Journal*, 36, 1–21.

Zhao Renwei 1993: Three features of the distribution of income during the transition to reform. In Griffin and Zhao (eds), 74–92.

Zhe Xiaoye 1995: Pluralization of village boundaries: openness of economy vs. seclusion of society. Paper presented to the Fourth European Conference on Agricultural and Rural Development in China, Manchester, 10–12 November 1995.

Zhou Daming 1995–6: On rural urbanization in China. *Chinese Sociology and Anthropology*, 28 (2), 9–46.

Zhou Daming and Zhang Yingqiang 1995–6: Rural urbanization in Guangdong's Pearl River delta. *Chinese Sociology and Anthropology*, 28 (2), 47–102.

Zhou, K. Xiao 1996: *How the Farmers Changed China: power of the people*. Boulder, CO: Westview Press.

Zhou, Xueguang 1993: Unorganized interests and collective action in communist China. *American Sociological Review*, 58 (1), 54–73.

Zweig, D. 1997: *Freeing China's Farmers: rural restructuring in the reform era*. Armonk, NY: M. E. Sharpe.

Index

Index

Index